TESTAMENT
of a TROUT FISHER

To the River Wharfe, to the trout that swim there, to those who fish for them and to all who find fascination and fulfilment in the way of a trout with a fly.

TESTAMENT
of a TROUT FISHER

Laurence Catlow

MERLIN UNWIN BOOKS

First published in Great Britain by Merlin Unwin Books Ltd, 2024

Text © Laurence Catlow 2024
Illustrations & cover photo © Merlin Unwin 2024

Merlin Unwin Books
6 Rural Enterprise Centre
Eco Park Road
Ludlow
SY8 1FF
UK

www.merlinunwin.co.uk

ISBN 978 1 913159 79 5
Typeset in 12 point Adobe Garamond Pro by Joanne Dovey,
Merlin Unwin Books

Printed by CPI Anthony Rowe England

CONTENTS

Chapter One

FISHING AT SEVENTY

When I look back to the earlier years of my fishing life there is certainly some sense of nostalgia: a regretful longing for a young body, for youthful days together with the vigour that belonged to them; days when I fished all morning and all afternoon and then, after forcing myself to stop for a gulped pint of beer and a guzzled supper, went out again in the evening and fished until the darkness told me that the time had come at last for more beer. And, of course, if I were on holiday, the next day would be no different; with brief and more or less unwelcome interludes, the whole of it would belong to the river until the light failed.

I should like the legs and arms that were mine even twenty years ago, limbs that were still slow to tire. Twenty years ago, a long day in the hills would, it is true, end in the contented weariness that comes to those of us who spend long days in the hills; but a longer day on the Wharfe, a day spent wading the rocky and jarring bed of an upland river seemed, even in my fifties, almost a trivial exertion. Whether it ended in contentment depended, of course, on whether or not it ended with any trout. Anyway, I should like younger limbs, I should like a back that does not complain whenever I slip or stumble in the river or on its banks, a back that, when fishing is over for another day, often tells me that it is getting too old for northern rivers with their rough beds and tangled banks. I should also like a neck that does not creak and ache in response to any abrupt or sudden movement, a neck that frequently adds its voice to my aching back's complaints. I am determined to defy these complaints for as long as possible, but undoubtedly it would be good to own a body that was not showing such obvious signs of wear. I should like something of the physical resilience of earlier years but at the same time I think that on the whole I prefer the thoughts and feelings that inhabit the fishing days of old age, even though this statement inspires immediate uncertainty as to whether or not I really mean it.

I can remember the easy rapture and the unquestioning joy that often came to me in early days on the Wenning and the Wharfe and how the marvellous beauty of my surroundings moved me to an entirely uncomplicated and passionate belief in the goodness of creation. And the years, years that I felt sure would be full of fishing, seemed to stretch ahead of me in shining succession to a horizon far too remote to pose me any threat at all.

Things are more complex now. We take our whole lives with us to the river, because the years have made us who we are, and by the time we are seventy the shaping experience of time points in several directions and often produces ambiguous or equivocal emotions; and yet, in spite of this and in spite of the ever-lengthening shadow of mortality, there are times now when I sit by the Wharfe at the end of a fishing day in possession of a peace that feels deeper and more serene and more important than anything I felt or experienced in younger days; and with this peace there comes a most profound feeling of gratitude to the river that has put another brace of trout in my bag and has brought with it this wonderful gift of peace.

This is something that I find chiefly on the Wharfe, but it comes to me on one or two other rivers, though never with quite the depth or intensity of stillness that I find on the Wharfe up at Deepdale or down at Black Keld and Spout Dub. Perhaps the main motive for setting out on another book is the desire to discover how a river and a few trout can do this for me, can produce in me a state of being that is undoubtedly the greatest and best of the innumerable gifts that fishing has given to me: a gift so precious, so nourishing that I treasure it beyond almost all the countless good gifts that my life away from rivers has given me.

It is indeed a most wonderful gift, the gift of the river Wharfe; but in spite of this just sometimes – not often by the river, more usually while drinking sherry before dinner or claret before bed – I cannot help thinking how exhilarating and at the same time how straightforward it would be to find myself an undergraduate again, coming to Watersmeet on the Wharfe for the first time ever and then fishing up the river all the way to Kettlewell, coming to Spout Dub, Black Keld, Knipe Dub without knowing their names but with my young fisher's heart already, on this my first encounter with them, stirred by unfolding love, coming to pools and runs of equal loveliness to which in later years I shall give my own names as the tribute of devotion, finding new beauty with almost every step, lost in wonder at each new revelation, intoxicated with the shining loveliness of flowing water and telling myself that I still have most of a lifetime to fish this river and to make it my own.

There was something glorious about my early contact with the Wharfe and how I recognised from the start that I had found my river, the river that I wanted to make the heart of my fishing life. We fishers fall in love with rivers and for me with the Wharfe it was love at first sight; it has also been an enduring love and, although there was a glory in those first raptures, I think I prefer the stronger bonds of long association and that precious gift of peace given to me so often now at the end of my fishing days. I shall return to the theme of my fisher's peace, because those few minutes that I almost always spend sitting by the river before packing up and going home can seem in their intensity of feeling like a sort of distillation of the whole day's experience, and there if anywhere I shall find why the Wharfe and its trout and the business of catching a few of them is so important to me. It is only occasionally that a brief longing comes over me for the thoughts and feelings of a young fisher, but it soon passes when I realise how rich I now find my fishing in old age. I would not choose to find myself an undergraduate of twenty summers again, but there is something from that time that I should love to be given back to me; I should love to be given back the river with which the undergraduate so easily and so sensibly fell in love. The Wharfe has suffered much in the intervening years.

I should love to go fishing in April and find that midday brought spring olives onto the river's surface, in a thin trickle at first but a trickle that soon grew into rather more than a trickle, bringing the first rings and splashes of hungry trout before swelling into a silent and teeming explosion of life from the bright currents of a pure and healthy river. I should love to go to the Wharfe in May, confident that the iron blues will hatch in the afternoon and confident too, especially should the day be cloudy and cold, that the hatch will be on a grand scale and that the fish will feast on the river's bounty. I should love once again to see summer blue wings floating down the river for hours on end, beginning about noon, floating down the river in unimaginable and ever-growing abundance with the trout all the time busy among them. These were once commonplace events but they occur now only at long intervals and you can now spend a whole season on the Wharfe without fishing through a great hatch. I have seen the Wharfe in late summer scattered from bank to bank with clustering droves of pale wateries; it is a sight that I have not seen for many years. All the flies that I have just mentioned are still there; all the flies that are meant to be there still hatch in their season but their numbers are drastically reduced. A long day on the river will bring odd specimens or a thin trickle of fly floating down the pools and just occasionally the Wharfe can still remind me of what she could once produce. Right up at the top of the river this past summer there came an afternoon that brought a hatch of blue wings comparable with the hatches of old, but on all my other fishing days I saw no more than occasional duns fluttering off the water.

The Wharfe, of course, is not to blame for this; it is we who are at fault: for the way we farm, the way we have drained the moors, the way we are changing the climate and the way we so scandalously discharge all sorts of rubbish and poison into our rivers. The Wharfe tries her best and we keep letting her down. Anyway, the steep decline in the population of invertebrates on the Wharfe, and for that matter on most other rivers, is a great sadness to me, for those great hatches of seasons past were not only welcome for the trout they brought up to feed and for the trout they put in my bag; they were wonderful in themselves, they were great spectacles of nature: a teeming demonstration of the power of pure water to produce life in unfailing plenty.

I should love to find the Wharfe the river that I fished in my early years at Kilnsey for, although I fish other rivers and find fulfilment and peace on their banks, my fisher's heart belongs to the Wharfe and my fisher's happiness depends on the Wharfe and how she treats me. Thank God that more often than not she can still manage to be kind. She may breed only a fraction of the flies that she once bred but there are still enough spring olives at the start of the season to interest a few trout and, early in April three or four seasons ago, I fished through a typically brief and thick hatch of march browns, which was a surprise and a delight, because march browns are not meant to inhabit the Wharfe, although the trout seemed to know all about them and to relish their taste. Late April and May often bring trickles of iron blues and olive uprights with enough fly to bring some trout onto the feed. Summer always sees a few blue wings and pale wateries but the great hatches have almost gone. The Wharfe is now predominantly a black fly river: a river where the trout stuff themselves with black gnats and smuts and midges. They also stuff themselves with the signal crayfish that now – our fault again – infest the river and are probably another reason for the declining fly life. Whether or not this is the case, the presence of crayfish in such numbers explains why there are now so many big trout in the river, why trout of two pounds and more are now ordinary trout rather than specimen fish pleading in death for the dignity of a glass case. When I first fished the Wharfe, a trout of a pound was a big fish. To my mind, by the way, it still is.

I set out just now to tell you how, in spite of her problems, the Wharfe still generally treats me well, for she still supports a big head of trout. It is true that on the main beats up to Kettlewell the river is fairly generously stocked, but these same beats also sustain a thriving population of wild trout and above Kettlewell, where there is no stocking at all, there are trout in abundance all the way to the first pool of the river at the tiny hamlet of Beckermonds. I catch plenty of trout at Kilnsey, plenty of stocked trout and plenty of wild ones, and because catching trout is very important to me I often come home from the river a contented man, a man at peace with himself and his place in creation, a man deeply grateful to the river that has once again fulfilled his wishes and put a brace of trout in his bag.

More than a brace is of course always welcome – I never tire of catching trout – but a brace is all that it takes to bring contentment, although it must be a brace that goes in my bag and comes home with me. I am happy to return most of the trout that I catch but there is enough of the hunter left in me to feel that a day that brings no fish for eating or just one of them has been a day of failure. I shall return to this matter of the brace in later chapters.

It is a great relief to me, anyway, that the Wharfe can still so often satisfy my longing for trout, but there is regret as well as relief: there is my already-mentioned regret that populations of upwinged flies have declined so sharply, but attached to this is a further regret, that this scarcity makes the method of fishing that I like best, the traditional upstream wet, much less effective than formerly. It is a beautiful way to catch trout, exciting as well as beautiful, and there is endless satisfaction to be found in lifting your wrist, lifting it in response to some subtle signal sent to you by line or leader, lifting it in response to some sign so faint that it was not consciously recognised, lifting your wrist and finding yourself connected with the solid weight of a surprised and angry trout. A skilful fisher of the upstream wet possesses a sort of acquired instinct for the strike. Perhaps, aged 70, I have finally developed something of the sort. The moment of connection brings me a thrill of which I never tire. That moment of connection is much more important to me than all the drama of the fight; and the thrill of connection is most intense for me when the fly that makes it is a wet fly fished upstream.

There are other reasons why the upstream wet is so precious to me: it appeals very strongly to my imagination because, especially when fishing this style at Kilnsey, I often tell myself that, not far short of two centuries past, Pritt and Cadman and their friends fished the same flies that I am now fishing through the same pools in the same way. It is a thought that appeals, establishing some sense of communion with long departed Kilnsey fishers. And I love the old and often very beautiful spider patterns of the north, I love their simplicity of design and they speak to my sense of history: flies passed down from generation to generation as the collective inheritance of northern trout fishers. They are part of our tradition and I have lost my thread because, in telling you why I so love the upstream wet, I have forgotten that I set out to tell you how I now fish it much less at Kilnsey and wish it were not so. I fish it less because the Orange Partridge, the Snipe and Purple, the Poult Bloa and their like are nymphal imitations of the various day flies (don't let anyone tell you otherwise). Spiders are nymphs and because numbers of day flies are so reduced, the Poult Bloa, the Snipe and Purple and the Orange Partridge catch me many fewer trout than they used to. Of course they still put fish in my creel and I think I should probably fish them rather more than I do, but they very rarely work when there are no olives hatching and so nowadays most of my wet flyfishing on the Wharfe is done with fancy patterns in a coloured and falling water. Spiders are still often deadly on the Tees and the Yorkshire chalkstreams and Pritt's Little Black is still a killing pattern at Kilnsey during a fall of black gnats or – dressed on tiny hooks – when trout are smutting their way through long summer afternoons.

These days the majority of my Wharfedale trout are caught on dry flies. I started my fishing life as a very ignorant dry fly purist; then, after finally acquiring a degree of competence in the art of fishing wet flies upstream, I became a fanatic for it, fishing no other way for at least ten years until, in the third phase of my fishing life, I gradually evolved into something like an all-round flyfisher. I shall not, in this final period, return to my beginnings by re-embracing an exclusive allegiance to the dry fly but, on the Wharfe at least, I shall probably continue to depend on it for most of my sport. It is, of course, a delightful way to catch trout.

There are several important rivers in my life and I find a different experience on all of them. I fish the top of the Tees above High Force, a wide river even so near the source, flowing through an open landscape of rough fields between high and rounded heather hills. I am a newcomer on the Tees but already I feel at home there and I find the moorland landscape tonic and exhilarating. I have fished the Foston Beck in East Yorkshire for over thirty years and I relish sport there with chalkstream trout. The beck is very beautiful, a perfect miniature chalkstream and the wild trout that you find on some of the beats are as beautiful as the beck itself. It must be at least twenty years since I first fished the Rea Brook in Shropshire and I love the days of shadowed seclusion that I spend there. On all these rivers I find fishing of very different sorts but of equally high quality and with it I find something else: something therapeutic and sustaining. On the Wharfe I find this same something but with this difference: that, on the Wharfe, I find much more as well.

On the Wharfe I find deep layers of experience, the deposit of more than half a lifetime, of two or three thousand fishing days, days coloured not only by themselves but by the events and emotions that lay on either side of them. I do not as it happens, sit by the Wharfe for hours at a time, watching the river and wading through deep streams of memory. I am too involved in the pursuit of trout, too eager to feel the weight of that brace in my bag to give myself over to meandering recollection. A day on the Wharfe is full mostly of immediate fishing thoughts, but the far-stretching hinterland is there and always I fish in its context and it makes my fishing something richer and more complex than I find on my other rivers.

On the Wharfe I feel a deep sense of belonging. Everywhere along its banks I meet what I have known since earliest manhood. There are trees that leaned over me as I fished in their shadow more than half a lifetime ago, there are grassy banks and wide green ledges above the water that through the years have been my riverside seat on days beyond number; there is a great boulder in the stream above Black Keld where I have propped myself time after time while changing flies. There is Black Keld itself and Spout Dub and Stepping Stones Pool. There is Knipe Dub and Watersmeet and so many other places that I have known for so long, beautiful places full of memories, places that look just the same and just as beautiful as on the day when they first saw me and that seem, whenever I come to them, to be welcoming my return. Every feature, every yard of the river has been part of my life now for half a century. Everywhere there is familiarity, everywhere there is intimacy and everywhere there is me.

But there are others too because, although I rarely fish in company on the Wharfe, in spite of this I never fish alone because, almost everywhere along the banks, I meet the kind ghosts of departed fishers and friends, encounters that bring some sadness but a much deeper sense of grateful love, love for the fisher-friends who can fish no longer and love for the river that first brought us together and made us friends.

Whatever else this book might be it will most certainly be an outpouring of praise for the river Wharfe, a celebration of all she is and all she has given me, an unworthy offering to the river that has been one of the most important shaping forces in the progress of my life. It will also, of course, be a celebration, not just of a river, but of the fish that swim there, of the brown trout of the Wharfe, especially the wild ones, for the native trout of the Wharfe are every bit as beautiful as the river from which they come. I shall celebrate the trout of my other rivers as well. I have been in love with trout since I caught my first one at the age of nineteen two days before going off to university. It is a love that has certainly developed and deepened over the years and there will be more to say of it. All I shall say here is this, that trout matter to me now more than ever, partly perhaps because I know that I have caught many more of them than I can expect to catch in however much of life remains for me. This makes every trout that now comes my way doubly precious. I hope my last trout of all is still some way ahead and, writing these words in late February, I hope that the first trout of another season is no more than a week or two away, although there will, of course, be no real contentment unless this first trout of the season is big enough to put in my bag and is then joined there, at some point in the progress of the day, by a second trout to make the brace. Perhaps the season's first trout will remain a singleton. I shall try to look on it as a promising start and not feel too dissatisfied. But the first brace will come, and on the evening of the day when the Wharfe gives it to me and with it gives me that most wonderful gift of peace, I shall celebrate the occasion with half of one of my better bottles of wine, although, on the evening of the season's first brace, the most ordinary wine in the world would smell and taste like one of the choicest and the best.

$$*****$$

A brief note. The pronouns I use to refer to the Wharfe are inconsistent. Mostly I think of the river as a 'she' and I am not sure why. But there are times when 'it' seems more appropriate, although I am at a loss to explain what lies behind this difference of attitude. 'He' never occurs to me, which is strange because throughout history, from classical times to the present day, personified or deified rivers have almost always, if not universally, been male, Father Tiber, for example and Father Thames and Old Man River. I cannot think of the Wharfe (or of my other rivers) in this way. Mostly I think of them, like ships, individually as she; occasionally 'it' seems more suitable. I apologise if this irritates or annoys you but there, I am afraid, it is.

Chapter Two

START OF THE SEASON

I used to greet the start of a new season with some sense of relief: relief that I had managed to make it through another winter and could now look forward to going fishing again. That was sometime in my fifties. I am seventy-two now, spring has come round again and the sense of relief is much, much greater, bringing with it a feeling of deep thankfulness that I am once again standing on the threshold of another trout season, stiff-jointed and slow it is true, but still feeling fit and strong enough to fish my way through the spring and summer and through another September's golden beauty.

For us fishers of the north-west, trouting begins in March. I am not sure that it should do, because March rarely brings ideal conditions for flyfishing. Even days in April often seem too soon, especially high up Wharfedale above Kilnsey and Kettlewell and way up the Tees above High Force. There are fishers who hold back until spring has moved on, warming up the water and waking up the trout. There are even fishers who somehow manage to wait until May and there are more fishers who are sensibly selective and, in March and April, only go to their rivers when the sun is warm, when the breeze is gentle and soft.

I am not a fisher who can postpone the start of his season for much more than a day or two and I am not a fisher who finds the sort of selectivity that I have just mentioned easy to achieve. I almost wish that I could but the truth is that once I am allowed to go out in search of trout I find it very difficult not to take advantage of the opportunity. You may be surprised when I tell you that guilt is one of the motives that sends me off to the river; if you asked me to explain what guilt can possibly have to do with it, I should explain how it comes from my half-conviction that God in his wisdom made me a fisherman, with a solemn duty to fish rivers and catch trout and celebrate the myriad beauties of doing so; piety therefore demands that I should go fishing just as soon as fishing is possible, and that cold winds and cold water should not discourage me from doing my duty and trying to catch the season's first trout.

Even if I leave God out of all this it is still beyond doubt that, as a fishermen, I feel something like a sense of vocation: something like a conviction that I was born to fish and to find joy and fulfilment through fishing and through trying to find the words to share with others something of the essence of those precious gifts.

I also feel restless when bad weather keeps me away from my rivers in the first few days of the season, restless and impatient for change, impatient to find myself on the Wharfe again, searching her pools and runs in the glorious hope of being rewarded for my efforts with the first brace of a new season. The start of the season also brings me something else that might surprise you, because it undoubtedly brings a nagging sense of anxiety, stemming from the fear that I shall go fishing and catch a trout or two and suddenly find that catching a couple of trout has lost most of its meaning, has lost its alchemic power to make the world and my presence in it seem twice as wonderful as they seemed before those two trout came my way.

There is this anxiety, made sharper by my knowledge that it once happened: that for something like two years, mental illness robbed catching trout of all its precious power to bring comfort, delight and fulfilment, at a time when my presence on a riverbank was so painful that, attempted once or twice, it was thereafter renounced. Undoubtedly there is this anxiety, but there is a much stronger feeling of hope: hope that I shall find everything that, with the exception of those two dark years, I have always found in fishing, everything and more because – with that same exception – as one season has followed another I have found that my experience of fishing has gained in intensity rather than surrendered any of its power. I tell myself this again and again but it cannot quite banish the anxiety that lurks somewhere in a dark corner of the mind, not even when I also tell myself that I am healthy again and that the season's first brace will surely confirm to me that being a fisher is as wonderful as ever. In the aftermath of that black period in my life it seems that I now have to relearn this marvellous truth all over again at the beginning of each season, although last year I managed to relearn it without the gift of even a single trout let alone of two.

I remember driving over into Wharfedale, late in March on the second day of the season. I cannot remember what had kept me away on the first and I was probably feeling slightly guilty. Anyway, as I drove up Mallerstang and then along to Hawes and over Cam Fell before dropping down into Wharfedale, I could not help wondering if fishing would be able to live up to my very high expectations. I was not thinking so much of the day ahead of me, which was more than likely to send me home with an empty bag, because it was so early in the season and the air was cold and even if fly hatched it might easily be ignored. I was thinking more of the whole season stretching away to distant

September and I was wondering if going fishing could continue to nourish and enrich my life in the way that it had done for the last 50 years. Yes, the specific anxiety that illness could once again take away my joy in fishing was undoubtedly there but I was more concerned with a possibility that had often suggested itself to me before: that the day might come when I suddenly found that I had caught enough trout, that catching more of them no longer mattered very much to me. I remembered pieces of music that once moved me very deeply and how I thought their emotional power could never fade, how I turned to them too often and then found disappointment and loss, finding that, although my mind still acknowledged their beauty, their hold on the heart was gone. Driving over to Wharfedale at the start of the season last year I could not help asking myself whether a similar thing might someday happen with catching trout, whether I might find all at once that the glory was gone from it, that I had done more than enough, had done too much of it and would be forced to acknowledge this sad truth with a sense of impoverished regret.

Five or six hours later, while driving back from the river with fishing now over for the day, I knew and rejoiced in the knowledge that I had nothing to fear. It was not that I had caught trout and found it just as wonderful, just as transformative as I had been hoping. I had never seemed likely to catch a trout and my failure, if it could be so called, had not made me restless with impatient longing for the season's first trout, because I knew that it would happen before too long. I had not caught any trout, but my time on the river had convinced me that, when the first brace did come along, it would mean every bit as much to me as it always had done, unless in fact it proved to mean even more.

The day had not been dissimilar to many first days of the season, which over the years have specialised in sending me home with an empty bag. It had been spent between Watersmeet and Black Keld, probably my favourite length of the club's main beats. This is partly because toward its top a fisher finds himself at Spout Dub, which is undoubtedly the place where my fisher's heart most truly belongs. You will hear much, possibly even too much, about Spout Dub in these pages. This doyen, anyway, this prince, this paragon of pools is one of the reasons why I so dearly love the beat to which it belongs; but it is also a beat where the river, it seems to me, is just the right size, is full of variety and of beauty and, for me, full of the richness that comes from long association. I was there, anyway, at the beginning of the season last year and it felt like an act of repossession, felt as though I was reclaiming an important and very precious portion of my life, taking it back for another half year until the end of another September asked me to resign it all again.

On that chilly March day last year, the end of September felt comfortingly far away and the narrow valley looked very beautiful. It was the beauty of early spring; it was a very spare beauty with pale colours beneath a patchwork sky. When the sun shone there was brightness in the water and on the outcrops of white limestone running in irregular and broken lines along the near skyline of the fells. In the grass there was the brightness of coltsfoot and celandines. The river flowed clean and very clear with a pale yellow light, flowing on its way through the faded pastures and beneath leafless trees. It was too early for any lambs.

In truth it was really too early to be fishing but I was very glad to be there and it was good to be casting a team of flies again, even though it was done without much hope of bringing up any trout. Round midday a scattering of olives appeared but I saw no rise. I enjoyed meeting my friends, Andrew and Kelvin, in the fishing hut at lunchtime, eating my sandwich with them, drinking a bottle of wine with them and being careful to pour myself just slightly more than my share. It was, after all, my bottle of wine. Anyway, we talked together in the easy way of old friends and then returned to our fishing, looking forward to meeting up again in May.

I walked up the river to Spout Dub and then fished my way to Black Keld. What mattered to me about this was the sense of reunion and restored intimacy. I sat by Black Keld for a time and looked at the river, at the inflow of the beck that gives the pool its name, at the pool itself and the long glide above it, flowing down from a small, restless pool beneath a leaning sycamore. Today they had given me no trout, but in the past they had given me dozens and dozens and I could tell myself that, with the coming of warmer weather and warmer water, they would almost certainly treat me with the old generosity. There was comfort in both recollection and expectation; it was a comfort that came from having known the river for so long. It was an old man's comfort. Without that relationship of half a century I should have sat there feeling cold and frustrated because the trout were asleep and there was no real prospect of catching any. As a young man I should have condemned the day as a tedious failure.

As it was I drove home unconcerned by the emptiness of my creel, feeling very glad that I had spent a fishless day on the Wharfe. It had, after all, been ritual rather than sport, a ritual which had established that the bond was still there, a simple and touching ritual of friendship renewed. Knowing that the bond was still there I knew too that it would be confirmed and strengthened by the trout the river would surely give me in the course of the season, a season that would bring joy and fulfilment to my old fisher's heart and would further deepen my long and very deep friendship with the river Wharfe.

Perhaps some of you are thinking that this talk of friendship is foolishness, is an illusion, and strictly speaking I suppose you are right, because friendship is something that grows out of a relationship between sentient and self-aware beings. But I miss the Wharfe when away from her, at the same time acknowledging that the Wharfe is unlikely to be missing me. In spite of this obvious truth, when I find myself standing on the banks of the Wharfe at the start of another season, I cannot resist the impression that the river is glad to see me and is welcoming me back into her valley and her life. And this is why I think of the relationship as one of friendship, one of the oldest and most fruitful friendships of my life.

But there is, of course, more to it all than this, because I do more than meet a river when I go to the Wharfe. I also meet myself. I meet the undergraduate fishing day tickets, not catching many trout but already in love with the river and longing already to join the world's most fortunate band of brothers by becoming a member of the Kinsey Angling Club; I meet the research student in the first two years of his membership, absurdly proud of his new status but increasingly alarmed by his immoderate appetite for alcohol; I meet him on the September day when he stumbled from the river in tears, tortured by the impossibility of self-control and by the guilt of excess and half believing that his fishing days are already over; I meet him the following spring on his return to the Wharfe, now a young schoolmaster who, with increasingly rare lapses, has turned drinking beer back into a controlled pleasure and is convinced that his love of the Wharfe and his longing to feel at home and happy on her banks was one of the chief motives that inspired reform and made it possible. I meet him at all subsequent stages of his life and of his progress as a fisher, until there is a gap of almost three years at the beginning of his retirement, and then I find him by the Wharfe again, slowly recovering from his grim struggle with depression and slowly fishing his way back to happiness and peace. On the Wharfe I do not fish through just a river; I also fish my way through a life.

*****

The first day of the season, because it is a day of such special significance, can bring happiness and something like joy even without any trout. This is not something that belongs to any other days spent in the company of the river Wharfe, days that will be felt as days of failure if they have not managed to send me home with a brace of trout. Some seasons back I spent three consecutive early-season days on the Wharfe, all of which were blank. I remember that on the last of these three days I hooked a good trout in the afternoon and told myself while playing him that on this occasion I did not need a brace, that on this occasion one trout would do just fine. When he dropped off the hook I roared out in pain and frustration, feeling most deeply miserable, feeling that I should have much preferred not to hook him because losing him was almost more than I could bear.

I then banished myself from the Wharfe for a whole week and somehow managed to stick to the almost impossible terms of this self-imposed exile. In a week, I told myself, the trout might just be beginning to move, there might just be a hatch of olives and I might, just might, be able to catch myself the season's first brace. Meanwhile I fished the Eden twice and on each occasion caught a trout. They were very welcome trout, they were the first trout of another spring but I should have much preferred to have caught nothing on the first day and both those trout on the next. You know how it is with me and the brace. You know how having two trout in my bag is immeasurably more satisfying than having just a lonely singleton.

Anyway, I returned to the Wharfe on a bright April morning with a gentle upstream breeze. The air was cool but there was no edge to it. It was a tonic air. There had been rain the day before and the river was big but it was falling and it was not dirty or brown. It was flowing with a dark lustre and it was unquestionably a fly water. It was the sort of water that, in late spring and summer, brings the possibility of a bulging creel; but so early in the season I thought it was the sort of water more likely to keep trout tucked in under the banks or hugging the bottom unless perhaps an untypical profusion of fly brought them up to feed. I half expected that, as a last resort, I should at some stage of the day be fishing weighted nymphs but, at eleven in the morning, that was still some hours away and I began the search for the first trout of another Wharfedale spring with my favourite early-season duo of Simple Simon on the dropper and my hackle Coachman on the point.

Even in a big water it is worth casting your flies into fast currents and strong runs, but you will probably find your best chance of success by searching edges and eddies and those trapped patches and rocking pockets of foam. I had been doing all this for perhaps half an hour when something told me to raise my wrist, some sudden twitch on the line or some slight pause or deviation; I raised it, anyway, and found that I was into a trout. He weighed 1lb. 11ozs., was an overwintered stock fish and was, of course, knocked on the head. He was a very special trout because he was the season's first trout from the Wharfe and he would, I hoped, be the first of many more. He was a special and very welcome trout but catching him brought an arguably unwelcome side-effect because it did not bring me satisfaction or peace; instead of this it provoked an immediate and unusually acute attack of brace-fever. I cannot remember breaking out into a sweat or feeling dizzy; I don't think there were hot flushes or a headache or sudden exhaustion or any new aches and pains; but there was most definitely a burning desire to turn one trout into two and I knew that, if only this happened, I should feel ridiculously happy, feel that God was in his heaven and everything in the world was just as it should be and that of all men I was undoubtedly the most fortunate and the most blessed.

I fished on and nothing much happened for about half an hour, at least nothing much apart from the whisper of my line and the fall of my flies onto the restless currents of the Wharfe.

I think there might have been a tangle that took a few impatient minutes to sort out, and there were certainly curlews floating over the fields and filling the sky with their sad and strangely thrilling music; there were floating curlews and there were wagtails fluttering over the water from rock to rock, and I can clearly remember a dipper flying upstream with what I thought were twigs or feathers in his beak. Now that I think about it there is, of course, always something happening in the vicinity of rivers and almost always it is good to see and hear. When I said that nothing much was happening, what I really meant was that the one thing that above all else I wanted to happen was refusing to happen, because no altruistic second trout seemed willing to attach itself to the end of my line and then stay attached until it had been tamed and brought safely to net.

It was almost time for lunch and I could not help thinking how my sandwich would taste twice as toothsome, my wine twice as fragrant and rich if only there were a brace of trout in my bag, but unfortunately it looked as though both my sandwich and my wine would be denied the transforming effects of the season's first brace, tasting like an ordinary sandwich and just ordinary wine rather than a sandwich and a glass of wine that had gone through some form of transubstantiation at precisely the moment when the second trout had splashed into my net.

It was almost time for lunch but there was just time for Spout Dub, that pool without equal which, as well as being the best and most beautiful pool in the world, is also the kindest of pools and seems to know when I most need a fish and to respond by persuading one of its residents to swallow one of my flies, which is, of course, one of the reasons why I love it so dearly. It is also the pool that, on a wild afternoon in September fifty years ago, put five out of seven trout in my bag, a bag that until then had never brought home from the Wharfe or from any other river more than a brace or (much more frequently) an unsatisfactory singleton.

Add to all this its beauty and its seclusion beneath a dripping cliff of white limestone, add some mysterious power of place and you may begin to understand my passionate attachment to this most wonderful of pools.

There is broken water at the head of Spout Dub, where the river rushes into the pool through a narrow channel in the rock and gravel, flowing hard and fast against what to an upstream fisher is the left bank. And it was here, just before lunch on that bright day in April a few years ago, that the line sent me its signal to strike. I knew at once that he was big and that he would take some taming in the strong flow. I was frightened, wishing him half the size that he felt to be, because then there would be less danger of losing him and losing with him the surpassing glory of the season's first brace. The dim, pale shape of him, twisting and turning in the dark water, confirmed that he was a big trout, almost certainly a two pounder, and he was very slow to tire. I thought for a few grim seconds that he had lodged himself beneath a ledge of rock and must surely break me, but the line held, pressure brought him out again into open water and at last he was drawn over the net. He weighed 2lbs 4ozs and was in fine condition. He was another overwintered stock fish, he had taken my Coachman and now it was most certainly time for lunch.

With the brace won, duly laid in the pale grass and admired with appropriate wonder and reverence, I now sat on a grassy shelf above Spout Dub and ate my sandwich, which tasted almost too good for an imperfect world, although the world's imperfections seemed to have no place on my grassy shelf above Spout Dub. I ate this sublime sandwich, which had been bought from the Co-op in Kirkby Stephen and may have been filled with two or three limp rashers of bacon and a few bits of salad, and after it was eaten I drank my very slow way through two metal beakerfuls of red wine. I cannot remember what the wine was, except that it was red, or where it came from, but I can remember that each sip seemed to confirm and deepen my sense of complete contentment, seemed to convince me more firmly that, if imperfection was part of the nature of things, it was so trivial as to be almost meaningless.

I looked at the tight green buds on the sycamores along the bank; I watched a dipper bobbing up and down on a rock across the water and saw that his beak held neither twigs nor feathers but strands of dry grass; I saw a wagtail fluttering over the water to seize a fly; I listened to the sound of the river; I followed the slow drift of clouds through the bright sky above me and, drinking all this in with grateful eyes and ears, acknowledging too that the brace in my bag made the revelation of this beauty twice as bright and my response to it twice as wonderful, I asked myself all over again how a couple of trout could so powerfully affect a man who had been catching trout for more than fifty years. How could two more matter so much?

For most of my fishing life, by the way, wine or, in younger days, beer belonged only to the end of fishing days. The wine became a lunchtime feature of days on the Wharfe almost ten years ago when I was recovering from my battle with depression, beginning to fish again, finding pleasure and purpose in it, but still often finding the prospect and sometimes the experience of fishing days daunting and difficult. It was then the lunchtime wine was introduced, because I used to tell myself that, if I got to the Wharfe and got through to one o'clock, I would reward myself with two glasses of wine, which meant, of course, that I then had to fish for two or three hours in the afternoon before I could think of driving home, and this in turn meant that I became gradually re-accustomed to spending long days on the river.

So it was that the indulgence of lunchtime wine was introduced – to begin with almost always at Spout Dub – an indulgence that has now become an essential element of a day on the Wharfe (or any other river). Anyway, as I sat there after Spout Dub had made the brace for me with a two-pounder, as I sat there sipping my wine while watching the dipper come and go with beakfuls of dry grass for its nest somewhere in the vicinity of Spout Dub's cliff, watching too the wagtail fluttering over the water and pouncing on an occasional fly, listening to the river and admiring the brightness of its flow, as I sat there with the blue sky and a few drifting clouds above me I felt quietly and very deeply happy and I suddenly saw something of what fishing gives to me with its gift of the brace; for this gift, I now saw, helps me for a time to live in the present: supremely content with Spout Dub and two trout and a metal beaker of red wine, with budded branches and a dipper and a wagtail, with floating clouds above me and with the sound of the river Wharfe in my ears.

This fisher's peace, this deep and grateful contentment in the conviction that the present and what belongs to it is all that I need for fulfilment and happiness, this is a very great gift and doubtless you will have known it yourself. You may have found it with just a single trout, you have probably found it without wine. For me two trout are needed and the wine certainly helps. Anyway, when on this particular occasion, the last drop of it was finished, when I had looked into my metal beaker and been forced to acknowledge that there was nothing left in it, I put my two trout in the cool and dripping shade of the miniature cave at the downstream end of my grassy shelf and began to fish my way upstream. A very thin trickle of olives was coming off the river but I saw no response from the trout and thought, in an unbothered sort of way, that I was unlikely to catch any more; the reason this scarcely mattered, of course, was that a brace of trout was already lying there in the shadows of Spout Dub's tiny cave.

In the event I did catch more trout. I caught two more of them, another brace in a typically short and profuse flush of

March browns. This second brace, of course, delighted me and confirmed the brightness of my mood but I say again that it was the first brace that mattered because it had brought me my fisherman's peace.

I came, anyway, to Black Keld and saw to my surprise that there were fish rising in the run above the inflow of the beck. I immediately – and unsuccessfully – attacked the lowest of them with a parachute Imperial. And then I saw that the hatching flies were not spring olives, saw that march brown was written all over their large and mottled wings. I should have caught a specimen to look for the femoral blotch that proclaims the true march brown but, to tell the truth, I was far too eager to catch another trout. The brace is enough but more is always welcome. I can never have too much of catching trout.

I was inclined to think that they were probably false march browns because the Wharfe has never been known as a river that produces the genuine article but, by appearing in a short and – as it turned out – abundant flush they were doing exactly what the genuine article is meant to do and it is true that I had never seen false march browns hatching so thickly of the Wharfe. These thoughts, anyway, occurred to me as I stood there watching the flies and the rising trout, but I was concerned much more with what fly would give me the best chance of adding to the brace in my bag.

I had no patterns tied with march browns – false or otherwise – in mind. Perhaps I should have looked for a Klinkhåmer of appropriate size and colour but I made no attempt to find a pattern even remotely imitative. For some reason, impatience perhaps or the suspicion that there was nothing in my fly boxes that looked anything like a march brown, for some reason, anyway, I tied a Simple Simon to the end of my line and in the next ten minutes I missed two trout, hooked and lost one and killed two more. And then the hatch failed and my day was more or less over. A better representation of the hatching fly might have held on to that lost trout and might have hooked one or other of the missed ones. I did not care. After fishing for perhaps another twenty minutes I finished and drove home in possession of the peace that only comes to me at the end of successful fishing days, deeply in love with fishing and with catching trout, with Spout Dub and the wonderful river Wharfe. The flies, by the way, turned out to be true march browns; I was back a few days later, there was an almost identical hatch, this time I bothered to pick a fly off the water and the clearly visible blotch on his femur immediately told me what I wanted to know.

Chapter Three

ON THE MAYFLY

Over the years I have caught several thousands of trout. In saying this I am not trying to impress you by implying that, with these thousands of trout to my name, I must be a fisher of extraordinary knowledge and skill. No, I have been at it for more than fifty seasons and I should be a poor fisher indeed if I had not by this time in my life caught lots and lots of trout. The reason I am telling you that thousands of trout have eaten my flies and been drawn over my net is because it is perhaps remarkable that, until the end of May came along five or six years ago, not a single one of those several thousands of trout had fallen to an imitation of the fly that takes its name from the most beautiful – but not as it happens my favourite – month of the year.

The Kilnsey water on the Wharfe produces a mayfly here and there, but the rocky bed of my beloved river will never provide a home for more than just a few of them and I have only once seen a mayfly taken by a Wharfedale trout. On the

Eden below Kirkby Stephen there are always a few mayflies to be seen in their season. Compared with the upper Wharfe, the Eden, even way up the river where I fish it, moves rather more sedately on its journey to the sea; there are beds of silt here and there and I have been assured that sometimes the mayflies hatch thickly enough for the trout to feed on them, presenting alert and suitably equipped fishers with the chance of an exceptional fish. I have never witnessed one of these thicker hatches, probably because I have always favoured the club's higher beats where silt is in much shorter supply and, anyway, it is probably for the best that I have never found Eden trout feasting on mayflies because I should certainly not have been suitably armed with a range of appropriate patterns. For most of my fishing life there has been nothing even remotely resembling a mayfly at any stage of its development in any of my now numerous fly boxes.

The lovely little Wenning is another river that gives birth to a scattering of mayflies, at least it used to when I fished it many, many years ago. I remember how, just once, on a hot afternoon in early June, the duns, looking huge and very bright in the sunshine, came floating down the stream in threes and fours together and how the trout suddenly decided to help themselves. For my part I found the whole business hugely frustrating because I had nothing to show them that could possibly be mistaken for a mayfly. I drove home telling myself that I was a careless and negligent fisher and I vowed to dress myself some mayfly patterns just in case they might some day be needed. It goes almost without saying that I did no such thing.

And so it was that five or six years ago, at the moderately ripe old age of 67, in spite of a lifetime total of something like five thousand trout, I was still, if you will excuse the metaphor, a mayfly virgin. I knew lots about mayfly fishing, because in dozens of books I had read all about the wonderful sport that fishers enjoyed with the nymph, with the emerging or sitting dun and with the laying spinner or the spent gnat. I knew all about duffers' fortnight and the huge trout that it sometimes put in duffers' bags, but it was all book-knowledge. Far from catching a trout eating mayflies I had never even tied an imitation of one to the end of my cast, and to tell the truth I was not much bothered. It is of course good to see trout gulping down flies in a frenzy of greed and to try your hand at catching them but, although I enjoyed reading about sport with the mayfly, I was inclined to think of it almost dismissively as probably too obvious and too easy. I also thought that the smaller day flies, olives and iron blues and pale wateries, were in their understated way more beautiful than their much larger, much brighter and somewhat ostentatious cousins and that sport with them was more delicate, more subtle and more satisfying than anything provided by the mayfly carnival. These were my views before, right at the end of May five years ago, and specifically with mayfly in mind, I went down to Shropshire to test these same views against personal experience. I was hoping at last to catch my first trout on the most famous of fishers' flies.

I love the little river Rea. I love how you get to it through a maze of narrow, twisting lanes and how this winding journey somehow strengthens the impression that, on reaching the Rea, you have found your way into a different and secret, a secluded and a much better world. Once or twice, when I was new to the Rea, I almost failed to get there. By the time of my visit in search of trout on the mayfly I knew the way well enough but, even when you know how to get to the Rea at Duddlewick Bridge, it is easy to imagine, even when you have got there, that you are lost somewhere deep in the middle of a sequestered valley, far from any habitation or human contact. On the first day of my visit, anyway, I came to this lonely and very lovely little river, winding its way through the heart of England; I came through bright sunshine with my friend Merlin Unwin's box of mayflies in my fishing waistcoat. Merlin could not fish with me but he had assured me that Shropshire's mayfly season was in full swing; on the nearby Teme a couple of days ago he had caught five good trout in no time at all.

The day was uncompromisingly hot, hot and still, and I told myself that I had undoubtedly chosen the best river for such a day, for the Rea flows well beneath the level of the surrounding fields and almost everywhere beneath a thick and sheltering canopy of leaves: leaves of alder and birch, of hawthorn, ash and, most notably, of huge and ancient willows with deeply scored bark, willows that tower into the sky and lean possessively and protectively over the little stream flowing way down there below them. It was a hot, still day but down in the river there would be the comfort of cool water and cool shade. And the banks were white with the may and the air was sweet with its smell. And the tangled grass was bright with red campions, with blue speedwell and white parsley, and already at eleven in the morning there were mayflies coming off the water and gleaming palely as they fluttered through the shadows. In the dim light beneath the trees they looked almost like the ghosts of mayflies rather than substantial and edible beings that would appeal to hungry trout.

I walked downstream as far as I wanted to before sliding into the water with one of Merlin's huge artificials on the end of my cast. I heard a rise, a slurping sound that spoke of a big fly and possibly of a big fish. Mayfly, I thought and when it happened again I saw where it had come from, which was seven or eight yards upstream beneath the trailing branches of a willow. My fly avoided the branches, fell just where I wanted it to fall and soon afterwards I had caught my first ever trout on the mayfly, a wild and beautiful trout of about twelve ounces, which is a decent trout for the little Rea (and in fact for any other river). If I had still been a smoker I should most certainly have put a match to my pipe and inhaled a few triumphant lungfuls of smoke. If there had been a hip-flask in one of my pockets I should without doubt have pulled it out and taken a few swallows in celebration of the great event that had just occurred. There was nothing to smoke and nothing to drink (until I got back to the Land Rover) and so I went on fishing, convinced that I was sure to catch trout on the mayfly from every corner, every run and glide and every pool of the wonderful Rea Brook. I had only caught a single trout; the brace was not yet mine, which as you know is necessary for satisfaction. But I was so certain of more trout that I already felt the satisfaction and contentment that usually comes only with my second trout. There were surely going to be ten or twenty of them.

The naturals were coming off steadily in ones and twos, but it was some time before I saw a rise. I covered it with Merlin's wonderfly and, of course, it was taken, but the fish departed the hook after a splash and a brief wallow on the surface. He had felt and looked like a good fish and the next one felt even better until contact was once again lost before it had been properly established. And that was more or less it until I found that I had fished my way back to the Land Rover, surprised and disappointed that the expected bonanza had not happened and by now most definitely deeply unsatisfied with the solitary trout in my bag.

I ate a pork pie, in fact I ate two of them because the first was so good that the second just had to follow. I told myself all over again that Ludlow pork pies from Mr. Griffiths (the butcher at the top of Corve Street) far surpassed the best that even Melton Mowbray could produce in challenge. Anyway, as well as eating two pork pies (very quickly), while marvelling at the crisp richness of the pastry and the delicate and succulent spiciness of the meat, I drank two much slower glasses of claret, which I did not proclaim quite the best that Bordeaux produced but it still smelled and tasted more than good enough, even though there was still only one trout in my bag. It was a comfort and it helped me to believe that the brace would surely come in the afternoon.

While drinking this wine, anyway, I pondered the morning's sport. There had, I reflected, been a regular trickle of mayfly and my single trout had undoubtedly been eating them, because I had seen at least one mayfly disappear into what I had taken to be his mouth. But even at the time I had wondered if those two pricked trout had been swallowing something else. I was, of course, a mayfly tyro but the rises that had drawn my attention had been delicate and gentle, suggesting smaller stuff, and there had also been one or two rising trout that had gone down as soon as my huge fly had floated over them. I declared myself a fool, seduced by those fluttering giants and by my eagerness to catch trout on the mayfly, seduced into fishing for rising fish with a fly designed to frighten rather than attract them or to make any inspection of it tentative and uncertain. I determined that in the afternoon, unless the mayfly came thickly and the trout greeted them with obvious approval, I should fish with a much smaller fly. The trout of the Rea had always shown a decided fondness for my own Dry Simon, a pygmy of a fly when compared with Merlin's enormous things, a fly dressed on a hook no bigger than a size twelve.

And so it was that, after finishing my wine and, as always, regretting that there was none of it left, I tied Dry Simon to the end of my leader and fished my way slowly upstream, fishing through green shadows and shafts of moted sunlight, fishing with those high and tangled banks rising above me on either side and bright all along with campions and speedwell and cow parsley, fishing beneath those huge and ancient willows while dancing swarms of damsel flies turned the air shimmering purple and green. And here and there a trout rose and almost always, liking the look of Dry Simon, he sucked him in, and most of them were good trout for the Rea between ten ounces and a pound, and all of them were wild and all of them were very beautiful, filling my fisher's eyes with admiring delight and filling my fisher's heart with a very quiet joy. And yes, it felt to me down there in the shadowed river beneath those sheltering trees as though I was fishing my way through the shy and secluded heart of England and that I was half lost in a place almost too lovely to be true.

In the course of a long afternoon Dry Simon caught me nine trout. After three or four hours I had to force myself to call it a day, fighting my way up the bank, through twining briars and brambles, accepting the stings and scratches and the odd trickle of blood as the price the Rea extracts from those who have entered her secret world, drawn there by the allure of the spotted treasure that swims down there in the brown water. The price, anyway, was paid and, as I wandered downstream through the sunshine, filled with all the thoughts and feelings that belong to the end of a trout-filled day, I had almost forgotten that the first of my ten trout had also been the first trout of my life to have taken a mayfly. If I did perhaps acknowledge this, it was probably with a shrug of the shoulders and thoughts roughly along the following lines: 'Who needs mayflies anyway?'

It was almost exactly the same the next day, except that this time none of my trout fell to a mayfly pattern. Again the naturals hatched in ones and twos throughout the day, again they were largely ignored and again the trout thought very highly of Dry Simon. Again there were two pork pies' for lunch with two glasses of red wine, although there was a difference here, because by lunch the brace had been secured and so the pies and the wine tasted even better than the day before. Once again I caught ten very beautiful wild trout and once again I finished almost unwillingly and drove away from my fishing thinking grateful thoughts about the Rea Brook.

Looking back on those two days, with a few more years' experience of mayfly time, I now realise that I must have been on the Rea right at the beginning of the hatch when the trout, perhaps unaccustomed to flies of such size, are slow to start helping themselves to what nature is providing,

They were, anyway, two delightful days. On the morning after the second of them, I left Shropshire and drove south, inadvertently driving away with Merlin's box of mayflies still in my fishing waistcoat. I was heading for more fishing, but on a very different sort of river. I was heading for Hampshire, for Chilbolton and for my first ever day on the most famous trout stream in the world.

I went from a little river that almost no one has heard of to a river that everyone, at least every fisher of flies, knows by reputation if not through personal experience. My knowledge was of the former sort. I loved the chalkstreams of East Yorkshire, having fished them for something like forty years, but I had never wet a line on any chalk water south of the Humber. My acquaintance with the Test and the Itchen was through the writing of Hills and Skues, of Plunket Greene and Viscount Grey; I had read them all, repeatedly and with enormous pleasure, but without expecting that I should myself ever fish the rivers where they had caught so many trout, finding at the same time such fulfilment and delight.

The Test is undoubtedly the most celebrated of trout streams and now I was going to spend a day there in mayfly time as the guest of my friend Christopher Tinker, fishing a private beat just below Wherwell on Chilbolton Common. I arrived the day before, booked in at The White Lion in Wherwell, drank a lunchtime pint and ate a sandwich before wandering out to take a look at the world's most famous chalkstream. It was very hot indeed. There were paths that led down to the river, where I stood sweating on low brick bridges, looking up and down stream at waving weed and gin-clear water; and in spite of the heat there were mayflies coming off the river and trout rising to eat them. And there was a waterside fringe of tall reeds and long grass with mown paths behind it and there were signs insisting that the fishing was private. I thought that it would almost certainly be very expensive as well.

That evening after dinner I sat outside with the last of my wine, loving the cool air that had come with the setting sun, loving the stillness and the pale, bright sky and watching swarms of mayfly spinners flying above me with shining wings. I hoped the duns would come thickly tomorrow and wondered what sport I might find given a decent hatch. I told myself that I should almost certainly enjoy myself and I admit that I expected fairly undemanding sport with oversized and unsophisticated trout that were recent arrivals in the river. I sat there sipping Rioja and I confess that I thought condescending thoughts about the river Test, thinking of it as a river for corporate entertainment, as a sort of playground for multi-millionaires, providing put-and-take fishing for men rich enough to pay for it. Thoughts such as these flitted through my mind until I found that my Rioja was finished and it was time for bed.

Christopher, who by the way is most definitely not a multi-millionaire, joined me for breakfast next morning. The sun was bright; it was already warm by half past eight and by the time we reached the water at ten it was boiling hot. The Test was flowing full and clear over the weed and there were already fish rising, although they were not rising in the manner of big fish and they were certainly not eating mayflies. I could not see these fish because of the reflected light on the water but I suspected grayling. I could not confirm my suspicion because I could not catch any of them. Already I was beginning to think that the fish of the Test, whether trout or grayling, might be more of a challenge than I had previously fancied. Unable to catch any fish I did however manage to catch myself, embedding the hook of a small Klinkhåmer deep in my thumb when the willow branch, from which I had just released my fly, sprang back from my grasp, pulling the line tight, at the same time driving the iron into my flesh and over the barb.

You fishers of barbless hooks will have no sympathy; you may even think that it served me right and that I thoroughly deserved a taste of my own medicine; it did occur to me at the time that a hook with an unbarbed point would not have so stubbornly refused to release its unwelcome hold on my flesh. Anyway, I sat down on a bench and tried to ease the Klinkhåmer from the inside of my thumb. It hurt and the Klinkhåmer refused to budge. I wandered back to the hut, found a small knife and began excavations in the vicinity of the barb. It hurt even more and the hook stayed put. And then I screwed my courage somewhere not too far from the sticking place, seized the hook and pulled it as hard as I could. It hurt like hell, but it achieved its objective, because I was relieved to find that I was no longer attached to a size 14 Klinkhåmer, which meant that fishing could resume.

I spent the rest of the morning licking my thumb and revising my opinion of the trout – or grayling – of the Test. By now there were a few mayflies coming off the water; I tried two or three of Merlin's artificials; I did not expect them to work – because I knew the naturals were being ignored – and my expectations were not disappointed. Lunchtime wine seemed an enticing prospect; in the event it was a delight. We sat in the shade of the hut, with the Test flowing almost at out feet and with mayflies now fluttering more frequently from its surface, we sipped our wine and ate our sandwiches and wondered how to approach our sport in the afternoon. We did not rush, we took our time and I feel obliged to confess that, when the last drop of wine had been finished and Christopher had returned to his fishing, I remained for a time in the shade of the hut: stretched out in the grass with closed eyes and no conscious thoughts of trout or mayflies – or anything else – for something like half an hour.

It was probably about three o'clock when my eyes opened again and I turned back into a fisher, wondering if it had perhaps been disrespectful to spend part of my first ever day on the river Test lying asleep on the bank. Anyway, I resumed my attempts to catch my first-ever Test trout. It was very bright and very hot but, in spite of this, the mayflies were now hatching in good numbers and were clearly being taken; and so it was with Merlin's flies that I sought to deceive the trout, but without immediate success. I began to wonder why mayfly time was sometimes called duffers' fortnight and then I covered a rise and found that I had hooked a trout.

He was slow to tire but he came to net, he weighed one and three quarter pounds and pleased me enormously: my first trout from the Test and almost certainly, it seemed to me, the first of several more, for the hatch was getting thicker all the time and all over the river there were slashing rises from what were indisputably big fish. I thought that the next two or three hours would be likely to provide easy sport even for a duffer; I thought that duffers' fortnight was about to live up to its name.

It was perhaps an hour later that, for all my fifty years as a fisher, I felt like a duffer myself, felt in fact like the prince of duffers: a duffer incapable of catching or even rising a trout when every fish in the river was gorging on what was by now a huge hatch of mayflies. The air had turned yellow with their teeming plenty and I had cast at least half a dozen of Merlin's flies over at least twenty large and gulping trout. I decided that they must be taking the emerging rather than the sitting duns; I could not find anything in Merlin's box that looked remotely like an emerger and so persevered despondently with high-floating flies. It never occurred to me – proof I suppose of my dufferdom – to soak an artificial in the river, turning it into a semi-submerged fly that might just have brought me a trout. I covered fish after fish; I no longer expected them to show any interest in my flies and I was absolutely spot on.

You could have seen me, towards the end of the afternoon, sitting in a yellow mist of mayflies, sitting there on the bank with a dejected and defeated look on my face. I had almost, but not quite, given up hope. I was wondering how on earth

I might manage to make the brace, I could not see a way until desperation turned my mind to Klinkhåmers, not of the size and colour of the Klinkhåmer that had so cruelly buried its barb in my thumb, but of much bigger flies, for I seemed to remember, three or four years earlier, tying a few Klinkhåmers on largish hooks, flies with bodies of yellow wool and with a badger hackle. I couldn't remember why I had tied them and was pretty certain it had not been with mayflies in mind, but it now seemed to me that, if I could find one of them, it might look to a trout something like an emerging mayfly. It was a long shot but it was worth a try.

There was a time when I went fishing with two fly boxes, one for dry and one for wet flies, but I long ago left behind such admirable simplicity. I still have a box of wet and a box of dry flies housing the patterns that I use most frequently, but there are now at least half a dozen other boxes in my waistcoat, filled with a confusion of flies of every sort, flies that float and others that sink, some of them big and bushy, others slim and indisputably tiny, others somewhere in between. There is no order in these boxes. I know that one of them began its life in my waistcoat as the box reserved exclusively for black flies but there are now black flies scattered through all my boxes and I could no longer tell you which of them started out as the black box. I have forgotten the distinct function of the other boxes, if they ever had one. They have turned into the boxes where I store – and too often forget about – flies for which I have only occasional use. There are lots and lots of patterns of this sort. I was now hoping that somewhere among them I might find a large Klinkhåmer with a yellow body and a badger hackle, unless I was deceiving myself and had never in fact tied them. And even if they really existed, even so they might still be beyond reach because they might be in yet another box, in the box where I abandoned flies that had refused to catch me any fish, a box that was three hundred miles away at home in Cumbria.

I found them in the last box that I opened; there were three of them and they were not just as large as I had fancied, although they were big enough to suggest a stunted mayfly and the Klinkhåmer effect might just suggest an emerging dun. The first two trout to which I showed one of them were both unimpressed. And then there was the third trout; he looked big and he also looked at my fly. And then he rose towards it and slowly sucked it in; and then all hell broke loose, as he charged round the river and shook his head and slapped his tail. In fact he did all the things that big trout do in books when they take exception to being hooked by fishermen; he did everything an angry trout is meant to do and he did it repeatedly and he did it well.

Meanwhile the 67-year-old heart of the fisher attached to him was thumping away more violently than was good for it, for I knew that this was a trout that really mattered to me. He had come right at the end of the day, for we could not fish into the evening; if landed he would make the brace which, for me at least, brings much more than double the satisfaction of a singleton; he was moreover very clearly a big trout and, if he stayed for the net he would turn my first ever day on the river Test into a day to remember with deep gratitude and satisfaction. He would turn a day of general failure into a day of final triumph.

And, God bless his memory, he did stay for the net, although he was so big that it was difficult to persuade him into it. But in he went and I lifted him from the water, knocked him on the head and sat there on the bank feeling exhausted and dazed, also feeling certain beyond doubt that I had finished fishing for the day. He was a beautiful trout, fat and full-finned and he weighed three and a half pounds. The world's most famous trout stream had confounded me; looking for easy sport I had been humbled, I had been taught respect and then rewarded with a gift that I had not really deserved. It was a gift that made every sip of wine that evening taste doubly and trebly wonderful. Sitting outside

in the delightful cool of the evening and watching the shining
spinners dancing away up there in the bright sky, I now I lifted
my glass, lifting it firstly in honour of my host Christopher,
lifting it then, of course, in honour of the river Test, in honour
of mayflies and Klinkhåmers, in honour of trout in general and
one trout in particular. I should doubtless have kept lifting it in
honour of other things, but I now found to my disappointment
that it was empty and was telling me that it was time for bed.

*****

I have never fished the Test again. I have been invited back but
things have got in the way and now I am beginning to dislike
long motorway journeys and think of a trip to Hampshire as a
journey too far. I have not returned to the Test but I cannot keep
away from the Rea, especially at mayfly time. I was there again
the year after my first efforts with the mayfly. I came about a
week later, early in June. I did not arrive until lunchtime on
my first day, which meant that, after looking over Duddlewick
Bridge and seeing that a few mayflies were already fluttering off
the stream, I ate a sandwich (the pork pies would replace them
on subsequent days after a trip to Mr. Griffiths in Ludlow) and,
of course, I drank two glasses of red wine, taking it slowly and
telling myself that I had the whole afternoon ahead of me for
fishing and catching a trout or two.

My first sight of the river, brown and hazy and moving out
ever so slowly from the bridge's single arch into the middle of
the broad pool where my fishing would probably begin, had
produced in me the usual response: a momentary feeling of
surprise, when I compared this sight with the bright and lively
waters where I spent most of my fishing days, that I was looking
at what, in spite of appearances, was most certainly a trout
stream, and a good one too, supporting a healthy stock of wild
brown trout, although I knew that there would undoubtedly

be even more of them if the river were fenced off and cattle kept away from the banks and from the water. Anyway, there are plenty of trout in the Rea and, as I sat in the Land Rover drinking my wine unhurriedly, I was enjoying the prospect of a long afternoon spent in search of just a few of them.

My search was successful and the three days that followed this first one all put trout in my net. It was my first sustained experience of mayfly fishing and it was interesting and instructive as well as very enjoyable. There was a decent hatch every day and the trout responded, but most certainly not in an indiscriminate frenzy of greed. On the first two days they would not take an artificial mayfly, although at the beginning of the hatch they would swallow a nymph, a great big thing that brought with its use some pricks of guilt, but it was still pitched into the spots where I had noticed the swirl of a turning trout. Once the fish were feeding at (unless it was near) the surface they would ignore my shop-bought floaters or merely nudge them before turning away, but they often helped themselves to the yellow-bodied Klinkhåmer that had turned my day on the Test to final glory. I had for once come prepared, for I had tied myself half a dozen more of these flies and had kept them on the small side, thinking that this might in fact be an important element of their appeal. On the third and fourth days, anyway, they were still eager for the nymph when the hatch was just starting, and I, of course, was ready to swallow any misgivings and tie one to my leader's end, but they later rejected the Klinkhåmer and took my smaller mayfly patterns fairly confidently.

After a cold spring the mayfly was late that year in Shropshire and was just getting properly underway on the Rea, where the hatch apparently starts somewhat later than on most nearby streams. I guess the trout preferred the Klinkhåmer until they became re-accustomed to the size of the naturals, unless they were eating emergers on those first two days and only later turned their attention to the floating duns. Anyway, it was new to me and it was absorbing and another thing that I noticed was how fish that were rising eagerly one day would apparently ignore a procession of mayflies the next, and how I would find trout stuffing themselves in places where none had been rising the day before. I did not stay for the spinner fall, although I did fish on into the early evening one day, when they were just beginning to get onto the water and the trout were already beginning to move. I suspect that, if I had stayed on for the main event, the rise would have been spectacular, but I find now that, if I have fished though the day, my body has had enough of it come six or seven o'clock and, anyway, my daytime sport brought me more trout then enough. Four days produced 27 of them, some of them big by the standards of the Rea, where any trout of a pound or more is a notable fish. I had half a dozen trout on either side of a pound and a half and, yes, I still think that the Rea trout are probably the most beautiful that I have ever seen, with their red spots and their red-rimmed tails and their shining amber fins. The few I killed were also wonderful to eat.

Last year I also came to the Rea early in mayfly time; I fished for four days and of the 20 trout I caught, not a single one fell to a traditional mayfly pattern, although the fish were very clearly eating the naturals, both as emergers and sitting duns. My first two trout, both really good fish, took the smallish yellow Klinkhåmer but thereafter it was consistently ignored. I caught eight on a Royal Coachman, or rather almost a Royal Coachman because I dress my version with a wing from a couple of white CDC feathers rather than of deer hair. This makes the fly wonderfully visible in almost all conditions of light. I think, without being certain, that I had somewhere read how trout eating mayflies sometimes look with approval on a Royal Coachman; I think this is why I tied myself half a dozen of them, unless it was just my vulgar fondness for gaudy flies, in which case the trout showed a similar lack of good taste. Perhaps even more surprising was the success of my CDC Sedge, which brought me seven trout. Dry Simon caught one and another is recorded as caught and returned without mention of the fly that put him in my net.

It is February now, almost a year later, and already I am looking forward to the Rea in June. I may delay my visit until almost the middle of the month in the hope of finding the mayfly season at its peak, which would allow me to see how this affects the behaviour of the trout and their attitude to my flies. Late in life, anyway, I have become an enthusiast for mayfly fishing. This is partly because it draws me to the Rea and the very special fishing world that I find there. Another reason may possibly rouse disapproval, for this other reason is that mayfly fishing does not call for flies tied on hooks so small that you can barely see them. Smutting and midging trout may be the ultimate challenge for fishers and flytyers. It is a challenge I would be happy never to face, a challenge I usually dodge by trying to persuade smutting or midging trout to grab something bright and shiny or temptingly large. This works more often than you might think.

I like big flies; I like them because they are easier to fish with than midgets; if they are dry flies you can see them much better; whereas when they are sunk I think the take of a trout is generally easier to recognise. As long, moreover, as they provoke a proper take I think they hook and hold on to trout more stubbornly than those microscopic patterns tied on 20 size hooks and smaller. I acknowledge that rising to the challenge of the difficult, on those occasions when I manage to achieve it, is very satisfying, but I like big flies and they not infrequently make for easy fishing, which is one of the reasons why I have so quickly become so fond of the mayfly season.

In my experience it has not brought sport for duffers. It has brought interesting sport demanding an open mind in pattern choice but, given this flexible approach, catching trout has not been particularly difficult. And there is this to be said for the mayfly season: that once the fly is up you are more or less certain to find feeding trout.

Many fishers value the mayfly because it brings up really big trout that very rarely feed on the surface at other times of the season. The chance of a monster is not something that matters much to me. I don't really want to hook a five-pounder (mainly for fear of losing it), and I know that such an encounter is very unlikely on the Rea, although I do commend the mayfly for persuading more of the Rea's pounders to reveal themselves and I have enjoyed the few larger trout that it has put in my net: trout of about a pound and a half which, to my mind, are as big as any trout needs to be.

There is this too in favour of the mayfly: that its season brings with itself a sense of occasion; it is a grand event, a spectacle of nature and it happens, moreover, at such a wonderful time of the year, when the leaf is still fresh, when riverbanks are painted bright with many colours, when summer seems to stretch almost indefinitely ahead of us and when for a time the world seems young again. The mayfly has a lot going for it; I am a convert, a devotee and my season would now seem diminished without it but it does, I think, have this serious failing: that it does not hatch in any numbers on my beloved Wharfe. Without this blemish I should love the mayfly and its season even more, although I should happily surrender my precious mayfly days and all the trout that they give me if, in return for this sacrifice, I could go to the Wharfe and find there the hatches of small fly that I found when I first fished the river so many years ago: huge eruptions of iron blues lasting three or four hours, blue wings in unimaginable abundance beginning at noon and still streaming off the river when I finished fishing in the evening, pale wateries hatching in teeming profusion throughout long afternoons. I had almost forgotten the spring olives and the olive uprights and how, between them, the smaller day flies used to give sport throughout the season and how those huge hatches of former years were themselves great occasions, albeit less obvious than the show provided by the mayfly which, after all, lasts for little more than a fortnight or three weeks. Yes, I have come to love fishing the mayfly on the Rea, but a big hatch of iron blues on the Wharfe at the end of May, or somewhat later a hatch of blue wings such as I witnessed regularly when I was still young: these it seems to me provided sport that outshone the best that the mayfly has to offer and I should love to find them once again a feature of whatever remains of my fishing life. They would put trout in my bag and they would also tell me that my river was pure and healthy again: a message that would make me feel very happy indeed.

Chapter Four

HIGH SUMMER
Six days on the Wharfe with some
reflections on the brace

In the second half of June a couple of seasons ago I fished the
highest beat of the Wharfe on three consecutive days and
then shortly afterwards I repeated the performance, except that
this time I did it down on the main beats on either side of Spout
Dub. They were days full of the special beauties of high summer;
at the same time they were days spared the high summer excesses
of savage sunshine and searing heat. None of them brought huge
numbers of trout but they all brought more than enough for
contentment; I thought that between them they gave me the
best of summer fishing and I should like to share them with
you, along with some thoughts on my obsession with the brace
and some reflections on the spirit of place and how, although I
love fishing up at Yockenthwaite and Deepdale and think that
the Wharfe there is at its most beautiful, I find some special

quality of experience in a fishing day spent in the vicinity of Spout Dub, something that I find nowhere else on any other river and nowhere else on that wonderful portion of the Wharfe that it is my high privilege to fish.

16 June

This afternoon I fished at Deepdale for the third day in succession. All three afternoons have been productive; in fact all three of them brought me eight trout and on all three I came home with the essential brace, although I have been wondering recently if I could try to rid myself of this burden, this conviction that a fishing day without a brace of dead trout to show for it has been an unsuccessful sort of fishing day. To catch one good trout, and perhaps return a few smaller ones, should surely be enough. I can remember days in my early years as a fisher when a single trout made the whole day glorious, but now a day that sends me home with only a single trout is a day clouded by disappointment.

On Friday, anyway, the first of these afternoons, I drove over to the Wharfe after spending most of the morning fiddling round on my shoot and exercising the dogs. It was a pleasant afternoon, with a sky of high grey cloud and a gentle breeze; it was a soft summer afternoon but there had been lots of rain over recent days and I thought the water looked too big and boisterous for much hope of sport. The flow was certainly exuberant, with the water pushing impatiently through the pools, cascading over shelves of yellow rock and rushing down narrow channels carved into the limestone. There were rocking sheets and rafts of foam in every eddy, and the voice of the river was loud between the steep and narrow sides of the valley; and yet, although high and hurrying, the water was clearly fining down and was already glowing from the peat. And, as it happens, the fish were moving.

I had soon spotted a rising trout or two and the CDC Sedge, which seems to be replacing Dry Simon as my first choice dry fly unless the conditions very obviously demand something else, the CDC Sedge had soon caught me a trout on the right side of a pound, meaning that in ten minutes or so I was already halfway to the brace. I did not even make a show, by the way, of pretending to myself that one good trout was enough for satisfaction. I knew that I needed two and my second trout was a long time coming.

There were plucks and pulls in every pool; there were frequent changes of fly but I could not find a pattern, wet or dry, that would produce a fair proportion of firm takes. You get days of this sort, most often I think when the water is on the high side, days when the fish seem to come at your flies without conviction, seem merely to toy with them and I am not sure we fishers can do much about it because I suspect the trouble lies with the trout rather than with us. I think they are not really hungry. Anyway, now and then a trout stuck, and the air was soft and the cloud had thinned and gave glimpses of the sun; and the breeze was upstream and the river was talking away in the language of running water, which is always wonderful to hear even if you cannot always understand it. Altogether it was a good afternoon to be high up towards the beginning of the Wharfe and I did make one or two feeble efforts to persuade myself that putting a brace in my bag didn't really matter, that there was virtually no difference between catching and returning a nine inch trout and knocking a ten-incher on the head. They were feeble efforts and I knew all the time that I was telling myself a lie.

I fished my way to the river's first pool, a restless feature no bigger than a bath tub, where I caught another eight-incher. Wandering downstream I investigated one or two likely spots a second time as I came to them, but they did not put a second trout in my bag. The calmness all round me softened my dissatisfaction but it was still there, I still felt that there was something important missing from my afternoon on the river. Early evening brought me to the pool where the pounder had been caught. I think I was fishing Simple Simon and the

Coachman and a trout splashed at one or other of them without taking hold. On impulse I knotted Simon Green to the point, spotted a rise and cast him onto the stream just above it. A minute or so later I had caught and killed a trout of roughly twelve ounces, which made the brace and mattered a lot more to me than perhaps it should have done.

I was happy to finish now, because now that there was a brace in my bag, the six smaller trout that I had returned no longer seemed a disappointment, but rather complemented the satisfaction that those two bigger trout had brought me. I walked down to Deepdale Bridge, took down my gear and stowed it in the Land Rover and then stood on the bridge for a few minutes, looking at the river as it poured in channelled spouts over white and yellow limestone shelves and foamed over rocks and ran darkly through the pools. The breeze had gone and the sky had clouded over again, bringing the deep sense of stillness that often gathers on the quiet grey air of a windless summer evening. Not a leaf stirred on the ashes by the bridge and the voice of the river spoke into the stillness without disturbing it any more than the small sounds of the birds among the branches.

I think I felt the strength and pressure of this evening peace more powerfully because the brace had been so late coming, because I had finally found my fisher's fulfilment and my fisher's peace little more than twenty minutes ago; it was a combination, a concurrence that brought me to the edge of tears and, if they had come, it would have been a very gentle flow; it would in fact have been the overflow of my thankfulness and my love. More and more often days on the Wharfe end like this for me. It is, as you already know, the best of all the river's gifts: a gift that I think can only come from a relationship stretching back through many years. I drove home over the hills in a state of almost perfect contentment.

*****

One o'clock on Saturday found me sitting by the river above Deepdale slowly reducing the contents of a metal beaker filled with red wine. I had yet to start fishing because I had spent the morning doing other things. These days I often choose an afternoon start, partly because I think that, except in prolonged periods of heat and low water, trout generally rise better in the afternoon, but also because I like to fish on into the early evening, hoping for the same early evening stillness that had blessed the end of my fishing on Friday. I could of course fish all day and then some way into the evening, but undoubtedly I tire more quickly than in the past and I also prefer not to leave the dogs unattended for too long. Five or so hours on the river is now about enough for me.

Anyway, it was one o'clock and I was sitting by the river drinking wine and wondering all over again whether it might be possible for me to unlearn the necessity of the brace, half convinced that it had become a millstone round my fisher's neck. I thought of yesterday afternoon and how, although it was far from being a red-letter day, it brought trout at regular intervals, how it was quiet and beautiful with a delightful sense of summer ease and summer comfort, but how contentment only came right at the end of my fishing with the coming of the brace. Would my contentment not have been deeper if it had begun with my first trout and settled further and further into me through the whole course of the afternoon?

I realised that, oddly enough, blank days do not bother me quite as much as days of just one trout. Days that have brought nothing or just a few midgets are most certainly disappointing but those one-trout days, perhaps perversely, distress me more. I think this is because, once my first trout is in the bag, immediately anxiety grips me with the fear that he will not be joined by another and that I shall therefore go home feeling cheated of a success that was already half mine. I find partial success somehow more frustrating than complete failure.

It is worst of all, of course, when the brace is almost achieved, when what would have made the second half of it drops off the hook or breaks me just when I am beginning to think it mine. What hurts, of course, when something like this happens, what hurts and leaves a mental scar that is often slow to mend is the feeling that satisfaction was so nearly won but was then so suddenly snatched away. Sitting there by the river with my second beakerful of wine it seemed obvious that I should enjoy my fishing much more if I could count every trout a blessing, however big or small, and if I could go home with no trout in my bag but happy with the memory of half a dozen small trout returned, or leave the river content with just a singleton to take away with me, in both cases telling myself that by catching trout I had done what a trout fisher sets out to do.

The importance of the brace brings a degree of strain to a fishing day, with relaxation impossible until it has been secured. Sitting there by the river with my beaker now only half full I half believed I could change and abandon the surely false belief that whenever a fishing day ends without a brace of dead trout in my bag it has by definition been a failure. I had friends, better fishers than me, who were perfectly content with a day that brought them only a single notable fish or a day when they had caught lots of small ones. Surely I could do the same? Telling myself that I should try my best to do just this, I finished my wine, tackled up and went fishing.

Very soon I had caught a trout easily big enough to knock on the head. Smaller fish followed and I could not help feeling disappointed each time I realised that they were just too small to kill. Yes, I admired their beauty, their streamlined gracefulness of form, the exquisite delicacy of their tails and fins, their patchwork pattern of red and black spots. They were perfection in miniature but at the same time I could not help wishing they were just a little bit longer. If I could have stretched one or two of them just half an inch they could have gone in the bag and undoubtedly they would have made me a more contented fisher. I told myself that changing an ingrained set of the mind was bound to take time.

It was an afternoon of heavy showers and there was often a sky of dramatic contrasts, with huge banks or towers of black cloud in billowing advance or slow retreat, with shrinking or expanding lakes of blue and with ever changing light. The background of climbing fields and forestry beyond was sometimes veiled by sweeping grey sheets of rain and sometimes shone with the radiant sharpness of definition that comes with bright sunshine after rain. And the river shone grey and white under the clouds and with a dark, glowing lustre beneath the sun. I like days of sunshine and showers; I like their variety and above all I like the extraordinary beauty of landscape in the marvellous brightness of rain-washed light. The trouble with Saturday's showers was that each one of them threatened to raise and discolour the river and so put an end to my sport, in which case I should at least try to drive home feeling satisfied with a twelve inch trout in my bag and the memory of five or six returned.

There were, by the way, a few mayflies coming off. There had been some the day before but I forgot to mention them. Although the Wharfe has always produced a few mayflies, I have never seen one eaten by a trout, not at least until yesterday when I came to the bottom pool of Greenfield Beck at Beckermonds, where I watched a large yellow dun sailing down the stream but could suddenly watch it no longer because a trout had pounced and gobbled it up. I did not put on a mayfly but I caught the trout; he was too small to kill but this did not matter because the brace had come ten minutes earlier in the form of a fat and beautiful trout at least eleven inches long. Almost in the act of writing this I have realised how, in doing so, I seem to have forgotten my resolution to make some sort of effort to put the cardinal importance of the brace behind me. I fear that progress may be slow and, since I did come home with a brace yesterday, it was not possible to put my feelings to the test, trying to find contentment in a bag of just a single trout. I came home early, incidentally, because almost as soon as that mayfly-eating trout had been returned to its pool, the river did come up and soon turned brown, bringing the early end to my fishing I had feared.

*****

The water today, the third of my consecutive days at Deepdale, was as near perfect as could be, flowing with a shining and restrained vigour that seemed to hold out the prospect of trout. My drive to the river had been unusually beautiful. It had been made in bright sunshine, which had shone down on two of summer's undoubted glories, on roadside verges covered with white and faintly stirring spreads of ox-eye daisies and on hedges widely scattered with pendant sprays of white and pink wild roses. I think the dog rose is of all flowers my favourite, hanging there with such careless, unfussy and delicate grace. Anyway, now I was sitting by the river and all round me in the grass was much shyer, much smaller beauty: blue speedwell, blue butterwort and milkwort, white eyebright and white bedstraw, yellow tormentil. Above me was the massive and mobile beauty of the sky, where huge white and grey clouds were marching slowly through the blue and almost at my feet was the matchless beauty of the river Wharfe, its voice telling me, whenever I bothered to listen, that it felt in the mood to give me a few more of its wonderful trout. My two metal beakerfuls of red wine tasted as good as they ever do; they tasted of summer on the edge of flowing water with the hope of trout to come.

Once again I caught a good trout almost as soon as I started, this one a twelve-incher caught on the CDC Sedge, which then seemed to lose its appeal. Dry Simon took over and the pattern of the two previous days was repeated with a succession of trout that were too small to join the trout already in my bag. I admired them and almost persuaded myself that it did not matter that all four of them had been undersized. I came to a bowl-shaped pool which the river enters through a narrow channel delved in the rock before running fast and broken hard against the bank. To the right of an upstream fisher quieter, smoother water extends to the curving line of sycamores along the far bank. The trout lie mostly on the edge of the turbulence and there are good ones among them. Once again a few mayflies were hatching. I saw none taken and there were no rises to anything else. Something told me to search the water with a mayfly nymph. I had almost finished my search and was thinking that this something had given me pretty lousy advice when the line jerked forward and a trout was fighting hard. He weighed perhaps two ounces over the pound, which is a good trout up above Deepdale. It is a good trout anywhere and it was impossible for me to deny that I was happier with two trout in my bag than just one. My re-education, I again realised, was going to take time. Anyway, I fished on for at least another hour, although my day now felt already complete. There were a couple more trout and one of them was certainly big enough to kill but we are only allowed two on the unstocked beats, a rule of which incidentally I thoroughly approve.

The breeze had been light all afternoon; by six o'clock it had dropped away almost completely and the early evening peace was bright beneath the sky. The light over the hills, as I drove home, was very gentle, smoothing out the hollows and wrinkles of the land, so that the rough fells looked as soft as velvet. I asked myself how often I must have driven down the steep road from Cam Fell on my way back from a day's fishing and, in asking myself a question that I knew I could not answer, I was seized by a sudden and unexpected longing to be young again and to be driving down the road to Gayle for the first time ever on my return from the Wharfe. It was not the preoccupations, the attitudes, the easy pleasures, the careless exuberance of youth that I wanted and, although it would be good to be given back some at least of the resilience of a young body, it was not this either. It was the broad prospect of the young that I so envied. I wanted to be able to tell myself that there were thirty or forty years ahead of me for fishing the Wharfe; I wanted to have time to catch all the trout I had already caught all over again; I wanted to do this and at the same time believe that there were perhaps twice or three or four times as many trout still ahead of me as were already behind me. Simultaneous with this brief but intense longing was the recognition that its realisation was, of course, impossible, which in turn brought a fresh determination: that in whatever time for fishing remained to me I should look on every single trout that came my way as a wonder and a blessing and feel deeply thankful for every day that I spent on the Wharfe or any of my rivers, even a day that sent me home without a brace of trout in my bag. I thought that progress had been made.

23 June

Friday was Midsummer's Day; it was midsummer weather as well, with warm sunshine and light winds and it was also the first of another three consecutive afternoons on the Wharfe, spent this time on either side of Spout Dub down below Kettlewell rather than way up the dale on the river between Deepdale and Beckermonds. On the way to my fishing I admired the daisies and dog roses again, deciding that I had never seen them more abundant or more beautiful. Farmers, seizing the opportunity of settled weather, were busy making silage. I drove past pale yellow fields already shorn and cleared, past fields strewn all over with cut and drying grass. There were fields patterned like corduroy with swath; there were fields dotted with big green bales waiting to be wrapped in black plastic and there were fields where machines were doing just this; and there were tractors rumbling along the road with high, swaying trailers full of grass and there were fields where the mowing machines were at work and my Land Rover was full of the sweet midsummer smell of it all.

The traditional hay meadows near Hawes and at the top of Wharfedale, which like my own meadow will not be mown for more than a fortnight, were at least half a dozen faintly stirring colours. As well as green grass there was the yellow of buttercups and the red of campions and sorrel, there were white daisies, there was red and white clover and in some meadows there were pink patches of bistort and pink splashes of ragged robin. It was all very lovely; and Spout Dub, when I got there just after noon and had settled down on my shelf with a beakerful of red wine, looked, to my admittedly partial eyes, even lovelier. The river was full and very dark from the peat, glowing with a touch almost of deep crimson or purple. Up at Deepdale the water had looked so beguiling that I had been tempted to stop, but after three recent days there the pull of Spout Dub, now unvisited for almost a fortnight, had been too strong to resist and so here I was, and I was glad to be here, looking at the keys that were already forming on the sycamores, looking at the dark flow of the river through the pool below me and the brightness of the sun on its surface, listening to the nervous calls of the sandpipers and the wagtails. There were occasional bursts of loud and rapid song from a wren somewhere on Spout Dub's cliff and there were swifts racing and screaming through the blue sky.

When I had finished the second beakerful there was the usual feeling of disappointment that there was nothing left in the small bottle that had brought my wine to the river. I did what I normally do and stowed the bottle in the miniature cave at the downstream end of the shelf. I noticed that there were already a couple of empty bottles carelessly left there from earlier fishing days; they were bottles of standard size and would have been drunk with friends at lunchtime, probably some time last season. I determined to take them away with me at the end of the day and felt almost guilty for not removing them on the day they had been drunk, but at the same time they gave me an idea.

While drinking my wine I had thought, among other things, how I should like knowledge of my deep affection for Spout Dub to survive me, how I should like some sort of mark, some sign left behind there to remind posterity how much the pool and my shelf above the water had meant to me. The thought was a serious one, although I knew while thinking it that it would never lead to anything. It seemed unlikely to me that, after my death, the committee of the club would decide to place a bench on the shelf with my name and dates and the inevitable inscription: 'He loved this place.' It would never happen, which was a relief because the thought of a bench on my grassy shelf appalled me. It would be a desecration and I realised that I did not want – and would not get – a plaque screwed to the face of the cliff, informing future generations that the eminent fishing writer Laurence Catlow had often sat on the nearby grassy shelf and drunk a couple of beakers of red wine at lunchtime on his fishing days. The plaque was definitely out and I also thought a statue would be inappropriate and, as they say, somewhat over the top. Statues, anyway, seem to be out of fashion these days.

But those carelessly abandoned bottles pointed me towards a much humbler form of memento, one without any ostentation or pride, that I thought entirely appropriate to both the place and my affection for it; I should like an empty bottle of wine, perhaps two of them, to take up permanent residence in the furthest recesses of Spout Dub's miniature cave, as a modest memorial of a departed fisher who dearly loved Spout Dub and the Wharfe and loved drinking wine at lunchtime on his shelf above the water. It would be a tribute more to a place than a person. And then I remembered that my books would tell anyone who read them all about my feelings for Spout Dub, and, if my books could do this and give some pleasure to a few fishers after my death, this would I thought form my most fitting memorial. I still thought, by the way, that the two empty bottles were a good idea. And then I went fishing.

I started, of course, in Spout Dub, which gave me one small trout and a wet left leg for which I blamed a sagging wader top. I did admire the spotted beauty of this troutling before I slid him back into the water; I was glad that I had caught him but at the same time I knew that I should have been much gladder if he had been big enough to kill. Sport was slow. I fished my way to Black Keld, searching the long pool there and the inflow of the beck and the lively run above it. Almost always there is a fish or two rising somewhere here but on Friday there was no sign of a trout and nothing touched my flies. The day was threatening to prove itself one of the sort with a full water when trout seem to be hugging the bottom or tucked in their lairs with no interest in either sunk or floating flies.

I came to another long pool which I call Two Barn Flats, where again it is very unusual not to find at least a few trout feeding, both in the slow glide under the sycamores and again in the long run at the head of the pool, a run that flows in the shadow of much taller and more stately sycamores. There was no sign of a rise anywhere. I was beginning to feel resigned to the prospect of an empty bag and was even beginning to wonder whether, with the river so quiet, it might be best to finish early. I told myself that I was not unduly bothered, which was almost true. I told myself that blank days are part of fishing and that the good days would be nothing like as satisfying without just a few fishless ones. I told myself these half-comforting truisms and I more or less believed them. I left the glide unfished and searched the run with the CDC Sedge, hoping that it would provoke a trout into eating it. Almost at the top of the run it did. I guessed his weight at one and a half pounds and suddenly there was no more thought of an early finish and I made not even a token effort to resist the violent brace-fever that, with the capture and killing of this trout, immediately took hold of me.

I now realised, as I walked back to Spout Dub and then further downstream to the Willow Run, that my feeble efforts to overcome this obsession with the brace were at an end. It was quite simply an essential part of my personality as a fisher and it now seemed good to me that fulfilment could not come with the capture of a single fish, because the tension of waiting to secure that second trout, and sometimes being denied it, made its achievement so much sweeter, made the fulfilment so much more fulfilling. I could not remember the initial cause of this central feature of my fishing life or whether it had appeared suddenly or taken only gradual possession of my fisher's mind. I could not remember how far it went back, although I knew it had been with me for a long time, certainly for thirty years. I also knew that it was now ineradicable and I was glad that it was so and determined that there would be no more attempts to cure myself of something that brought occasional disappointment but much more frequent satisfaction and peace. Marching purposefully down to the Willow Run, I was very hungry for the brace.

The Willow Run gave me an eight-incher. Yes, I thought how beautiful he looked but I also thought that he was at least two inches short of bringing contentment. I did not even pretend to find satisfaction in his capture. He was a disappointment, because he had risen and I had set the hook and felt his first pull; I had felt all the excitement of connection and then the almost immediate deflation of realising that he would be too small to kill. I came to the Sycamore Glide below Mile House, where I saw a trout rise in a tricky spot under the far bank: a spot where low-hanging branches threatened to claim any fisher's flies rash enough to attempt passage between them. I managed the throw rather neatly for once, my sedge was taken immediately and for a second or perhaps only part of one I felt the thrilling pull of an undoubtedly big trout, until the fly came back to me and the trout, of course, was gone.

This is the worst way not to catch the second half of your brace: to rise and hook it, to know at once that it is more than big enough and simultaneously to know that the line is loose and the contact has gone, although perhaps, on reflection, worse still is to lose contact when the victory seems all but won and the net is ready to lift the fish triumphantly out of the river and onto the bank, where you would have laid it next to your first trout before feasting on their beauty and feeling ridiculously happy. Anyway, that brief contact left me brooding morosely on what had been denied me. I fished on somewhat mechanically, more or less convinced that my chance of the brace had gone. You can sometimes watch a dozen or more trout rising busily along the Sycamore Glide, all of them big fish. This time my pricked fish was the only riser that I had spotted. I began to search the run that flows into the glide, more or less certain that my chance of contentment was gone, and then, glory be, the sedge disappeared and a good trout was fighting hard and every second of the fight was a torment to me; but he stayed for the net and he weighed well over the pound, was most certainly a wild fish and, in making the brace, brought me the contentment for which I had been searching all afternoon.

I caught and returned a small trout in Mile House Dub and another in Spout Dub and you know how it is: because there were two trout in my bag I could admire their beauty and thank the river for the gift of them and return the gift with no disappointment or regret. And then I sat for ten minutes at Spout Dub with the thoughts and feelings that come to me on my shelf above the water at the end of a successful fishing day, until it was time to put those empty bottles together with the brace in my bag and drive home serenely over the midsummer hills, where beds of white cotton grass were bright in the evening light; and, because of the two trout in my bag, the hay meadows in Wensleydale and the spreads of daisies and the wild roses along all the hedges looked twice as beautiful as when I had passed them in the morning. The farmers and their machines, by the way, were still busy with their grass and I thought, as I drove down Mallerstang, how temperate was my appetite for trout, given that I only needed two of them to feel that it was enough. I thanked God most sincerely for making me a fisher with such moderate needs and thanked him all over again when I had filled my glass with sherry and taken a few reverent sips.

*****

It was Spout Dub again on Saturday for wine and a sandwich before fishing through the afternoon. At eight in the evening I was drinking *fino* again and just the thought of how wonderful the day had been immediately had me on the point of crying into my glass. It had been the same most of the way home, except that, if the tears had come, there would have been no sherry to receive them. I think grown men are allowed to cry these days, which is, of course, something that they have always done. Anyway, I love fishing and I love the river Wharfe and when the river gives me a particularly wonderful day along her banks and when later I drive home over the hills full of quiet and grateful thoughts it seems entirely natural that this mood of serene thankfulness should sometimes provoke very gentle tears as the tribute of my love. I look on them as a blessing, but perhaps, in order to spare the feelings of all the strong and silent alpha-male fishers among you, I should try to stop banging on about them all the time. I make no promises.

I am not sure why Saturday was so wonderful. The river was quiet again with few rising fish. I killed three good trout of about a pound and a half, all on my CDC Sedge. They were good trout but they were in no way exceptional and there was nothing particularly notable in the process of their capture.

Beneath a broken sky with the slow alternation of shadow and sunshine, the river and its valley had both looked very beautiful. They usually do. The breeze had been light and upstream, which always makes my fishing more enjoyable. The prevailing wind at Kilnsey is upstream and a kind breeze has drifted through most of this season's fishing days. Yesterday afternoon was a fairly typical afternoon of fairly productive sport, but it produced an untypical – though by no means unusual – response.

*****

I fished again today, fishing the same stretch of water in very similar conditions with almost identical results, with another bag of three trout, two of them caught on yesterday's fly and one with Pritt's Little Black. There was very little to separate the two days but this evening I drove home over the bright hills in a contented and peaceful state of mind, thinking to myself how kind my beloved Wharfe had been to me once again, but without ever feeling the emotional pressure that finds its outlet in tears, and so the sherry that I am now drinking is in no danger of dilution and the keyboard of my laptop is very unlikely to need wiping dry, unless of course I manage to spill my glass all over it, which would be a criminal waste of sherry and might in fact produce a few tears.

It is interesting, at least it interests me, why two outwardly very similar days on the Wharfe have affected me so differently, why the first of them brought a flow of much deeper feeling. The answer is perhaps more straightforward than I was assuming and applies to most areas of our experience, where we find that the same things work on us differently on different occasions. One day a piece of music seems sublime; play it again the next day and it may sound pleasant enough but it refuses to possess you so completely. Food that one day tastes glorious may seem almost dull when you repeat the recipe again a week later. In the same way, although my latest two fishing days both brought pleasure and satisfaction, the first of them produced something deeper and more moving, and this deeper something surely came from me, came from some subtle difference of sensibility that accompanied me to the river, somehow connecting me more intimately to the river and the trout and the surrounding landscape, making me more sensitive, more susceptible to all the beauty that belongs to a fishing day. These days of deeper feeling and response happen more frequently now. Perhaps it is because I know that they cannot keep happening for too many years more.

Anyway, at about five this afternoon I was sitting on my shelf above Spout Dub, drinking a beaker, not of red wine, but of lukewarm tea from my flask. I had cleaned my trout and I was more or less ready to head home, but there was that now-customary reluctance to drag myself away from a place that I so love, especially since in tentative evening sunshine it looked even more lovely than usual. While sitting there I was suddenly visited by an idolatrous fancy, which turned my mind to a Wordsworth sonnet that I once knew by heart, unless perhaps it was the other way round and the sonnet had inspired the idolatry. The sonnet begins, anyway, with 'The world is too much with us', before the poet goes on (even back then) to condemn the rampant consumerism of his times and to lament man's growing alienation from nature. Sitting there drinking tea I could no longer recite the whole poem to myself but I could remember Wordsworth half wishing that he had been born a pagan and 'suckled in a creed outworn' so that he could have seen Proteus rising from the sea and could have heard old Triton blowing 'his wreathed horn.'

I mention this because, sitting there above Spout Dub, I felt a flow of agreement and sympathy with these sentiments. It wasn't that I suddenly found myself raging inwardly against the excesses of the consumer society or hating callous humankind for ravaging trout streams; it was rather that, sitting there by the Wharfe, I thought how I should rather enjoy being able to acknowledge the river's godhead and offer appropriate worship. I remembered how to the classical world rivers were ruled by horned gods who ruled the flow of their waters and lived in rocky chambers beneath their streams. It seemed to me that the Wharfe would be an exception, for the Wharfe would surely be the realm of a goddess, a very beautiful goddess, and nymphs (almost but not quite as lovely) would inhabit her tributary becks and acknowledge her sway. And I would erect an altar to the goddess, I might even proclaim myself her priest and I should most certainly bring her weekly offerings of smoked trout and bend low over the altar in reverent prayer and praise. And perhaps, just once or twice, I would catch fleeting glimpses of her as I sat by the river at the end of fishing days.

But here was the question; where would the altar stand? I thought of the first pool of the Wharfe up at Beckermonds and as soon as I thought of it I knew that it was wrong. I knew immediately that the goddess dwelt in a limestone cavern delved beneath the waters of Spout Dub and that her altar must be built where I was now sitting, on my shelf above the pool. I knew too that, if ever I did catch sight of the goddess, it would most certainly be at Spout Dub, probably as for just a second she raised her fair and gold-wreathed head from the waters of the pool.

It was all an absurd and entirely innocent fantasy but it made something important suddenly very clear to me. Recently I have been wondering whether the focus of my devotion to the Wharfe has moved upstream from Spout Dub and is now fixed upon the river between Deepdale and Beckermonds, with the river's very first, and very small but very lovely pool recognised as the most sacred moment in the river's whole course.

Now it is, as it happens, my belief that the Wharfe is at its most beautiful in the first few miles of its journey down the dale, where the young river and its narrow valley seem to belong so intimately to each other, where the bedrock shines at its brightest and most beguiling through the water hurrying on its way through a swift and continual succession of different features, pool and glide and fall and run, each one as lovely as the last, hurrying on its way between those steep meadows and those climbing pastures criss-crossed with their irregular pattern of dry stone walls. And somehow, up there on the high beats of the river you seem near to the sky; there is a brightness, a tonic openness of mood which finds its way into a fisher's heart and the air seems nimbler than it does below Buckden and Kettlewell and Kilnsey.

Down at Spout Dub the river and its surroundings are still very beautiful but there is some sense of separation; there is also a feeling of depth and some slight suggestion of confinement, there are times when the air hangs heavy and, although the river is in fact still flowing through its upper reaches, it has already slowed down, and, compared with the quicksilver grace of its flow up at Deepdale and Beckermonds, it is beginning to take its time. There is already a touch almost of solemnity to some reaches of the river round Spout Dub; there are long pools and glides and the secluded beauty of Spout Dub can still take my breath away. But I know that, if beauty were all that mattered to me, I should declare the river above Yockenthwaite dearer to my heart than Spout Dub and its neighbouring beats.

But there is more to the spirit of place than place itself; there is your presence in it, your connection to it, your sense of closeness and belonging, and this is why, in pursuing a frivolous line of thought about the goddess of the Wharfe and where to build her altar, I knew as soon as I had thought of the river's first pool that I had thought of the wrong place; it had to be Spout Dub because of what I find there and because the beats of the river that extend above and below it are the beats of the river where I first realised that I had fallen in love with a river and where in subsequent years I fished that river deep into my heart.

I was a Kilnsey member for at least ten years before I discovered that we had the fishing below Yockenthwaite and between Deepdale and Beckermonds, fishing that had for whole decades been completely neglected by Kilnsey members, discovering too, once I began to explore it, just how foolish that neglect had been.

I fished the main river between Watersmeet and Kettlewell hundreds of time before first I ever fished up at Yockenthwaite and Deepdale. Up there, moreover, the water drops away so quickly that there are long periods in a dry or even a normal summer when the river is unfishable. There have been more than a few seasons when I have fished the high river on less than a handful of days. There may even have been seasons when I have never fished there at all.

Anyway, for every time that I have fished up at Yockenthwaite and Deepdale I must have spent more than half a dozen days in the neighbourhood of Spout Dub and my long acquaintance with that place has made it very dear to me; it is an old friend of a place and its seclusion only deepens the sense of intimacy. Spout Dub has shared my life for more than fifty years. I have been there and sat above the water on days of strong emotion, finding comfort in sorrow or finding joy confirmed simply by being there. These have been important days, but perhaps the days when I have brought no special happiness or pain to the river have mattered even more, days when I have fished up from Watersmeet or walked back from Black Keld or Knipe Dub before resting for a time at Spout Dub, alone or with friends, eating a sandwich, drinking lukewarm tea or decadent and delicious red wine, looking at the water and thinking how lovely the place is and how lucky I am to be sitting there with a brace of trout in my bag and to be a fisher of the Wharfe. It is these hundreds of ordinary days that have built the bond and made Spout Dub, even though it is not the home of a goddess, the one place where I feel the effect of all that the Wharfe means to me most deeply and most gratefully and where, when it visits me, I feel the fisher's peace with a healing force that I find nowhere else.

If asked to confine my Kilnsey fishing to a single stretch I should choose the river between Watersmeet and Kettlewell and think of Spout Dub as its heart. It is a most marvellous piece of water, both in it varied beauty and in the quality of the sport that I often find there. And it is, quite simply, the stretch of the river where I feel most at home and which I most certainly love best. Fishing the top of the river is often wonderful. The days I spend there are special days because the river there is so often too low to fish. And I often find my days above Deepdale very moving in their beauty, in the fulfilment that they bring me and the peace that they inspire, but they cannot quite give me what I find at Spout Dub, where I seem to breathe in the distillation of all the feelings that I have ever brought to the river or found waiting for me along the banks, and these same feelings are somehow infused with all the brightness and beauty that the Wharfe has given me in the course of our long relationship; there is so much happiness, so much contentment, there is so much joy in beauty and sport and friends and love and life; inevitably there is also sorrow and pain and loss and there is guilt as well; there is all the sweet sadness of departed and irretrievable time and there is, of course, the common burden of mortality, which will some day take me away for ever from Spout Dub; but somehow, when I am sitting there on my shelf at the end of a fishing day that has brought me a few trout, somehow I can acknowledge the burden and find in doing so that it quietly lifts away while I sit there watching the water, leaving me in serene and thankful possession of the present with its supremely consoling gift of peace.

Inevitably the day will come that gives me my last trout of all. It would surely be best if I could catch it in the shadow of Spout Dub's cliff and if it could also make the brace. Failing this I hope that it comes from the next pool down, from Mile House

Dub or further upstream from Black Keld or Two Barn Flats or the Stepping Stones Pool. I also hope that it is far enough away for me to fish these places at least a few more times and to learn, if indeed it is possible, to love them even more.

Chapter Five

SEPARATION
AND REUNION

Weather matters to fishers; I suppose it matters to almost everyone, but it perhaps matters rather more to us fishers than to some others because it so profoundly affects our sport. Of all adverse conditions, roaring spate is, I think, the worst because, for flyfishers at least, it makes fishing impossible. But there is this to be said about the conditions that produce raging floods: that, even in periods of unsettled and sometimes violent weather when there are only relatively brief lulls between bouts of intemperate wind and rain, there is often a day here and there when a falling water can bring outstanding sport.

I much prefer wet and stormy summers to the settled sort when high pressure dominates for weeks on end, when day after day the sun beats down, when rivers shrink down to the level of their springs, reduced to a dusty trickle between the stones so that more rock than water glares back at the midday sun.

It is undoubtedly true that, until it turns stale, low water can produce absorbing fishing with sometimes surprising results. But there comes a point, if dry days turn into weeks and weeks without rain, there comes a point when the trout more or less refuse to look at our flies during daylight, when only late evening brings them out in search of food, in search of the duns that have delayed their appearance for the cool that comes with the sun's setting, eager too for the summer sedges that will keep them busy well into the darkness.

I have almost never fished at night and I no longer fish the evening rise. I am too much of a coward for night fishing. Mysterious noises in the black darkness fill me with misgiving and wading in the darkness fills me with dread. I used to fish in the evening often enough. Sometimes it produced trout and there is, of course, a very special beauty to calm summer evenings, particularly those that follow long hot days and come with the blessing of slanting light and cool air . I used to enjoy my evening fishing but – except occasionally in September – I no longer fish on into the evening or go out specifically in hope of the evening rise. Come six or seven o'clock I am usually feeling tired and old age, anyway, has turned me into a helpless creature of habit, which means that by the time the evening comes along I am ready to sit down with a glass or two of sherry before enjoying my dinner with a glass or two of red wine.

I now fish in the daytime or not at all, which can make a drought summer a frustrating experience, especially because the Wharfe, flowing over limestone, is quick to drop low. This means that it takes only a few rainless weeks, especially if the days are bright and hot, for the Kilnsey trout to become uncooperative during the heat of the day. Away from the Wharfe there are compensations in the form of the reservoir-fed Tees and the spring-fed Foston Beck, but a summer without the Wharfe at the heart of my fishing is a summer of deprivation because, as you know, trout from the Wharfe mean much more to me than trout from anywhere else. And, now that I am in my eighth decade, weeks on end without the Wharfe hurt me much more than in the past because I know now that my supply of Wharfedale summers will run out before too long.

Last summer was the sort of summer that I most dread: endless heat, weeks and weeks without rain with the Wharfe on its bones from June to September. It mattered somewhat less than it might have done, because the ravages of covid and the privations of the several lockdowns made the restored and unfettered freedom to fish seem a most marvellous gift, which of course it was. Yes, it mattered less than usual whether I was on the Wharfe or the Tees or down in Shropshire on the Rea; just to be by a trout stream with a rod in my hand and a trout or two in my bag was an inestimable blessing. I missed the Wharfe and in particular I missed the high beats up in Langstrothdale, but I missed the Wharfe much more a couple of years earlier when, once the drought had really taken hold, I paid not a single visit to my favourite river for more than six weeks.

It was a summer that saw the Wharfe, from May until deep into August, consistently lower than she had been for at least twenty years. For week after week the becks that make the river were given barely a drop of water beyond what came in a couple of torrential bursts that fell very briefly on the top of the catchment and brought small and transient rises of dirty, peat-clogged water. There was one such early in June and I fished at Kilnsey two days later, where I found the river already back down on its bones with no more than a lingering trace of all that peat. I did not expect much sport. After booking my beat I sat in the Tennant Arms, where members used to gather for a while before going off to the river in search of trout. Nowadays we gather somewhere else but, on this particular day I sat in the Tennant Arms with a cup of coffee listening to unremittingly gloomy talk: talk of hard days and hot days, of days on end without any rain and – much worse – days on end without any trout. And when at last I was told a brief downpour had come, it had at first left the river too dirty to fish and now, just a day later, the river was once again no more than creeping on its way. I had, as it happened, fished one of the lower beats four days earlier and managed a decent brace; even so, sitting there in the Tennant Arms surrounded by all this despondency, I could not help wondering if I should have done better doing something other than fishing, working on the shoot or going walking in the hills or perhaps even cleaning up my back yard.

The truth is, of course, that I had come to fish the Wharfe because I could not help myself; I had come to fish the Wharfe because it seemed to me, as so often it does, that the river was almost demanding my presence on her banks. And so there I was on a Tuesday morning early in June, sitting in the Tennant Arms drinking coffee and being assured by two or three members that there was no prospect for any fisher, however accomplished he might be, of catching any trout. They were not even going fishing but, living in the village, they had popped into the pub to demoralise any members foolish enough to be entertaining any hopes of sport. They did a pretty good job.

Three or four hours later I was no longer sitting in the Tennant Arms. I was sitting in a much lovelier place, sitting in the partial shade of a leaning sycamore on my grassy shelf above Spout Dub, sitting there drinking red wine rather than coffee and telling myself that the members in the pub had got it just about right. There were no trout in my bag and it had never seemed likely that there would be. It is true that I had caught one of five or so inches and I had come across a couple of much bigger trout eating something tiny in the shade of the trees, where my little floaters and my little damp or indisputably wet flies had been completely ignored. The wine was a comfort, making the prospect of a blank seem somewhat easier to bear. My wine promised to be the highlight of the day. While drinking it, I remembered how, twenty years ago, I should not have needed, at the end of a hot and troutless morning with the river so shrunk and so thirsty, to consider my strategy for the afternoon, because twenty years ago, whenever the Wharfe was down on its bones, I came to Kilnsey armed with a bag of worms and, if the fly failed in the morning, the worms came into service once lunch was over and it was time for fishing to resume.

For a few seasons I enjoyed fishing the upstream worm, which is undoubtedly a deadly method in a shrunken river flowing, or at least trying to flow, beneath a savage sun. In spite of this I renounced its use because I came to believe that flyfishing is the only truly satisfying way of catching trout. The upstream worm demands no little skill and still more rivercraft; but flyfishing demands much more skill and much more knowledge and is altogether much more involving; it asks a fisher to observe and interpret the behaviour of the trout and it is so much more beautiful than fishing the worm that I finally decided it was all I wanted to do.

And so I was now sitting there on my shelf with my beaker of wine and without a bag of worms, even though the (recently revised) rules of the Kilnsey Angling Club, perhaps surprisingly, still allowed members to fish the upstream worm in low summer water. I remember, between sips of wine, asking myself what would happen if the drought continued right through the summer. Would I finally be driven to desperate measures, bringing my long rod out of retirement and declaring myself a born-again wormer? I insisted that this would never happen, that my worming days were over for good and I began to wonder how to set about catching a trout or two in the afternoon.

In the morning I had been fishing with small flies down to something like size 20. I wondered if their failure had been because they were not small enough. They were, anyway, the smallest flies in my boxes, which persuaded me as I sat there above Spout Dub, to try a very different approach in the afternoon, for I decided to start my afternoon with a much bigger fly in the form of Simon Green, who, you may remember, is a close relative of Dry Simon, differing from the latter only in the matter of his tail which is fashioned from green strands of Shimmer and Shine rather than gold Krystal Flash. The plan was to fish my fairly large, very fancy and arguably repulsive fly through the pool heads, where there was still in places a passable imitation of running water, in the hope that he might shock a trout or two into eating or attacking him.

I took the wine slowly, because the day was hot and it was lovely sitting there on my shelf with what was left of the Wharfe slipping very quietly on its gentle way a few feet below me. I may have dozed off for a few minutes, unless perhaps it was more like an hour, before I roused myself, walked down from Spout Dub for about five minutes and started fishing again, exploring a much-diminished neck of fast water through the medium of Simon Green. And then it happened: after six or seven casts Simon Green disappeared and very soon I had drawn over the net a wild trout of almost a pound. I fished the moving water right at the top of Mile House Dub without success before returning to Spout Dub and fishing the remains of the run below the inflow very carefully. I searched every inch of fast or broken water and was just beginning to think that Spout Dub was for once – and almost certainly unwillingly – going to let me down, when Simon Green repeated his disappearing act and in due course brought to my net another wild trout a few ounces heavier than the first. You know that a brace of trout always makes me a happy man. This particular brace – two indisputably wild trout drawn from the trickling remains of the river Wharfe – made me very happy indeed.

Walking upstream I came to Black Keld, where the beck that flows in on the corner was much smaller than usual, with the slide of its motion so slow that it was barely perceptible, but there were fish rising here, three or four of them, clearly taking something very small indeed, but as soon as Simon Green had settled into the rings made by the lowest of these trout, he was taken and I had soon released a trout of something like twelve ounces. Simon Green next settled on the weary creep of water below the trailing willows just upstream from the beck's entry. He brought me another trout of almost identical size and appearance. And then he put two more trout in my net and they were all wild fish with perfect fins and tails and they pleased me inordinately. They were so beautiful and so unexpected.

In more normal conditions the run above Black Keld is a lively affair; not so on this occasion; it was more like a shallow trickle than a run but there were trout rising along what was left of it and, although some of them nosed at Simon Green or splashed at him, none wanted to take a firm hold. I should have changed him for something much, much smaller, but I only thought of this on the way home and, as soon as I thought of it, I felt certain that one or other of them would have worked and so I determined to give them the opportunity to prove themselves on my next Kilnsey day.

Three days later I was back on the Wharfe. There had been no rain and the river was even lower. There was the same litany of despair in the Tennant Arms. I came to Spout Dub when it was almost time for lunch. I came there fishless. I had seen very few rising fish and they had disdained my F-flies and IOBOS and the little black things that are my usual choice for sipping trout in a thin river. Dry Simon and Simon Green had failed to bring up any trout in the remains of fast water. I wondered whether they were perhaps developing the rudiments of good taste and I was also beginning to wonder again whether the prophets of gloom in the Tennant Arms had perhaps got something of a point. Anyway, I could see the splashes of one or two rising trout right at the head of the pool. Simon Green was already attached to the end of my leader and, being a lazy fisher, I was tempted to leave him there. He had, after all, done the trick the other day. I was tempted to give him a go but some unaccountable impulse drew my eye to a small deer hair sedge with a thickly palmered body and a twist of flat gold thread instead of a tail; it was a shop-bought fly given to me, I seemed to remember, by a friend one or two seasons past.

Twenty minutes later I was sitting on my shelf with a celebratory beaker in my hand and raising it repeatedly to my lips in honour of Merlin Unwin, the very friend that I felt certain had given me the little sedge a couple of years back together with half a dozen other flies. I declared Merlin the very best of friends and his little sedge the very best of flies, because in no time at all it had caught me four trout from the trickle at the top of Spout Dub, with two twelve-inchers big enough to kill and make my brace.

In the afternoon I forgot all about IOBOS and F-flies and searched likely spots with the little sedge, which caught me one more trout, a trout well over the pound that joined the brace already in my bag. I thought that the F-flies and IOBOS would probably come into their own on my next day on the Wharfe and at the same time, incidentally, I fell to wondering where all the stock fish had gone, for on all recent visits every fish that I had caught had been the river's own. I came up with no theory but, since I much prefer catching wild trout of ten inches to stock fish of two pounds, I declared myself well satisfied with this state of affairs. And then I remembered sitting by Spout Dub at lunchtime just a day or two ago and wondering whether adversity might drive me back to my long rod and a bag of worms. I realised that between them the little sedge and Simon Green had settled the question once and for all, by proving that there was no need.

A day or two later there was an afternoon on the Tees, which, thanks to the reservoir at its head, seemed like a raging torrent compared with the Wharfe and gave me a few trout. Then it was back on duty by the remains of my favourite river after first calling in at the Tennant Arms to drink a cup of coffee and at the same time drink in the accompanying dose of despondency and despair. The river was very weary indeed and, already at ten in the morning, the sun was hostile. I started in the shade of tall sycamores, in water that was still somehow managing to move, and in no more than ten minutes Simon Green had hooked and lost two fish, one of them big. And then, for the rest of the day, I fished dusty, trickling runs and shrunken pools that had more or less turned into stillwater, fishing beneath a merciless sun with no sign of rising trout. The Simons, Merlin's little sedge, my F-flies and IOBOS and my little black wet, dry and damp things all proved equally ineffective.

By lunchtime I had more or less abandoned any hope of a trout, although I fished on for a couple of hours in the afternoon because it seemed too early to go home. And all this time the hard, glaring light and the burning heat and the scorched brown fields were trying to persuade me that I was fishing in Greece or in Sicily rather than in the Yorkshire dales. If I had found myself sitting with fellow fishers in the bar of the Tennant Arms I should have been busy announcing that fishing was a complete waste of time, that anyone planning to head off for the river was a fool who was deceiving himself if he fancied he had any chance of catching even a single trout.

I fished into the afternoon but I gave up earlier than usual and drove away. Up at Yockenthwaite the water had disappeared completely for long stretches on either side of the road and, even where there was still a hint of wetness down there among the rocks and stones, there was so little of it that I found it difficult to believe that I was looking at a river. And it was now that I realised, almost guiltily, how I felt unwilling to fish the Wharfe again until she was flowing and full again. There was no thought of worming, because I did not want to go back to the river and see it so diminished, so shrunk and shrivelled, almost like a skeleton of the living river that I so loved. I did not want to return to the Wharfe until she had turned back into the wonderful river that flows through my imagination at all times, so bright and healthy and so beautiful. And for this to happen the weather would have to remember how to rain and then make up for lost time.

I did not go back to the Wharfe. I fished the Tees and caught trout. I fished the Foston Beck and caught more trout. I went down to Shropshire, where the Rea was still somehow managing to flow and gave me some surprisingly good trout. You will read about them in this book's final chapter. There was comfort in all this but, as the weeks passed without rain, apart from a few very brief and completely useless thunder showers, I came to realise that, for me, high summer without the Wharfe was somehow incomplete. It had happened before, but for some reason this time I felt the deprivation more sharply. Once back from Foston and Shropshire, anyway, I kept fishing the Tees and kept waiting, not very patiently, for my fishing life to be made whole again. It proved a long and weary wait.

*****

At the end of the second week of August I remember telling myself that I had not fished the Wharfe since the beginning of July; it was difficult to believe that six weeks of the trout season had passed without a single day on a river that had been at the heart of my fishing for almost fifty years. I have just told you how, on my way home from that last visit early in July I had sworn that I would not fish the Wharfe again until she was once again the bright and lively ribbon of beauty that I saw with the mind's eye whenever I thought of her. I did not realise just how long the separation was going to last and it was painful; I felt that something important, something central to my happiness was missing from my life. I wanted that something restored to me. I wanted it to rain.

Right at the end of July there was a brief rise of water while I was catching nothing in what was left of the Irfon and one or two other Welsh rivers, but by the time I returned home its influence had disappeared. Almost every morning during the trout season, while finishing the day's first cup of coffee after breakfast, I check river levels on the national website. Every morning in the first week of August I found that the Wharfe was almost as low as when I had last fished there, far too low for me to return. On the 10th of August there was a brief shower in Brough with talk of downpours elsewhere. When I looked online the next morning I found the Wharfe at the perfect level for the main Kilnsey beats. I had multiple commitments and fishing was impossible. There was heavy rain forecast overnight which would bring the river up in spate. On Monday I had to present myself at a speed awareness course. There seemed some chance of fishing the Wharfe on Tuesday and the forecast suggested that the river might be in good order and that the day itself would make for a pleasant fishing day.

I began to dream of favourite beats. If there was enough water then without doubt I should fish the very top of the river. I had only fished there once in the season, back in March when both the air and the water had been cold. I had not expected to catch fish and my expectations had not been confounded. The Wharfe is at its most beautiful in its beginnings and the trout that swim there, red-spotted and wild, complement the beauty of the river and of the steeply folded landscape through which it flows. If the Wharfe was full and glowing from the peat then I should head for those first pools and runs between Deepdale and Beckermonds. Less water would send me down the valley below Kettlewell to the river on either side of Spout Dub; there would be two glasses of red wine with lunch – there would, of course, be the same allowance up at Deepdale – and on either side of lunch I should search all those familiar and much-loved pools with my flies, feeling relieved and happy to see the Wharfe flowing full and bright again. And every time I caught a trout – if indeed any were caught – I should whisper my grateful thanks to the river for so wonderful a gift, telling myself – and, of course, the river – that something essential had at last been restored.

*****

When I checked on Sunday morning the Wharfe had dropped back a little. I went to feed my pheasant poults and found that my beck had barely stirred. I waited for the heavy showers that the weathermen were promising and in Brough there were none, but the Wharfe was up again on Monday morning. I spent my speed awareness course wondering whether the heavy showers beating on the roof were also falling on Cam Fell and the surrounding hills. Driving home, with the strictest regard for all speed limits, I noticed how rivers and streams were high and dirty. My computer had soon told me that the Wharfe was now a raging torrent. On Tuesday morning it told me a slightly more cheerful story: that the water was still high, but just fishable and dropping away steadily. Unable to fish on Wednesday or Thursday I now decided to spend the morning among my pheasant poults before driving to the top of the river to fish through the afternoon and into the early evening. As soon as this decision had been made I found that I was nervous; I had been dreaming of fishing the Wharfe again for six weeks. I had been telling myself how wonderful it would be to find myself back at Spout Dub or Yockenthwaite or Beckermonds; now it was going to happen and I was worried that failure and disappointment might poison all the joy of reunion.

At one o'clock you could have found me in my Land Rover, parked by the iron bridge at Deepdale and drinking a beaker of red wine before drinking another one, drinking Dutch courage before facing the innumerable uncertainties of sport. When we think about fishing, especially when we cannot be doing it, we tend to imagine ideal conditions; the water is just the right height and colour, while under a bright sky with a gentle movement of white clouds the breeze is drifting cooperatively upstream; the air is pleasantly warm and, of course, flies are hatching, the trout are busy eating them and we soon find the artificial guaranteed to put them in our net.

The scene revealed to me through the windows of my Land Rover did not match up to this fisher's dream, although the water was certainly fishable, flowing with a dark peaty glow, perhaps an inch or two above perfection, and it was, of course, wonderful to see the Wharfe so full and so lively again after those weeks when she had been more rock than water and been creeping on her way like some crippled, enfeebled thing. My side-window was half open and I could hear as well as see the river, hear a sound so different from the faint and thirsty whisper of July; it was a sort of improvised and exuberant celebration of health and strength restored.

The river was not far from ideal; not so the wind, which was gusting very inconsiderately downstream, bending leaves and branches to its force. It was also blowing grey sheets of drizzle over the fields and hills, while dark clouds sagged down over the fell tops. It was a dank and dreary scene and even inside the Land Rover it felt like autumn in August. Through my window I could see two or three pools and their connecting runs and nowhere could I see any signs of feeding trout. I lingered over my wine because it seemed that I was likely to struggle once I got round to going fishing.

However much you linger, two glasses of claret cannot last for ever, not at least if you are as keen on the stuff as this fisher, and so it was not too long before I was making my first cast onto the waters of the Wharfe for more than six weeks. I had not made many of them when a fish plucked at one of my flies, was felt and then felt no more; it was an omen of things to come and I suspect, by the way, that when rivers are on the high side trout are often prone to snatch and grab at flies without taking

a firm hold, especially when they are not feeding visibly. I tried
a variety of patterns both wet and dry and eventually decided
that my favourite combinations for a big coloured water – my
Coachman on the point and Simple Simon on the dropper –
had as much chance as anything of bringing a fish or two to net.

The wind blew but most of the time I managed to persuade
my flies into it and from time to time there were short periods
of relative calm. And now and then a trout was securely hooked.
The first such must have been at least four inches long and was
followed, after three or more frustrating tugs, by a monster of at
least six inches. I thanked the Wharfe for these gifts as I shook
them free in the water and wondered aloud whether she might
be generous enough to put a brace of ten-inchers in my bag,
telling the river at the same time that I should try to be content
with little trout if that was all she was able to give me. And, by
the way, I almost always talk to rivers when I am fishing them,
encouraging them to be generous, thanking them for the gift of
a trout and just sometimes asking them why they are feeling so
mean and so ungenerous. I don't think this admittedly strange
habit indicates serious mental instability, and by the way, I talk
to myself as well.

The wind, anyway, kept blowing and the trout kept plucking
at my flies; and then I hooked a better trout, thought he might
be breakfast and was disappointed to find that he was a bare nine
inches, a whole inch too small to kill. The wind kept blowing;
those sheets of drizzle kept sweeping over the fields and across
the fells. After a fashion I was enjoying myself, mainly because
it was such a relief to see the Wharfe so vigorous again; and if
those tugging trout were frustrating they also reassured me that
the top of the river had coped with the long drought and still
carried a decent head of fish. Once or twice there were brief
encounters with trout that felt bigger than eight or nine inches,
but I was more or less reconciled to an afternoon of midgets
and I kept telling myself that it was good just to be back on

the banks of the Wharfe with a fishing rod. And of course it was good, although it would undoubtedly have been better if I had already caught a couple of trout to take home with me. I determined to persevere, fishing my way through wind and wetness to the beginning of the river at Beckermonds.

I came to that round bowl of a rock pool. I searched the edges of fast water; there were two or three of those annoying tugs and I was wondering what flies I should try next when a lively fish took hold of the Coachman and stayed for the net. He was a whole twelve inches long and, after knocking him on the head, I admired his shape and his spots and his fins, wondering what he had found to eat in the rainless weeks to keep him in such good shape. Of course I thanked the river very sincerely for this gift, but not without begging her very earnestly to find a way of providing me with a second one of roughly the same size. A second such trout would make my return to the Wharfe everything that I had been hoping for. Ten minutes ago I had been resigned to disappointment. Now I was suddenly very hungry for the brace.

In the next pool I thought it was mine. I felt the pull of a trout and it was a strong pull; I saw the turning gleam of his belly and saw at the same time that he was a good trout; I thought that he was firmly hooked but even as I thought this, the line went slack and I told myself bitterly that my chance of the brace, and of the fulfilment that would come with it, had almost certainly just disappeared. Through the wind and the drizzle I fished on round the next corner – rather disconsolately – coming to a run where I have caught a decent fish or two over the years; there was another annoying pluck and then suddenly the line went tight and a trout leapt clear of the water, indisputably a good trout and shining silver through the gloom. Perhaps a minute later contentment flooded over me as the net lifted him from the river, complete contentment and deepest gratitude. The beauty of trout still strikes me as something miraculous, something for

the eyes to feast on with thankful wonder, and I believe that
trout of about twelve inches, trout approaching three quarters
of pound, are often even more beautiful than fish twice their
size and more. Lying there in the grass, bright beneath the dark
clouds, my brace looked incomparable, looked beautiful beyond
words; they were all that I wanted, they were the river's gift to a
returning pilgrim, telling him that all was well, that communion
had been restored, that he was welcome back and welcome to
return just as often as he chose.

The very last stage of my pilgrimage had soon brought me
to the union of Greenfield and Oughtershaw becks and the first
pool of the Wharfe. I did not catch another trout here, but after
making the day's last cast I sat happily on the bank, looking at
the little river with deep affection while my wadered legs, trailing
in the stream, were washed and cleansed by the murmuring
embrace of holy water. I thanked the river for becoming part of
my life again and for giving me a brace of trout. I told her that I
should return in three days and then I walked back to the Land
Rover and drove home. And the trout, by the way, tasted every
bit as beautiful as they looked and, yes, my life felt whole again.

Chapter Six

SEPTEMBER

September is undoubtedly my favourite fishing month, which may seem strange given that it is also the last month of the trout season, given that the first of October brings almost six months of separation from the Wharfe and its trout and from all my other rivers and from everything that I find along their bank. The thought of this imminent separation actually sharpens the delight of September days on the Wharfe, at the same time infusing them with a poignant sadness that is all their own and perhaps it is this September sadness, which even away from the river is an undeniable element of September's personality, that speaks so powerfully to the deep vein of melancholy that runs through me. I cannot listen to the wistful singing of September robins or to the restless twitter of those gathering swallows, I cannot look at the changing leaves and the dying flowers or mark the shortening days or breathe in the sharp morning air without thinking unavoidably conventional thoughts about change and decay, about transience and mortality. If you are a connoisseur of the bitter sweet, September is unquestionably the month for you. And still, bright days in September are very beautiful and somehow there is a fragility to their loveliness that I often find almost painfully moving.

But there is more to the month than its sadness. I think the main reason I like September so much is that it is a month of ambivalence, a month of fullness and fruition but also of fading, with the plenty of berry-laden trees and corn-filled granaries but with the sun declining, a sun that now shines on falling leaves, on dry and withered grasses and on only a few last flowers. And September calm seems calmer, quieter than the calm of any other month, but it also brings other days which the September wind spends tearing those dry leaves from the trees and whirling them through the unquiet air. September clings to summer but most certainly belongs to autumn. It is a month of celebration, of harvest festival, but it is a month of sorrow and regret because summer has almost gone and dark winter lies ahead.

September is a complex sort of month. Think of sunny days in the middle of May, of their brightness and unqualified optimism, of their assertive vitality and their irresistible impulse towards life and growth. There is a wonderful simplicity about the mood of spring. Autumn is more complicated and there is a richness to it that I find gently compelling, and autumn, of course, although it has been my favourite season for whole decades, speaks its message more powerfully to a man of seventy than it did to a man of twenty-one.

Even away from the river September is my favourite month. But the essence of the month is certainly experienced most intensely by running water, which flows with a complementary symbolism, especially when carrying a cargo of fallen leaves. I love September fishing very much indeed and I should like to share with you some September days from a couple of years back. Most of them find me on the Wharfe, but they begin on the banks of Foston Beck.

6 September

Yesterday evening I returned from four days' fishing in East Yorkshire. For some reason I feel tempted to tell their story backwards but I had better begin at about one o'clock in the afternoon on Monday 2nd, when I reached Lowthorpe Road Bridge, ate a sandwich sitting in the Land Rover and then drank the holiday half bottle with slow relish, relaxing from a journey of almost three hours and looking forward to rather more than three hours fishing on the beck.

Outside the Land Rover, September was looking sad and restless, with a sighing wind fortunately blowing straight upstream. I could see tall stacks of straw bales in the shorn stubble fields, which were the only places that looked tidy. The roadsides were full of confusion and decay, with half fallen and matted brown clumps of seeded meadowsweet, with withered brown thistle spikes and lanky patches of nettles, with rotting clusters of sweet cicely. There was fruit in the hedges, red hawthorn berries and rose hips and purple sloes, but they were hanging there among torn and withered leaves, between dead, dark flower heads. There was no brightness in the sky.

Sadness is part of September but this was the gloomier sort without the blessing of calm air and golden sunshine; this was dark melancholy and when, with my wine finished, I started fishing, it seemed likely that the mood of the day would seep into me.

I went upstream looking for trout and spotted none. I fished a favourite corner pool in the hope of bringing up a trout but there was no response. And then, on the next corner, I saw a fish over the chalk in a narrow run of open water between the weed. He was not rising but he was certainly on the fin and he ate my CDC sedge as soon as he saw it. He was a lovely wild fish just over the pound, he went in the bag and immediately he lifted my mood. Perhaps twenty yards further on I spotted a second trout. He too liked my fly; he too was wild and beautiful; he looked a couple of ounces heavier than my first trout and had soon joined him in my bag. The all-important brace had been secured in less than half an hour and my mood had forgotten all about September sadness. I now went back to the first corner pool and knotted on Dry Simon, which immediately took the fancy of a stock fish that had soon been knocked firmly on the head.

Returning to the bridge I set off downstream, crossed the railway line and walked down to yet another corner, where I would slide into the water and fish my way slowly back to the Land Rover. I was walking under grey clouds with a mournful wind moaning in the willows and alders along the bank; I was walking past dead and dying grasses, past withered flower heads on the edge of the stubble. I was walking through the weary remains of summer but I was walking all the while in a mood of quiet rejoicing. The message of September was all round me but, because there were three trout in my bag, I felt reconciled to its burden of mortality. I was a happy man and I acknowledged all over again that the thought of death loses almost all of its often sharp sting when I am walking by a river with a brace or a leash of trout in my bag.

I caught nothing below the railway bridge but just above it on my way back I saw a rise without being able to see the fish. A big trout lunged at Dry Simon when it floated over him, lunged and was missed unless he turned away without taking the fly. He lunged again when I had changed to a CDC Sedge and this time he was hooked, landed and killed: a stock fish not far short of two pounds. And so it was that I returned to the Land Rover with two brace of trout in my bag and then drove off to my friend Oliver's house in Pocklington, blithely untroubled by the inevitability of my own end. It is a wonderful blessing to be a fisherman. 'Man, I'm an angler', said Stoddart the lawyer when asked his occupation. So say I and I say it with deepest gratitude.

On the next day, Tuesday, I spent the morning right at the bottom of the club's water on a short stretch below Foston Road Bridge. It is a place where you fish from the berm with a high bank behind you, a bank where tall thistles and brambles and stalks of parsley and sweet cicely, even when brown and withered, lie in wait to grab your fly on the back cast. Across the beck willows stretch swaying and drooping branches out over the water; these too are eager to take hold of your sedge or your spider or your Dry Simon. Most of the fish down here are stock fish but getting your fly into the small pockets of water where they lie, playing them when hooked and then bringing them to net in the rush-choked margin of the narrow stream is a tricky business and demands no little skill.

I managed it three times on Tuesday morning and felt inordinately pleased with myself. I felt even more pleased because two of these trout, if not wild, were most certainly overwintered fish. Their fins and tails were almost perfect and their flesh, when I cleaned them before lunch, was salmon red. It is twice as satisfying to catch trout that look as trout should look rather than trout bearing the scars and imperfections of their early life in a confined and crowded rearing pond. Both these fish, anyway, were poised visibly between beds of weed; they were not rising but looked ready to feed. Both rose very slowly and absorbed my CDC Sedge very quietly before reacting to my deceit with commendable vigour. It was smash and grab when my third trout helped himself to the sedge in the open water just below the bridge. He was an obvious stock fish and he told me that it was time for lunch, time for a sandwich and a first beakerful of wine, as soon, that is, as I had driven a few miles upstream to the beat I wanted to fish in the afternoon.

The short journey was soon done. I had soon walked over a wooden footbridge always for some reason called Donkey Bridge and was sitting by the edge of the beck, eating a sandwich and taking the first sips (unless they were rather more than sips) of red wine. The sun was shining, which somehow made the wind, similar in force to the day before, seem a bright and lively rather than a mournful wind; the willows were streaming green and silver in the wind and the brightness of the sun and the restless sky drew my eyes to the brightness below them, drew them away from dullness and decay to the red glow of the hips and haws thick along the branches over the beck, to the loose white bells of convolvulus twining between the red fruit, to those quicksilver leaves on the willows and to the shining flow of the beck just below me. Yesterday September had told me gloomy things and the trout I caught had persuaded me that September was wrong. September had now changed its tune, because it was telling me that life was beautiful and good, while the trout in my bag – not to mention the beakerful of red wine – were confirming that September was most certainly telling me the truth.

It was quiet in the afternoon but shortly before it was time to finish, a trickle of blue wings came down the beck and with an F-fly tied with blue wings in mind, I added a fourth trout to the bag and so I drove away from my fishing feeling very grateful indeed that God in his compassionate wisdom had decided to make me, along with Thomas Tod Stoddart, first and foremost an angler.

On Wednesday the wind, which had been mostly my ally on the two previous days, most definitely turned into an enemy and it was the wind I blamed for sending me away from the beck with an empty bag. On Wednesday it was no longer an upstream wind and it was also much stronger, roaring in the willows and rushing intemperately across or down the beck.

I spent a large part of the day at a pool below a little wooden weir where the trout were visible and, in the morning at least, rising to eat blue wings. I failed with all of them and, if it was partly my fault, it was also the fault of the wind. The trouble was that I kept thinking my fly was somewhere where it was not. I would strike a rise and find that it had not been to my fly, which turned out to be six inches to one side of it or a foot downstream. I did this more often than I care to remember and just as often I thought a rise to my fly had been to one of the naturals and so made no response at all. The trout were slow to go down and so this incompetent performance went on for what seemed a very long time before I gave up and sought solace in a sandwich and red wine. The wine worked better than the sandwich.

I had briefly hooked a big fish in the morning but the strike had not been properly timed and it was a very brief encounter. It happened again in the afternoon and it was all very frustrating and dispiriting. I am sure that a better fisher, a more skilful caster would have coped better with the adverse conditions, but the truth is that flyfishing in a hostile wind is to my mind not much of a pleasure. If I had not been on holiday I should most definitely have left fishing alone; I should have split logs or got out the chain saw and put dying ash trees out of their misery. I should have taken the dogs for a long walk and might have found the wild air exhilarating. I should not have gone fishing to be made a fool of by a howling gale. I was out of love with September when I drove away from the beck on Wednesday afternoon.

Our relationship was repaired on Thursday, which was the last day of my excursion to East Yorkshire. It was a much quieter day and it was spent with Oliver as his guest on the Yorkshire Derwent. It was also a delightful day and an important element of this was that it brought me most of September's moods in the course of four or five hours on the river. There were periods of hazy autumn sunshine when September seemed serene and reflective; there were times when a gentle sadness gathered in the stillness beneath a grey cover of cloud; now and then a breeze sprang up from nowhere and sighed restlessly in the trees but at lunchtime, sitting with Oliver in warm sunshine and listening to the swallows, September had taken us all the way back to summer.

My wine tasted of summer too and in the best possible way it also tasted of the three trout in my bag, not because there was anything fishy on the nose or palate but because the thought of them brought out the savour of the bright cherry fruit with its attractive touch of astringency and beneath this the gentle grip of soft tannins. I like the Nero d'Avola grape and the modest price of the wines made from it. Occasionally too I like to make pretentious comments about my experience of a particular wine. Anyway, though cheap it was a well made wine and the pleasure of sharing a bottle with my host was certainly enhanced by the sunshine and the swallows, by the pleasure of Oliver's company and most of all by the three trout already in my bag.

I had once had a day on the Derwent at the end of a visit to East Yorkshire when the three days before it had brought me just one trout. It was a tense and anxious day for me because I was very eager to make a bag and because success was long delayed, although it came at last and brought powerful feelings of fulfilment and relief. Think of a batsman who finally scores a century after months of poor form and this may help you to understand something of my response to the limit bag I caught in the afternoon of that day on the Derwent. I mention this because it was, for a day on the Derwent, an unusual experience. Fishing there is normally of the relaxing sort. The water is well stocked, fish are almost always rising; find a fly that appeals to one of them and the likelihood is that it will appeal to others as well. On that particular day it was an ancient and miniature Wickham's Fancy; on an earlier visit this season it was – and often is – Dry Simon; yesterday it was a size 14 CDC Sparkle Sedge.

Usually on the Derwent it is not too difficult to catch yourself a trout or two and because of this, the stronger emotions that sometimes visit fishers are less likely to be encountered. Yesterday brought an early brace and the rest of the morning and then the afternoon were punctuated by more trout. It did not really matter that one or two dropped off or were missed at the strike. It was a tranquil sort of fishing day spent in a beautiful place at the beginning of my favourite of the year's four seasons. Instead of the elation that sometimes comes with particular trout there was quiet satisfaction when another was drawn over the net. There was no bitter despondency when I lost or failed to make contact with a fish, just a gentle feeling of regret and the feeling that I should have preferred to catch him and see how big and how beautiful he was. Just before lunch I caught a rainbow not far short of two pounds, a fish that fought with all the savage energy of his kind. He was a superbly conditioned, fin-and-tail-perfect trout and, in a quiet sort of way, I was delighted to catch and kill him, but it would not have spoiled my lunch or soured the taste of my wine if he had broken me. I used, by the way, to disapprove very strongly of stocking brown trout rivers with rainbows but, now that all stock fish are – absurdly – infertile triploids, I don't suppose it really matters one way or the other.

It was, anyway, a restful sort of fishing day and I drove home in a mood of very quiet satisfaction, reflecting on the different feelings that I find on all my rivers: on the Rea, the Foston Beck, the Derwent and, of course, the Wharfe. I thought of favourite composers, of the mood and spirit running through their music and how this corresponded to the mood and spirit that waits for me on my several rivers. The Rea, I decided, with its brown water and deep shadows beneath the trees, was Brahms in sombre and brooding mood. The Foston Beck, fringed with monkey flowers, pellucid, with those beds of waving and rocking weed and with the white chalk shining through, was, of course, Mozart, fluent, graceful and tender but perhaps not Mozart at his most profound. The gently winding Derwent was Mendelssohn, relaxed and full of charm. And what of the Wharfe? Well, the Wharfe was Mozart in every mood, it was Brahms and Mendelssohn on top form. It was Bach and Schubert and Beethoven as well, all at the height of their powers; it was Schumann and Elgar and every great composer that I could think of and it was wonderful to think that within a couple of days I should be there on my favourite river in this, my favourite month. I also decided, by the way, that The Clash, Led Zeppelin and Queen captured the spirit of none of my rivers or the experience that I found in fishing them.

I'm not sure how long this ridiculous exercise took me. I think I abandoned it just west of Pickering after the sad realisation that the Eden, once the second river in my fishing life, had been left unconsidered because in the last few seasons it had been left unfished. Anyway, I abandoned composers and, to while away the journey, began to fashion a sort of litany extolling the innumerable blessings that flow to me from catching a brace of trout. It went something like this: two trout, bringers of deepest contentment, two trout, bringers of fulfilment and peace, two trout, bringers of grateful joy, two trout, gifts of beauty beyond compare, two trout, balm to the weary and sad, two trout, transformers of perception, opening eyes to the beauty and goodness of the created world, two trout, transformers, not, it is true, of water into wine but capable of changing a pretty humble bottle of Italian stuff into nectar fit for the (non-existent) gods on Olympus, two trout, reconcilers of man to his mortality, two trout, alchemy of the soul, two trout, blessing be upon the good God who gives them to me.

I think this took me down Sutton Bank and through Thirsk and, yes, I acknowledge that it was frivolous and self-indulgent, but quite a lot of it is true. Anyway, once out of Thirsk I more or less forgot about composers and litanies and drove on my way feeling delighted with the fishing that I had found in East Yorkshire and looking forward to opening the bottle of sherry that was waiting to be drawn from the fridge almost as soon as I had reached journey's end.

9 September

I managed to stay away from the Wharfe for three whole days, although it was not really through choice. Partly it was because there was work to be done with the pheasants on my little shoot but mainly it was because Saturday brought heavy rain and on Sunday the river was too big. This morning, anyway, the 6.30 reading on the Kettlewell gauge told me (online) that the top of the river would be in perfect order for the fly and so, once the pheasants were fed, it was over to Yockenthwaite for midday wine and a sandwich before walking half a mile downstream and beginning to fish.

I realised as I wandered down to my starting point that this would be my first day of the season on the Yockenthwaite water; I also realised that the reason for this is that I have become completely besotted with the higher stretch between Deepdale and the river's beginning at Beckermonds, and that I was only at Yockenthwaite now because a friend was fishing above Deepdale and I did not want to invade his beat, even though he would have been more than happy to share it with me.

I should not neglect Yockenthwaite. Everything about it is beautiful, above all the river itself, with its deep rock pools where the white and yellow bedrock shines through, with its miniature falls over limestone slabs and ledges, with its shining and singing stony runs. There is the river and there are the steep meadows on either side with their seaming pattern of walls. There are willows, alders and ashes spaced along the banks and standing sentinel over many of the pools. And this afternoon everything was bright beneath the sun and the trees were showing their first signs of autumn colour and robins were singing their sad September song and the sky was restless with the shape and sound of swallows. The swallows were restless but the air was almost still and the sun was warm: warm with September restraint rather than that enervating midsummer excess

The fishing was slow. I started where a now-dead sycamore stretches its gaunt branches over a long and lovely glide with a lively run at its head. There were a couple of plucks either at Simple Simon or my Coachman but nothing took a firm hold and there was no response at all in the deep basin of a rock pool just beyond. This brought me to another long and even lovelier glide with another run at its top and, beyond this, a turbulent pool beneath one of those miniature falls. It is among my favourite places on the whole river, partly because over the years it has given me lots of trout but also because the long glide carries and somehow transforms the colours and patterns of the sky in a way perhaps more beautiful than anywhere else on the Wharfe.

This afternoon the long glide was as beautiful as I have ever seen it and it gave me a trout to my Sparkle Sedge, a trout that was certainly nine and a half inches long but equally certainly not half an inch longer. It cost me a struggle to return him, because he was fit and beautiful and would doubtless have eaten very well indeed, but the struggle was won and I gave him back to the river and fished on through a delightful and very fishy succession of small pools and runs and glides without seeing a rise or bringing a trout up to my fly.

I now came to a difficult pool with sycamores stretching their branches low over the water, sometimes dipping them in, from both sides of the stream. There were fish rising here, three or four of them. I managed to flick my sedge over the lowest of them and his response was immediate. He felt heavy. I feared that my line would snag in one of the branches but I won the battle and he weighed one pound twelve ounces. It goes without saying that, instead of this single impressive fish, I should have preferred two of them, each roughly half his size. Unfortunately our contest had put those other trout down.

Next I came to a long and wonderful rock pool, another place that has been very kind to me in the course of our long acquaintance. I always expect trout here but there were none today. Round a slight bend in the river I came to a glide and above it a run where I also expect trout and was also disappointed. I expect trout in the pool below Yockenthwaite Bridge but today my expectations were confounded and, reaching the bridge with only one trout in my bag, I could acknowledge the beauty all round me in the September stillness, in the glowing burnish of the river, in the now slanting light and in the steep and shadow-patterned fields, but my heart could not quite go out to it all in the silent praise that would have filled my heart if there had been one more trout in my bag. You know how it is with me in this matter.

Anyway, I knew that Rob would by now have left Deepdale and there was time for something like two hours' more fishing. It seemed almost as quiet up there as at Yockenthwaite. I caught two small trout, seven- and eight- inchers; they were beautiful and at the same time they were a disappointment. I only draw real pleasure from catching small trout when there are already two bigger ones in my bag. And then the brace came from the bowl-shaped pool which you have already fished once or twice with me in the earlier course of this book. It is a pool – just to remind you – that the river enters through a narrow channel of limestone and where the current runs, foaming and broken, hard against the true right bank. It is a fine pool, where the trout lie on the edge of the turbulence and are often good ones. It is indeed a fine pool and, early this evening it seemed a pool that deserved some sort of award or some grand title or some other high honour. I wonder if the monarch could give the pool a knighthood or perhaps an MBE. You will have guessed, anyway, that this pool gave me the brace: with a red-spotted trout that weighed at least twelve ounces: a trout that, lying in the grass beside my first fish, lying there in the low radiance of the sun with the pale sky above, filled my fisher's heart with peace and with all those other feelings that, as you already know, come to me from gazing at a brace of trout as they lie in the grass on the edge of the river Wharfe. There was delight too in the cool air and the evening stillness and the sound of the river and in the yellowing leaves that hung motionless on some of the trees, and I fished on for another half hour, caught nothing and then drove home over the quiet hills.

13 September

At Yockenthwaite this afternoon I realised that I am not your intellectual or cerebral type of flyfisher. I have friends who love nothing more than a problem, who love the puzzle of rising fish that refuse their flies, because this gives them the opportunity to think and analyse, to solve the puzzle by working out which the right fly might be before finding that they are right and catching lots of trout and feeling rather pleased with themselves. The trout are almost a secondary pleasure; the solution of the puzzle is what really matters.

I am not a member of this breed of flyfishers. There are, of course, times when circumstances force me to adopt something of their approach and, yes, it is satisfying to feel that I have managed to interpret the signs by choosing the right fly, but I would much rather catch lots of trout without any frustrating preliminaries, much rather find trout eager to take my Dry Simon or CDC Sedge without the need for deep thought on my part or intelligent and informed experimentation.

Today I thought the trout were going to behave as I like them to behave by thinking my initial choice of Simple Simon and the Coachman just what they wanted, because I hooked, landed and killed an eleven inch trout with my second cast. I had decided to fish the three pools below the bridge before walking downstream to the dead sycamore and fishing my way back. This first trout had come from the lowest of the pools, the long and beautiful rock pool that I mentioned in my last entry. There were three fish rising above him and in the course of half a dozen casts I had risen or pricked or failed to connect with all three of them, which forced me to acknowledge – too late – that those three fish had come short because they were unconvinced by my flies. Your intellectual fisher would have realised this after just one failure and he would probably have gone for something small and black. I thought it would be worth trying a Sparkle Sedge and it didn't work. I reached Yockenthwaite Bridge perhaps twenty minutes later without having interested another trout. There was one rising in the bridge pool. He went down as soon as he saw my fly and so I trudged off downstream, knowing that the brace should already have been mine and feeling as disconsolate as the blue and silver of the sky, as the bright stillness of the afternoon and the dark shine of the river would allow.

I was not disconsolate for long. In the absence of any more rising fish I had restored my Coachman and Simple Simon, and it was Simon who brought me another eleven-incher from the run by the dead sycamore, a trout that suddenly made the blue and silver of the sky both brighter and more beautiful, that made the shining stillness of the afternoon even more serene and also deepened the glowing lustre of the river's flow. I put on Dry Simon and fished my way upstream; I returned two small trout and enjoyed both of them because there was already a brace of trout in my bag.

Things fell quiet for a time. When I reached the long rock pool, which incidentally should have a proper name, instinct rather than intelligence told me to try a Greenwell Klinkhåmer through the fast water at the top of the pool. Another small trout went back. The trout in the bridge pool was still rising. He liked the look of the Greenwell and was a whole twelve inches long. As soon as I had killed him I realised that I had just broken the rules of the Kilnsey Angling Club, which allow fishers to kill three brace of trout on the stocked beats but only a single brace on the wild water above Kettlewell Bridge. It is a good rule and I have managed to remember it all summer. I cannot explain why it slipped my mind this afternoon and I was more or less untroubled by guilt because it had not been an act of disobedience or defiance. I had simply forgotten that, up at Yockenthwaite, I am only allowed a brace.

I am not a cerebral but rather an emotional fisher, which I say, incidentally, with no sense of self-congratulation. I am not suggesting to you that I am blessed with a specially sensitive, artistic or creative temperament. I make the statement as a plain fact, because I often find my days on the Wharfe very moving indeed, and you already know that I am most often and most powerfully moved when, with fishing over, I sit by the river in a sort of grateful reverie, inhaling the spirit of place and all its countless beauties and associations. And September, with its infinitely suggestive ambiguities, is the time when this end-of-fishing experience is often unusually intense, which unsurprisingly is how it was this evening.

This evening shortly after five o'clock, sitting in the shadow of Yockenthwaite Bridge, I felt the pressure of tears and felt no inclination to resist. There were not many tears but they were called up by powerful feelings, because everything about the September evening all round me was so painfully beautiful. The stillness hurt because it could not last and the beauty all round me made my heart ache because I knew the day would come when I should leave it for the last time. And it was so fragile too in its brightness and there was such love within me for this place and for what it had given me today and on so many other days and now it was steeped in the September sadness of fading and decline. And there was pain too because I knew that I should never find words to do justice to the beauty of the sky and the fields and the rock and the water or to penetrate the complexity of my response to them. And then a robin sang from a cottage garden just over the river while the swallows talked restlessly on the wires crossing the water to the farmhouse on the bank above me, which was already sending a column of white smoke climbing from one of its chimneys and then slowly dissolving on the still air. I thought how sad and lovely it all was and how long it had been a part of me and how much I loved it. Then I got up to go, took myself and those three trout to the Land Rover and drove home.

It occurs to me, after writing this paragraph, that some readers may find my talk of tears annoying. I don't think it's because they look on them as necessarily unmanly. Rather they regard them as an absurd and tedious emotional self-indulgence on my part, as a ridiculous overreaction to the circumstances that see them shed, because what have I been doing is nothing except going fishing and catching a few trout. These same people probably dislike much more than my tears; they think my whole approach to fishing and writing about it is overwrought and in particular they hate what they regard as its false spirituality, they think that I inflate what is no more than a bit of fun into a quasi religious experience.

I think fishing is a whole lot of fun and I also think it is much more than that and again I think that most fishers think something similar without always realising what they think. Fishing is my way into nature, where I find a world of fascination and beauty that feeds the soul and puts me in touch with something fundamental beyond myself. I take fishing very seriously and for me it is most certainly a religious experience because I happen to believe in God and believe that I discover something of his goodness on the banks of the river Wharfe. I think perhaps this is why some of my fellow fishers hate my work so much, because they regard any form of religious belief with suspicion or secret contempt or open animosity.

Through fishing I forge an intimate and special bond with nature; in nature I find the work and love and beauty of the creator God. This is so old fashioned that it is almost embarrassing, which is perhaps what has held me back from an earlier confession of it and from telling you that there are times on the Wharfe when fishing turns into a silent prayer of thanksgiving and praise. Thanks be to God for making me a fisher. Glory be to God for rivers and trout, for the river Wharfe above all and for the trout that swim there. Praise be to God for all the beauty and comfort and joy that I find there. And so there you have it and, in order to avoid offending modern orthodoxy, I shall say little more about this very simple conviction at the heart of my fishing life. Regard it as a given and disapprove or, if you prefer, try to forget all about it. But it is there and I suppose my regrettable metaphysical leanings are obvious on every page of this and my other books because their influence colours almost every thought that comes to me and every sentence that these same thoughts inspire.

18 September

At four o'clock today I was sitting by the Wharfe some little way above the Stepping Stones. It was a cloudy afternoon beneath a ridge-and-furrow sky of white and grey. It was completely still; the trees stood along the banks with unstirring leaves, leaves just touched here and there with hints of yellow and brown. Now and then a dry leaf fluttered silently down onto the grass or the water. There was that autumn feeling of gathered calm. It was intensely September and, sitting there beneath the trees on the edge of the water, I was visited by a succession of September ghosts, almost all of them kind. They were ghosts of time and place, of fishing days from earlier years on different beats of the Kilnsey water; they were the ghosts of dead members, friends and fellow-fishers; there was one in particular that often visits me at Kilnsey, the ghost of the man who brought me to the club, who made me a member and in doing so brought me more than I can ever adequately explain. I turned up as well, of course, at all stages of my relationship with the river Wharfe.

And all these Kilnsey ghosts, moving through the September stillness, somehow reinforced the September symbolism, bringing a soft sadness and some sense of regret at the passing of so many years and the loss of so many friends; but they brought something else as well, they brought a much deeper sense of profound thankfulness for all that the Wharfe at Kilnsey has given me. And here is the marvel; that there were no trout in my bag and yet I was untroubled by its emptiness. I should, of course, have preferred the comforting presence of the brace but just this once I was sitting by a river with no trout to my name, not even any small ones returned, and I was telling myself that I was a fortunate and very happy old man.

The mood of the afternoon, so still, so soft, so persuasive, was the reason for this unusual contentment, for it somehow seemed to present to my mind the whole wealth and depth of my long association with the Wharfe, which was something wonderful and against which the experience of a single day was insignificant. It was good to sit by the river with an empty bag and feel grateful in spite of it. I shall be very surprised if, when I fish the Wharfe again in a day or two, the presence or absence of the brace will not have resumed its customary importance.

25 September

This morning I fed my young pheasants; I feed them almost every morning and it is a good way to start the day, at least when things are going well, which they have done during this release. I enjoy the daily routine of pheasant care. My friend, Tony Smith, a retired gamekeeper, helps me with the shoot, which means that now and then, quite often in fact, at least three times a week if the Wharfe is in good order, I can leave him to do the afternoon feed and head off for the river. The mornings when I enjoy feeding pheasants the most are the ones when I know that, as soon as I have made my circuit of the feed rides, I can climb into the Land Rover and go fishing. This is what happened today.

I fished up above Deepdale. I ate my sandwich and drank my two beakerfuls of wine before starting and then fished through the afternoon. The river was slightly bigger than I would have chosen, but it was falling and clearing, flowing with a deep peaty shine. It was restless and beautiful; it seemed to me a water for wet flies, not for two or three graceful spiders, but for my less lovely Coachman and Simple Simon; and so it proved. I never saw a rise but now and then some movement of the line told me to raise my wrist and once or twice the fish was only pricked – pricked fish, by the way, almost always feel big – but more often he was firmly hooked. I kept telling myself how much I loved fishing wet flies upstream. All afternoon I fished in a windless calm beneath a layered grey sky and all afternoon the river spoke to me of our approaching separation.

Shortly before six I was sitting a pool or two down from the beginning of the Wharfe. The brace was in my bag, four had been returned and honours were even between my two flies. I had tried some changes but none had worked and so the original team had been restored. All afternoon the river had been reminding me that September was almost over and that the season would end with its passing. Sitting there I now told the river that my season might in fact already be over because heavy rain was promised for the coming days, which would probably bring it up in flood and make fishing impossible until it was too late because by then it would be illegal. I told the river that I would not blame it if this happened because it would, after all, be the fault of the weather rather than of the river itself. I think, by the way, that talking to rivers is perfectly normal behaviour. I'm not sure we fishers shouldn't do more of it. Anyway, the thought that my fishing might already be over concentrated the still, quiet September sadness and brought with it the temptation to surrender myself to self-indulgent September melancholy.

The temptation was there; sometimes I give in to it but this time it was resisted. I felt that the light was too soft, the air was too still, everything was too calm and too peaceful for anything but a restrained sadness. I told myself that, if this was in fact my season's end, then it had ended quite as it should have done, on a calm, grey afternoon of very gentle and unassertive beauty, an afternoon that had seen my slow progress from pool to pool, bringing me at last to the Wharfe's first pool of all, an afternoon that had brought me a succession of trout with two of them big enough to go home with me: the river's last gift to me until another spring brought us together again. If this was how it was going to end, it was an appropriate, a good way for the end to come.

I walked back towards the Land Rover and then sat down briefly on the edge of the river to gut and clean my brace. It was while I was busy with this that the low sun found passage through the grey clouds, and its slanting rays shone directly downstream, turning the water sliding blue and white like flowing silk, but when I looked upstream it was restless quicksilver all over. And up there on the steep sides of the valley the light found the scattered hawthorns, setting their red berries aglow and turning the dying bracken russet instead of dull brown. And it shone in the yellow leaves of the ashes and on the white rock and for a time there was brightness everywhere and the river, of course, was the bright heart of it all and brighter than everything else. And it seemed to me, given that this might well be my season's end, might be the beginning of a long separation, that I was being given shining images of the river and its valley to take away with me and to sustain me through the months ahead. They were with me all the way home and they are with me now.

30 September

I did not really expect to be writing this entry because, anticipating rain, I thought that I had probably already fished the Wharfe for the last time this season. And there was rain, lots of it, and the Wharfe came up and was far too big for me to think of fishing, but it falls as quickly as it rises and yesterday's early morning reading suggested that by early afternoon the level at

Deepdale would be more or less perfect, a message that seemed to be confirmed by my drive over to Wharfedale, which took me past stretches of the upper Eden that were flowing full and shining bright; and the Ure above Hawes looked beautiful and Gayle Beck looked even better. There had been showers through the morning but it looked as though they had not produced enough rain to bring rivers up again and, when I had crossed Cam Fell and parked the Land Rover on the side of the road just below Beckermonds, the Wharfe seemed to be promising me a brace of trout at the very least and I felt fairly confident that it would give me more. I was looking at the sort of water that we fishers of upstream flies dream about, flowing with controlled exuberance and with that wonderful glowing stain of peat. Before tackling up I ate a sandwich and drank a beaker of wine; there had been pheasants to feed in the morning and dogs to exercise and it was already one o'clock. There was another heavy shower while I was doing this.

When the beaker was empty I filled it again; when it was empty for the second time I climbed out of the Land Rover and began to get ready to go fishing. After putting my rod together I glanced impatiently at the water and thought it had come up a little. When I had tied on my team of flies I looked more carefully and saw beyond doubt that the river was two or three inches higher than when I had arrived. It was at least another inch higher when I made my first cast. It was not unfishable but suddenly it was big and, although the last heavy shower had fallen some time ago, it was still rising and already my earlier confidence had drained away, for I have rarely done much good in a full and rising water. I did little good this time. I caught one trout about an inch long and never felt so much as another pull. I fished until five and then I gave up and drove home, once again thinking that my season was almost certainly over, because tomorrow was of course my last opportunity to go fishing and there was more rain forecast overnight. And this time I drove home, not with shining visions to delight the mind's eye, but feeling frustrated and downcast and cheated of a last day's sport.

It was true that, whatever the weather and the state of the water in the morning, I should be driving back over to Wharfedale after pheasant care because I had arranged to join friends for lunch. In honour of the season's last day we should certainly meet and drink a glass together but it seemed unlikely that we should do much fishing, much more likely that we should do none at all, that we should meet somewhere on the river, chew a sandwich or two together and drink a glass or two of wine in acknowledgment of season's end, unless we preferred to perform this solemn ritual in the pub. With food eaten and wine finished and farewells made I expected that I should then drive away from the season's last day without ever wetting a line.

Pheasants and dogs came first again. It was about eleven when I set off for the Wharfe. I had checked its level before breakfast and it had not seemed hopeless. You will find me, on another last day of September, looking anxiously at the Eden and the Ure on my way to the Wharfe. Today their message was gloomy; they were both big and dirty, too big and dirty for a team of flies. I feared I should find the Wharfe unfishable, but Gayle Beck gave me tentative hope, because it looked just right, suggesting that there might have been less rain over Cam Fell (where it rises together with the becks that make the Wharfe). It seemed possible that I might yet go fishing and, glory be, when I pulled up above Yockenthwaite Bridge a few minutes before noon, the water was just about an inch on the high side of perfection. And the day was soft and almost windless; and the sky was grey, a kind and gentle grey, and there were yellowing leaves stirring very faintly beneath it, yellowing leaves and golden leaves, and there were clusters of red berries on rowan and hawthorn and, best of all, there was the amber glow of the water; and the slip and slide, the rush and ripple of the river were the loudest sounds on the quiet air and, in the twenty minutes

I had for fishing before I met my friends, I caught a trout of almost a pound, a beautiful wild trout, and I began to hope that, in spite of the troutless months that stretched ahead of it, the last day of the season might send me home a happy man.

Then there was lunch – a pork pie and a sandwich – with a glass of wine in the company of four friends, sitting together on a high bank above the Wharfe and looking down on the single arch of Yockenthwaite Bridge. It was a simple meal but, in recognition of the season's last day, there was just a touch of solemnity about it all, there was a bitter-sweetness on the air because trouting was again almost over and because five friends, brought together by a shared love of fishing, would soon be going their separate ways and might not meet up again until the beginning of another spring brought them back to the river. Anyway, we did not sit there too long because most of us were keen to be back fishing. After we had toasted the river and said our farewells I confess that I poured myself another half glass and sat there for ten minutes, looking at the river, at the changing leaves and the steep pastures rising up through brown spreads of bracken to the near fells, looking at all this and thinking grateful thoughts and thanking God that he had made me a fisher. And then I got to my feet and went fishing myself.

It began to rain, but it was soft and gentle rain that made no sound with its falling through the still air, patterning the sliding water with a myriad tiny, evanescent dots. One or two big autumn sedges were flying clumsily over the river; a few small olives were fluttering through the air but there were no rising fish. I was fishing my fancy pattern, Dry Simon, because it will often bring up trout when they are not feeding. It did. I had fished my way almost back to Yockenthwaite Bridge when, from a flow of faster water at the top of the long and very lovely rock pool that you have visited with me several times, Dry Simon disappeared and I had hooked a good trout. He weighed one pound four ounces and was just as wild and just as beautiful as the day's first and somewhat smaller trout. The rain had faded away by now and, while I was admiring the shape and the spots and the silver gleam of this second fish, the sky turned blue and all at once the sun was shining down on glowing leaves and pale grass and the river's bright slide.

I moved further upstream, above Deepdale, because I wanted to end the season right at the top of the river. I wanted to pay homage to the beginnings of the Wharfe and I hoped to catch just one or two more of the lovely wild trout that swim there. The early evening was very quiet and very beautiful, with a pale blue sky and cool air, with slanting light and shadows slowly stretching themselves, with those yellow and golden leaves briefly aflame in the low rays of the sun. And the climbing fields seemed somehow softly to cradle the infant Wharfe, so that the little river flowed at the heart of the landscape, flowed with a peaty shine, flowed silver and blue and silky white beneath the pale sky, flowed darker and sometimes almost black beneath the arching trees and the deep shadows of the steep land. I fished through a pool or two, then sat for a few minutes, drinking in the cool air and the peace before starting to fish again.

All day the trout had been quiet and it now seemed that they had caught the mood of the evening and fallen fast asleep. I felt almost certain that those two earlier trout were the season's last and that I should have to wait almost six months for the next one. But I was content; there was a brace in my bag and I found both pleasure and satisfaction in the whisper of rod and line and the soft falling of my fly; just as on the first day of the season it was ritual as much as sport, a ritual performed to mark not the beginning but the passing of another season; and, even without rising trout, it was delightful fishing through those miniature pools and runs in the thickening shadows and the fading light and the deep evening calm, through pools and runs all stored with memories of trout from earlier seasons. There was thanksgiving in every step and in every cast.

So it was that I came in sight of the Wharfe's first pool, where Oughtershaw Beck and Greenfield Beck come together to make the river that means so much to me. It is a restless pool; in fact it is perhaps a run rather than a pool, a disturbed movement of water on either side of the big rocks that lie between the inflow of the two becks. It may be a pool, it may be a run; indisputably it is the beginning of the Wharfe and as such to me it is hallowed and holy water. Over the years I have caught a fair number of fish from this first feature of the Wharfe and they have not always been the seven- and eight-inchers you might expect from such a place.

On the last day of the season, anyway, I sat on the bank below this pool or run for a time, thinking sad and grateful thoughts as should every fisher at the end of another September when he sits by the water and acknowledges that there are only a few casts left. I thought such thoughts, more grateful than sad, and then I fished the pool – to me it will always be a pool – and on the third or fourth cast Dry Simon disappeared again and a minute or so later I had caught a trout of about twelve ounces, a trout every bit as beautiful as the day's two earlier and rather bigger trout. I gave him back to the river and immediately I knew two things. First of all I knew that I should not cast a fly again until the beginning of another spring. It was the end of fishing for the day and for the season. And secondly I knew that my season could not have ended in a better way. A five-pounder from a different place would not have been as good as this three-quarter-pounder from the beginning of the river that I love beyond all other rivers. It was the perfect end to the season and, since you cannot improve upon perfection, I whispered a few words of thanks to the first pool of the Wharfe, blessing the water on the start of its journey to Yockenthwaite and Buckden, to Kettlewell and Kilnsey and beyond; and then I walked downstream though the gathering shadows, took down my tackle, thanked the river all over again and drove away over the darkening hills.

Chapter Seven

HOLIDAY FISHING
A tale of two rivers

There may at times come to us more assertive, more aggressive and consuming pleasures, I mean the sort of pleasures that possess the whole being and admit no thoughts or feelings beyond themselves; doubtless we at times experience more savage delights, more transporting raptures than the pleasure with which I am now concerned. I am thinking of a soft, a very gentle but at the same time a very deep pleasure, a pleasure that leaves the mind free to roam wherever it fancies, to lose itself in recollection of this same pleasure found in earlier times, to dream of similar pleasures on days yet to come or, which is probably the best choice, serenely to contemplate present pleasure and present contentment.

I am, of course, thinking of the pleasure to be found by sitting in the sunshine on a grassy bank by the edge of running water, sitting there with a beaker of red wine in your hand, with your fishing rod and bag lying beside you, sitting there and from time to time raising the beaker to your lips and taking from it slow, reverent and very grateful sips. For me – with or without the sunshine – this has become one of the essential (and most enjoyable) elements of a fishing day and it is a pleasure that I enjoy very frequently, because during the trout season I can never stay away from running water for more than a few days at a time. A day between fishing trips is sometimes a good idea, whetting the appetite for more fishing after this single day of rest; two days is tolerable, three days is already too long and any more days is something that should most definitely be avoided.

Anyway, it is, of course, Spout Dub on the Wharfe that most often sees me sitting under the sky occupied with my thoughts and with a beaker of red wine. On the Tees there is a spot some way below Cronkley Bridge that also, sometimes as often as twice a week, sees me similarly engaged; and there are favourite places on Yorkshire's Foston Beck and Shropshire's Rea Brook that several times a season play host to me and my thoughts and my beaker of red wine.

I am telling you all this because I recently found myself sitting with my beaker in the Highlands of Scotland by a river two or three hundred miles away from my usual haunts. It was a miniature sort of river, scarcely more than a beck or a burn, which was something that pleased me because I am particularly fond of becks and burns and little rivers. The bottom few beats of the Kilnsey water on the Wharfe, for example, are already just beginning to be too big for me, whereas the scale of the river up at Yockenthwaite and Deepdale is to my mind just about perfect. And a big part of my pleasure in the Foston Beck and the Rea Brook is that both of them are small. But this time I was sitting there by my little Scottish river, sitting there alone and thinking that on the whole, even when as now I was on holiday with a group of old and precious friends, I preferred solitary to sociable fishing: not, I immediately insisted, because I was tired of these priceless friends, but because it has always seemed to me that we absorb the beauty and spirit of our fishing more deeply when we fish with only ourselves for company. My friends would be there in the evening and their company would be its chiefest pleasure. Now I was alone, and happy that it was so, partly, it must be admitted, for the questionable reason that the absence of my friends relieved me of the very difficult and deeply unwelcome duty of offering them some of the contents of the half bottle that I had just opened and from which I had just poured myself the first glorious beakerful. Being temporarily friendless meant that the half bottle would be all mine, every wonderful drop of it. Half a bottle, by the way, means an extra glass, or beaker of wine, because my usual lunchtime ration on a fishing day is just two of them. Half a bottle is a holiday indulgence and I relish every sip. Sitting there in the sunshine by my little river I was relieved and delighted that the whole of the half bottle, down to the very last drop, was destined for my lips alone.

I took my first sips, each one of them inducing in me a state of deeper and deeper contentment. I was thinking how wonderful it was to be a fisher sitting by a little river with a beaker of red wine in his hand and with the prospect of two beakerfuls still to come. I was also thinking that fishers – at least if they are like this fisher – rarely hear the music of running water when they are actually fishing because they are too absorbed in the pursuit of trout. It is when we sit down at lunchtime with half a bottle of wine that our ears are suddenly opened to the sweet singing of the water flowing between the banks. I do not, as it happens, believe that the sounds of water on its way to wherever it is going are as beautiful, as moving or as profound as the sounds that Bach and Mozart have woven into sublime creations that somehow touch the very essence of what it means to be a man. The music of Bach and Mozart has more to tell us than the music of running water but it would be out of place for a fisher sitting on the edge of a little river in the sunshine, while making slow and grateful progress through half a bottle of red wine, to bother himself with this comparison. The music of running water makes the perfect accompaniment for a fisher resting after his morning's sport while sipping his wine and seeing where his thoughts decide to take him.

The sound of the water, anyway, was delightful and there were other sounds to be heard and enjoyed. There was, to begin with, a stonechat sitting on a fence post and chatting away. He was, I suppose, telling me that he would have preferred the view without me in it and doubtless the golden plover somewhere to my left was sending me the same message in a much sadder and softer and less obviously indignant sort of way. The chirping and parachuting meadow pipits were probably more bothered by the nearby calls of a cuckoo than by my presence among them, while the larks – and there were plenty of them – seemed infinitely remote somewhere high above me in the blue sky, infinitely remote and entirely unconcerned with the human figure sitting so far beneath them by a winding silver ribbon of water; I fancied that the shiver and tremble of their song was their tribute – the tribute of imitation – to the plash and murmur of my little river.

Towards the end of the first beaker I spotted an eagle floating through the sky way, way above even the larks. The wide horizon was ringed with mountains, with Ben Klibreck, Ben Hope and Ben More Asynt, all three of them still patched with high snow even in the third week of May. I was further north than I had been for many years and I was delighted to be there. I was not sitting by a famous river, celebrated for its run of salmon or its head of big trout, but I would not have exchanged my humble highland river for one more renowned. I was glad that my little Scottish river had, as far as I knew, received scant attention from any earlier fishing writers; it would be my honour and privilege to be perhaps the first fisher to sing its praise.

I filled my beaker for the second time, took a sip or two and told myself that the little river had been kind to me and that the wine, the sunshine and the drowsy midday peace were not the only reasons for my contentment. The river, by the way, had been a creeping trickle when we arrived on Saturday. But it had rained all through Monday and, although this had been frustrating because we fishers do not come to Scotland to sit in a hotel reading novels (or fishing books), two days later I was, of course, grateful for the rain. The river was much cleaner now and there was also much more of it. It was not big but the flow was vigorous and the water was the colour of a pint of bitter beer lifted to the light. The river was in more or less perfect trim and in the morning its generosity had surprised me, which meant that the fisher now piously sipping his second beakerful, was, as already indicated, a serene and contented fisher. When you have caught nothing, lunchtime wine consoles; when your morning sport has exceeded expectations it helps you to celebrate and tastes twice as sweet. For both situations I recommend lunchtime wine by the river very warmly indeed.

On this occasion the wine was wine of celebration, which may just encourage you to form a false impression because, when I tell you what the morning had brought me, you may feel that there was in fact little cause for it. There had been no two-pounders, although I had, as it happened, caught a brace of two-inchers, parr-marked tiddlers that had seized my fly greedily. I had caught no two-pounders, no pounders, nor even a trout weighing three-quarters of a pound. But I had caught seven or eight seven-or-eight-inchers, fat little trout that had fought beyond their size and pleased me no end. Better still, and perhaps the chief reason for my mood of quiet festival, apart from the wine and the sunshine and the birds and the sweet sounds of the little river, had been the brace of indisputable and very lively ten-inchers that had seized my dry fly and bent my rod and been briefly admired and then returned to the river. Earlier experience had told me to expect the seven- and eight-inchers, just a few of them, but I had not thought to catch a brace of trout at least two inches longer and probably weighing each of them a whole half pound.

They had been a surprise and a delight and an additional satisfaction had been that all my trout, the two-inchers, the seven-and-eight-inchers and those two monsters not far short of a foot long, had all been caught with the help of Simon Green. I have already told you about him in my chapter on flytying; how he is the offspring of Dry Simon and looks just like him apart from his tail of green Shimmer and Shine, how in some respects I am almost ashamed of him, most especially on account of his name, but also because he is undoubtedly slightly more vulgar even than Dry Simon. Both the Simons are overdressed and gaudy, but both of them have given me outstanding service and both are my own creations, factors that temper any inclination towards disapproval or disdain.

Something, anyway, had suggested to me that one or other of them would be likely to appeal to the trout of a small and peaty highland stream; my choice had fallen on Simon Green and he had indeed appealed to the trout and he had done it repeatedly, which helps to explain why my mood was so contented, so benign, as I sat by the little river drinking my wine. And far from feeling ashamed of Simon Green, I now felt almost proud of him. I was, at any rate, very glad that I had decided to attach him to the end of my leader and that he had done such a good job.

In the couple of hours before the half bottle had started telling me that the time for opening it was approaching, there had been large numbers of egg-laying stone flies fluttering through the air before settling on the water: there had been needle flies, also some slightly larger species with faint mottling on the wings and two sizes of yellow sally. Simon Green bore no obvious resemblance to any of these flies but the trout had not been bothered by this and nor had I. Sitting by the river, anyway, about half way through the second beakerful, I was now thinking of something else. I was thinking how delightful it was to be fishing for small, wild trout, to be fishing in a river where a ten-incher was a good fish and a twelve-incher would make my day. Everything seemed in proportion. Here was a river, a small river with a very healthy stock of small trout and a scattering of larger ones. Everything was as it should be. The river was sustaining a thriving population of the sort of trout that were designed to live and prosper in such a river. This sense of appropriateness pleased me, especially because there are so many rivers today where you can recognise and enjoy no such thing.

Finding that my beaker was now empty I filled it for the third and final time, took a sip or two and realised that there was something else about the sort of sport offered by the little river that I found entirely to my taste. It is something that may surprise you, because it was the acknowledgment that I was very unlikely to encounter a really big fish. We fishers are meant to find a special sort of fulfilment in the capture of exceptional trout and, of course, we do. But, as I grow older, I find myself increasingly uncomfortable with the violent emotions that belong both to catching and losing unusually big trout. Enough to say here that, while sitting by the river drinking my last beakerful of red wine, I was relieved to reflect how unlikely it was that the course of the afternoon would confront me with the extremes of either triumph or disaster.

If I caught a twelve-incher I should of course be absolutely delighted and would most certainly get out the mobile phone and take his photo before putting him back where he came from. If, on the other hand, I hooked and lost one I should be disappointed but the experience would not darken the day, or would only do so very briefly; in ten minutes I should more or less have recovered and an eight-incher or two would complete my convalescence. Fishing sometimes upsets our mental balance and this state of mind can linger: an experience that I thought unlikely to afflict me here on my little river, where as it happens the day's most demoralising moment was now beginning to loom: the moment when I should have to acknowledge that my beaker was empty and that the half bottle no longer had anything to pour into it. Perhaps ten minutes later the grim moment came; I felt as nearly sad as it was possible to feel on such a day after such a morning; I also felt drowsy, felt that my eyes were wanting to close themselves, felt that my back and head were wanting to stretch themselves out on the grass; and then for a time I felt nothing at all.

Consciousness was restored after something like half an hour and I began to fish my way slowly back to the hotel. There were one or two six-inchers; there was an eight-incher that pleased me and a fat nine-incher that pleased me rather more. And the sun was shining and the mountains were shining back at the sky and the larks were singing their hearts out. I came to a deep rock pool below a little waterfall and told myself that here if anywhere the elusive twelve-incher might be waiting to seize my fly. I put on a Coachman and cast it out and seconds later the rod was bending to the pressure of what felt like a big fish. He was not a two-pounder; if he had fallen off or broken me it would not have poisoned the memory of all the pleasure that had come before him; he was not a two-pounder but he was an indisputable twelve-incher and may well have been a whole inch longer. Indisputably he made the day, except that the day had already been made before he became a part of it. The day had already been made. He made it even better and he persuaded me that it was in fact time to call it a day and return to my hotel.

You can fish my little highland river if you stay at the Crask Inn about twenty miles north of Lairg. It is called the Tirry and your day will cost you all of £5. The Crask Inn, by the way, is almost certainly the finest inn in Scotland, although I admittedly make this claim with minimal experience of Scotland's other inns, but I cannot bring myself to believe that there could be a finer one. The Crask Inn is now owned by the Episcopal Church of Scotland and one of the delights of staying there is that you can come off the river at about five o'clock and join your host for evening prayer; and then, having given thanks for a day that has seemed in its own way not unlike heaven on earth, you can lie in the bath for a time, after which you may well find that it is time for a glass, rather than a beaker, of red wine before dinner. After dinner it will be time for coffee and a small dram and before long you will probably find that it is time for bed.

*****

I first fished the little river Tirry and stayed at the Crask Inn, way up north in Sutherland, something like four years ago but before that I fished with friends on the river Annan, that famous river in the Scottish Borders and very soon I shall tell you about it; but, since this chapter is called *Holiday Fishing*, I think I should first explain what I mean by the term, explaining at the same time how my attitude to holiday fishing differs in one very important respect from the spirit that informs my fishing on home waters. If I do not catch any trout on holiday fishing days, then – very unusually for me – I do not care too much. I am, of course, delighted if holiday rivers put plenty of trout in my net, as did the little river Tirry, but failure bites nothing like as deeply as it so often does on home waters. And home waters, by the way, are not necessarily particularly close to home. The Wharfe is an hour away; it takes me almost three hours to reach the Foston Beck; and the Rea Brook is at least four hours distant, but these three trout streams are home waters, waters of long acquaintance, waters that I visit repeatedly in the course of each season, waters where catching trout is very important and where catching no trout breeds deep disappointment. These are my 'home waters' and perhaps, given the distance I travel to fish them, they should be called something else, especially because some of my holiday rivers are considerably nearer home than some of these supposedly home waters. The Annan is just such a river; it is little more than an hour's drive from my front door. It is where I spent a week for five consecutive springs fishing with friends and catching virtually nothing.

Success was certainly very limited on the Annan but I found that, after a blank day on its banks, I could return to our cottage and enjoy the convivial pleasures of the evening, pleasures surprisingly untarnished by a brooding sense of failure. And if my friends had caught three- or four-pounders when I had caught nothing at all – which happened fairly frequently – I could rejoice in their achievements without feeling even a hint of jealousy or resentment, knowing at the same time that things would have been different had all this happened on my home waters.

On the Wharfe and the Foston Beck and the Rea Brook, catching trout matters to me and failure hurts. It may well hurt more than it should to a fisher who has been catching trout for over 50 years. Failure on my home waters sends me from the river sullen-faced and demoralised. On the Wharfe, on the Foston Beck and the Rea Brook, I am prepared to make strenuous efforts to put a few trout in my net. One trout is a relief, two, as you already know, bring contentment; three or more almost certainly mean a sense of deep fulfilment at the end of the day. A complete absence of them inspires a suddenly deep-rooted conviction of incompetence and – very frequently – the grim determination to fish all day tomorrow in order to get even with the trout that have got the better of me today, in this way proving to myself that I can after all still catch a fish or two.

On home waters there are just a few days that put nothing in my bag when I can honestly tell myself that even the best fisher in the world might have struggled to catch a trout. But usually – and this is much more dispiriting – usually I can look back through the dark history of a blank day and remember how two or three fish sailed up to my fly and were missed at the strike or how another trout that was firmly hooked and then lost at the net. Or perhaps I pricked trout all day long or consistently put them down before I could properly fish for them. Perhaps I lined them or showed them a dragging fly or fished for them with a floater when they were busy with sub-surface food. Perhaps I persisted too long with a pattern that I knew was wrong for the conditions and the behaviour of the trout. Perhaps I failed to cope with moderately troublesome breeze. The reasons for failure in fishing are so many and so various that it sometimes surprises me that we ever catch any trout at all. Anyway, it is chastening to survey the opportunities of a fishless day and acknowledge that, if only you had done things differently, there would be trout to your name and the world would seen a much better place. It goes without saying that the worst possible ending to such a day is to meet a friend and fellow angler, only to find that he caught three two-pounders before lunch and then lost count of all the fish that came his way in the afternoon. It does happen; it puts a strain on friendship and can even make the prospect of golf seem almost enticing.

Blank days depress me and I try hard to avoid them, which means that on my home waters I am moderately resourceful. I have never been a compulsive changer of flies but a day on the Wharfe with the trout in a picky mood may coax seven or eight wet patterns from their quarters in my fly boxes and may attach a similar number of floaters and emergers to the end of my leader. You already know that, in search of trout, I occasionally sink as low as a copper wire nymph or even a beadhead. And occasionally you could have seen me, even in my arthritic sixties, crawling very slowly along the rough banks of the Wharfe in pursuit of a difficult trout, although this is something that will now never happen again. As a matter of course, anyway, I avoid obvious blunders such as parading my outline above the bank or throwing my shadow over the water that I plan to fish. On

my home waters I try hard and fish hard and I attempt to fish
with a degree of enterprise and intelligence. On holiday streams,
up in Scotland or down in Wales, my attitude is almost light-
hearted; I will, of course, change flies if the trout refuse what
I am offering them but I will probably decide that enough is
enough if a trout has looked at three or four of my patterns
and been unimpressed. I will go looking for a less challenging
opponent and will not be too bothered if I cannot find one.
Sometimes I think of my holiday fishing as interludes between
the more important business of food and wine; undoubtedly the
best thing about my holiday fishing, even better than the food
and the wine, is the friends who share it with me every year.

The Annan, of course, was completely the wrong river
for so frivolous an approach; it is unquestionably a great
trout stream, breeding enormous and discriminating trout;
it is a river where expert fishers, drawing on deep reserves of
knowledge and skill and, unlike me, trying their very best,
often struggle to catch trout, which makes it unsurprising that
fishing the Annan in my holiday frame of mind brought me
very small rewards. The Annan is a noble river but, in the five
years that I fished it, I never really grew fond of it. By contrast
I loved the little river Tirry from the start; it could even turn
into a 'home water' for me, although I should prefer to keep
it on the holiday list so that I can continue to fish it in the
relaxed spirit that delights in success and regards failure as
no more than a trivial disappointment. There are fishers who
would think the Tirry, with its population of small wild trout,
barely worth fishing, at the same time declaring the Annan
the sort of river where proper fishermen spend difficult days
engaged with worthwhile trout. To me the Annan seemed a
grim sort of river; we fished it ten or so miles below Moffat,
where it was already rather too big for my taste. And I did
not find it particularly beautiful. It seemed to me that it was
a river that just got on, in a somewhat unimaginative sort of

way, with its business of flowing towards the sea. And then there were those enormous trout, which were undoubtedly a challenge worthy of a committed and skilful fisher, and I did try to catch them, but I think that I rarely tried hard enough because I was never entirely sure that I wanted them on the end of my line, knowing as I did that, if I hooked one of them and, as seemed almost inevitable, lost him in the fight, then even on a holiday river the hurt would go deep. The Annan seemed too big for me; its fish were definitely too big for me and I never felt any prospect of intimacy, never felt any sense of welcome, not even when returning to the river for the fourth and then the fifth time.

The friends who fished with me on the Annan fished her as she should be fished – seriously – and, although they often struggled, caught big trout. I fished her casually and disrespectfully and caught almost nothing, although I relished the food, the wine, the company and sometimes sleeping on the bank for an hour or two in the middle of a hot afternoon.

It is true that I caught a fish or two from one of the Annan's tributaries, from Kinnel Water, but most of these were midgets, although one of my friends managed a three pounder from the same stream. Kinnel Water was, in fact more to my liking, a river on the sort of scale that appeals to me. Kinnel Water and I could easily have become good friends and I remember a sunny afternoon when three of us fished it together taking turns to explore the rapid succession of features with our flies. It was lovely water flowing through a pastoral landscape, the trout seemed to be resting for the most part but here and there one rose and now and then one was caught. I managed a half pounder and a trout just over the pound and was more than content. A trout just over the pound is my kind of trout. Altogether it was a delightful afternoon, followed by a day or two back on the Annan, fishing there as usual in a half-hearted sort of way.

On what turned, anyway, into our last ever week on the Annan I came to our cottage looking forward to the food and the wine and the company, but at the same time telling myself that it would be a good idea to try just a little harder to catch a few trout. The Annan was very low and Kinnel Water had almost disappeared; it seemed to me that, even if I tried a little harder, there would still be no guarantee of catching any trout.

I did try harder. On the first morning of my fishing I caught a trout of about a pound, little better than a fingerling for the Annan but bigger than any fish that I had caught from the river in earlier years. I spent the afternoon failing to catch four or five very large trout that were feeding just below the surface on a long, wide flat. They were daunting fish with plenty of time to inspect my flies and find them wanting. If one of them had swallowed my fly I should have been so surprised that I should almost certainly have forgotten to strike.

The next day I fished the Annan again, caught nothing in the morning, drank two glasses of wine with my lunch and then slept in the green shade for an hour or so. After this short siesta I saw what I took to be the rise of a smallish trout under a willow bush, flicked Dry Simon over him and hooked a fish that was twenty yards below me within a second or two of feeling the iron. He was slow to surrender and, as I held him in the water before release, I reckoned him between 2¼ – 2½ pounds. I almost wished that I knew how to work the camera on my mobile phone. And then I returned contentedly to the green shade and dozed for a time before driving back to our cottage with my thoughts already turning towards sherry and the beginnings of a convivial evening.

There followed two days on the head waters of the Clyde: a winding stream with peaty pools and surprisingly choosy trout. Each day produced only a single fish and then, on my last day, it was back to the Annan with low expectations in stifling heat beneath a bright sky. The morning fulfilled these expectations, leaving me sweaty, blank and unsurprised. The afternoon confounded them and it was Dry Simon who once again worked the miracle, except that this time he did it twice.

There were few fish rising and so I fished Dry Simon through the runs in the hope of bringing up a fish or two. I had been doing this for no more than five minutes when he suddenly disappeared and immediately the reel sang. From the surging power of the first run I knew that, with 3 pound nylon on the end of my leader, I must lose this fish, but somehow the tackle held. He was too big for the net but, with a shake and a sort of shuffle and with my heart on the edge of my mouth, I managed to squeeze him in: 20 inches of trout that I guessed at 3 ½ pounds. And then an hour later it happened again: towards the top of a fast run Dry Simon disappeared and I found that I was fighting a trout I must surely lose, but the hook held and at last he was drawn over the net: one of the most beautiful trout that I have ever caught, perhaps five or six ounces lighter than the first. Once he had been revived and released I just sat on the bank, bewildered by the afternoon's rewards, only half able to believe that my casual and unscientific approach to a notoriously difficult river had given me two such noble trout, conscious at the same time that I should actually have preferred an afternoon occupied with more but smaller fish, with bright trout of half- and three-quarters of a pound and with a scattering of genuine pounders. I felt grateful to the Annan for giving me those two exceptional and beautiful trout, but at the same time, sitting there with no inclination to try for a third three-pounder, sitting there and waiting contentedly for my friend Kelvin to decide that he had fished enough, I could not help telling myself all over again that I was happier with the sort of trout that I found near the beginnings of the Wharfe up at Deepdale or down in Shropshire on the secluded Rea Brook.

We left the next morning, calling in at the estate office to return keys and book our cottage again for the following year. It was then we learned that it would no longer be available because it was being turned over to long lets, and we later decided that it was time to find some fishing further north, which is why, next spring, a bright day in May found me sitting in the sunshine on the banks of the Tirry, sipping a beakerful of red wine and telling myself that I was sitting in a special and very beautiful place where, although the little river flowing at my feet was indisputably a holiday river, my fisher's heart already felt almost completely at home.

Chapter Eight

WALES AND THE
SPIRIT OF PLACE

I am in Wales, in the twisting, deeply cloven valley of the
Irfon. It is a very lush valley, a very green valley. It is, in fact
a celebration of green in most of its many shades. Some of the
steeply rising and confining slopes are covered with bracken and
rough grass, with the almost emerald green of the bracken and
the much paler yellowish green of the grass. Others are planted
with dark and crowded stands of spruce and fir and pine. On
some of the slopes there is open oak woodland, with individual
trees choosing their own more delicate or slightly heavier
shade of green and, by the way, although I acknowledge that
vast plantings of conifers are very bad for rivers and generally
unbeautiful, I still find the contrast between the loose and
informal pattern of those broad-domed oaks, dotted here and
there over the rising ground, and the regimented lines of the
sharp-shaped, thrusting pines and spruces strangely pleasing.

The riverside pastures are much the palest green, spiked with purple-headed thistles and with, here and there, a haze of white clover, while up above the bracken there is further relief from green in the shapes of sheep grazing slowly over the rough ground between spreads of leggy brown heather and grey outcrops of rock or short slides of scree.

The sides of the valley are often precipitous. Its floor is very narrow and the Irfon winds along it, rushing between cramping slabs of dark rock, foaming down rapids and falls, lingering on wide corners, resting in deep pools and flats before setting off again down broken, stony runs. There are trees all along the banks, alders and willows and ashes, all again a different shade of green; often the branches are thickly lichened and ferns grow on some of them. Buzzards soar and mew, ravens croak, kites float through the sky and this morning, after thunder overnight, the laden air barely moves and the sun is at last beginning to burn off the clouds. I cannot see the river from the cottage where my friends and I are staying; it is a garden and a field below me, but I can hear its voice and I shall answer its call this afternoon. For now I am happy to be sitting here trying to write. My friends have already gone fishing. I am enjoying the silence and the opportunity this gives me to collect my thoughts about this valley and the powerful effect that it has on me.

I know of no other valley where the spirit of place is so immediately assertive. Almost as soon as I first fished in Wharfedale I realised that I wanted its river to flow through the rest of my life, but this first impulse of affection was felt almost exclusively for the river itself; the spirit of the surrounding place took only gradual, and very gentle, possession of me, over the years slowly strengthening its hold with ever more binding and very welcome chains of love. Sometimes I look at it differently, thinking that the spirit of Wharfedale has seeped into me, almost like a geological process, and I know that some part of its power comes from my long association with the valley and its river. It feels now like friendship, the old and loving sort, the generous sort, the sustaining and nourishing sort.

I think the spirit of Wharfedale is formed from more wholesome forces than those that make the spirit of Cwm Irfon, where the impact of the valley strikes me as something like an encounter with a dominant personality. We have been coming here for more than ten years now and I felt the mood of the valley just as soon as I inhaled it for the first time. There is a heaviness to it, a heavy calm, experienced most deeply if you walk down to the Washpool on a still evening under cloud, where it often seems to me that the essence of Cwm Irfon is gathered and concentrated and is felt as something like a pressure on the mind, a weight of brooding stillness. I suppose it comes from the sense of confinement down there on the floor of the valley by the brown pool, where like the river you are hemmed in by the steep sides pressing round you and sweeping up so high above you. You find a sort of peace down there by the river but you do not find serenity.

I love coming to Cwm Irfon and I particularly love those after-dinner strolls down to the Washpool, but I could never belong to this valley because I could never feel at home in this air, in this atmosphere. To breathe it for a few days brings the stimulation of difference, but over time I think that it might stifle and dull, might even suffocate, not everyone perhaps, perhaps just me. I say that brief contact is stimulating because it puts me in front of my lap-top, eager to explore and understand what I find here, unless the effect is in fact the opposite of stimulation, is in fact narcotic, unless the heavy air coagulates and confuses thought to produce the meaningless mumbo-jumbo that has filled the last few paragraphs. I am open to the possibility that I have just written a load of nonsense, but there is undoubtedly something special here and I am trying to make sense of it.

I know there is something special because the spirit of the place has a strange effect upon my attitude to fish and fishing.

I have already told you that holiday fishing makes catching trout less important. At Cwm Irfon it barely matters at all and I often choose to write rather than to go fishing. When I do go to the river I do, of course, like to catch fish, but the brace is of no significance and a blank day can send me back to the cottage without any sense of failure or discontent. I look upon the annual week in Cwm Irfon as a holiday among friends in a beautiful place, a place with a very powerful presence, and with the possibility of a few fish. Two or three years ago I caught lots of grayling and was delighted. Last year I caught virtually nothing and enjoyed myself just as much. This year, by the way, seems to be modelling itself on its immediate predecessor. At Cwm Irfon it sometimes seems that I have found my way into a different reality.

*****

There was something similar last week on the Rea, which I fished for four consecutive days before coming here, although on the Rea, catching trout, as I think you already know, matters very much indeed. It began anyway, this feeling that I had entered something like a world apart, just as soon as I got to the river after driving for more than four hours on busy motorways and congested main roads. I looked over Duddlewick Bridge and saw a rising trout, then very slowly I drank my holiday half-bottle of red wine, sitting in the Land Rover in the deep shade of the trees, and already it felt like a retreat, as though merely by reaching the bridge and the river, I had left behind the rush and stink of the modern world – not of course without having made my own contribution to it – and escaped into a slow, green, shadowed refuge where the loudest sound was the faint breath of the breeze in the leaves or the occasional and slightly discordant rasp of a crow or the high-pitched mewing of a circling buzzard. After the stress and frazzle of the journey I was being lulled into a much gentler state of being. The wine, of course, had something to do with it, but it could not have happened without the quietness all round me and without the beguiling prospect of a long afternoon beneath the trees in search of the wonderful trout of the Rea Brook.

And they came to me, those trout, drawn from the water down there in the shadows, down there beneath the trees in narrow shafts and rocking dapples of sunlight made brighter by the dancing shine of green and blue damsel flies and by the rare flash of a kingfisher. There were red spikes of willow herb and white flowers of twining brambles all along the banks between tall purple stalks of alien balsam. And, even in July, there were still mayflies fluttering from the water. It was as though, whatever season it might be beyond those high, tangled and sheltering banks, beyond the tall poplars and willows rising so high above the water, down there in the shadowed stillness the Rea was still flowing through an afternoon in early June; it was as though time had stood still, waiting for my return, and it strengthened the feeling that I was fishing in an enchanted place, that there was some potent magic at work in the enclosed world between the banks and beneath the trees. And every trout that I brought splashing to my net only deepened the spell, which took complete possession of me: a spell somehow formed from sunlight and shadow and sliding water, from spotted trout and seclusion and a powerful sense of otherness.

It was wonderful, and yet I should not want the Rea to form the staple of my fishing. Just sometimes, down there in its confined, shadowed and secret world, I feel that it is almost too much for me, feel something like an oppression of the spirit, feel suddenly ill at ease in the enveloping loneliness, feel myself an intruder in a place where I do not belong. This happens only rarely; most of the time I breathe in the deep solitude as a sort of healing balm and often I find it very difficult to leave the river, feeling something like a compulsion to try for just one more trout, to see if perhaps there is one rising in the next pool or round the next bend; and so it goes on, especially if the trout really are rising and if I am catching a few of them, until at last I somehow manage to tear myself from the river and return, half against my will, to common reality.

Trout matter very much on the Rea, for its magic depends on them, and more often than not the river is kind to me. It was kind to me last week. On the first day of my visit there were five trout, and some of them were good fish, which I realise immediately is the wrong thing to say, because of course they were all good fish: red-spotted and wild and very beautiful. All five of them were miracles of nature and three of them were bigger than the general run of Rea trout, which is what I should have said in the first place. None of them, incidentally, took an artificial mayfly, which is, I suppose unsurprising given that I never tied one to the end of my leader because I never saw a trout eat one of the naturals. All five of these miraculous trout ate my CDC Sparkle Sedge, which is a new development and seems very promising. I dress it just like my standard CDC Sedge pattern except that the two turns of gold wire are replaced by Dry Simon's tail of Krystal Flash. You should give it a go.

There were four trout on my second day; on the third I had to be content with three. I was in fact more than content and this was the day on which the Rea was formally recognised as the second river in my fishing life. I may already have told you that for many years it was the Eden and it is not the Eden's fault that it is no longer so. Back in 2015 Storm Desmond – what a ridiculous name for so destructive a force – devastated the river and she has yet to recover, although some of my friends tell me that this is at last underway. Others deny this. I have anyway broken all my promises to discover for myself which of them are right because I cannot force myself to risk the pain of finding that a river where I once caught four two-pounders in little more than an hour is now a broken ghost of her former self. The Wharfe, ever since I first fished at Kilnsey in undergraduate days, has been the abiding love of my fishing life but for many years the Eden, with those often enormous hatches of olives and those big wild trout and plenty of them, was in truth a finer trout stream. She was a finer trout stream but she never threatened the Wharfe's unshakeable hold on my affections. Now, anyway, I am frightened of the Eden, frightened of fishing where I once fished with such delight, frightened of finding, instead of fulfilment, only emptiness and pain. This is, I know, a danger to which I shall sometime have to expose myself, probably next season now, unless I wait for the season beyond next. It may never happen.

The Rea, anyway, for the time being at least, has been awarded the status of my second-favourite river. The elevation occurred on the third day of last week's fishing when, after no more than ten minutes on the water, I had already caught a brace of very beautiful trout. I took a photograph of them and at the same time told the river of the honour she had just received. Then I fished on gratefully, reflecting on my different feeling for different rivers and realising, among other things, that much as I love the Rea she would not, like the Wharfe, have been able to help me when I was most in need of it. For I believe that the Rea is a river for resilient fishers with healthy minds.

I have already written a book exploring the depression that overwhelmed me shortly after my retirement rather more than ten years ago, explaining how almost three years passed with virtually no fishing and with almost no pleasure coming from the little that I did do (or from anything else). There were many forces that helped my slow and erratic convalescence; there were dear and very loving friends, there was the devotion of a brother and a sister; there were two expert and caring doctors; there was my catholic faith and there was probably medication; but there was also the river Wharfe, where my tentative and very nervous resumption of fishing and then my growing confidence and pleasure in the prospect and experience of long days on the river was a chief element of the healing process: through finding that I once again belonged on the banks of the Wharfe, through finding that catching trout was important again and, just as it had always been until the time of my illness, was once again a source of delight and fulfilment and peace. And all this, together with all the beauty of the river and of its valley, together with that precious sense of restored intercourse and intimacy, brought new strength and healing joy.

I do not think the Rea could have performed the same service. I think that, in that season when I was slowly fishing my way back to health, days on the Rea might even have set me back. They might, I think, have felt like a confinement. Just occasionally the Rea provokes in me a feeling of unease. I think that, seven or eight years ago, the atmosphere that envelops fishers of the Rea might well have been too much for my fragile state of mind, might have disturbed and driven me away, might have persuaded me that I was still not strong enough to fish. I think the heavy stillness would have weighed me down, I think the deep shade would have felt like darkness, I think the loneliness would have inspired self-doubt and fear. Now that I am indeed strong again I can embrace the shadows and the seclusion and the solitude, finding peace down there in the brown water beneath the trees while searching for a brace or two of the spotted trout that swim there. The magic of the Rea is undoubtedly good magic, but it is also powerful magic, too powerful for a weak or damaged mind. The magic of the Wharfe is just as powerful but in a different way; it is healing magic, magic to nurse a wounded spirit back to health and happiness.

Anyway, on the last of my four days fishing on the Rea, I could only spend a couple of hours there and was given a fine brace: a gift that confirmed the new status of the enchanting Rea Brook. It was on the afternoon of this last day that I drove down to Cwm Irfon to spend a week in Wales, a week that included a couple of days on a mountain stream that tumbles down from the hills about an hour's drive from Cwm Irfon itself.

*****

It is a winding staircase of a stream, winding and very steep. The rough slopes rise, often almost sheer, on either side of the water, which soon falls and clears after rain but still flows with a glowing touch of peat, while the bed of the stream and the projecting rocks and the bankside cliffs that rise over some of the pools are all white and grey and often lichened or mossed. It is a slippery staircase and a narrow one but, as I struggle from pool to pool and from run to run, sometimes forced to abandon the watery stairway and clamber up through the rough surrounding ground, I feel no sense of confinement, no hint of the heaviness that comes to me at Cwm Irfon down by the Washpool; and there is no fear of the oppressive sense of loneliness that very occasionally visits me on the Rea.

I wonder if part of the reason is that fishing this lovely stream involves ascent. I am not just fishing, I am climbing to ever higher places, I am rising above the valley below me on my way into the hills. There is something that seems, for most of us, to be intrinsically invigorating and, yes, uplifting in doing this. We enjoy getting nearer to the sky, we enjoy the effort involved and we enjoy being able to stand and look down on the world that we have left below us.

And there is, I think, something else about fishing this stream that draws me, for it turns fishing into a journey with a destination, a destination that I shall soon reveal although, if you will permit me the old cliché, the journey is probably more important and more enjoyable than journey's end. And this particular journey's end, anyway, is moveable, because it is partly up to me to determine precisely when it has been reached, by telling myself that here is today's destination and then sitting down for five minutes to celebrate my arrival before standing up and heading back down to the Land Rover.

My destination, anyway, in so far as I have one, is the hanging valley that I come to when at last I climb out of the stream's narrow passage and find the water now winding its much gentler way towards me along more or less level ground extending some way from the banks on either side. I was hesitant in talking of a destination, but I realise now that it was appropriate, because I do not feel that I have fished the stream properly unless I have completed the ascent and reached the high valley from which it comes. How far I fish on towards the source depends on the weather and on my mood.

This year, on the holiday's last day, after reaching the level ground of the high valley, I fished on for perhaps another mile, much further than ever before. It was a hot day, hot and bright, but there was still a healthy flow of water from rain a couple of days earlier. I caught trout from start to finish and, as soon as one had been returned, I was eager for the next.

Most of them were midgets, parr-marked little jewels of four or five inches. On home rivers I find catching such trout unsatisfying, even though it tells me that they are still managing to breed their own trout. On my mountain stream these three and four inch trout are a shining delight and on this particular day there were lots of them. There were medium-sized trout of six and seven inches. There were big fish a whole eight inches long and there were one or two trophy fish at least an inch longer. All were enjoyed, admired and returned, which reminds me of another difference between my home and my holiday fishing: that on holiday waters I am happy with catch and release. And perhaps it is on my Welsh mountain stream where I am happiest of all in giving back every trout that I catch to the water from which it has just been drawn.

Fishing my mountain stream is in many ways like fishing the Tirry up in Sutherland. In both waters I am fishing for small, wild trout; on both waters I return all the trout that come my way and feel that this is somehow appropriate, although on the Tirry I might well feel inclined, were I making my own meals rather than sitting down for dinner in the Crask Inn, to keep and consume a brace or two of those nine- and ten-inchers that the river gives me when it is in the mood. The Tirry is so full of trout that killing a few of them would do no harm at all. Even on my mountain stream I suppose I could take back to our cottage a brace of breakfast trout, but I do not and I do not want to. Perhaps this untypical forbearance is bred by the mountain air and by the spirit of place that inhabits my mountain stream.

There are similarities to fishing the Tirry and fishing my Welsh mountain stream, but the landscapes through which they flow are very different. The Tirry, at least where I fish it, flows through an open landscape, rough and wild and wide, with a horizon of high mountains. There is an exhilarating feeling of space. By contrast my mountain stream is a secret water flowing in the cleft that it has made for itself on its steep descent from the hidden valley above. It is an intimate water that takes you to itself and somehow brings easy, but at the same time important, satisfaction.

On that last day of my recent holiday I fished the lower pools and runs for something like an hour, perhaps a little longer, which brought me something like half a dozen small trout, none more than six inches long and all very beautiful; and the sunlight was in the water and on the rock and the rough ground and in the sky above. Midday had passed and it seemed time for wine and a sandwich, sitting by the stream and feeling pleased that it had been so kind to me and that there was still lots of fishing ahead of me, at the same time acknowledging that on other rivers, like the Wharfe and the Rea, six similar trout would have brought frustration rather than fulfilment.

With food and drink finished I fished on under the sun through the steeply stepped pools, dark pools with a rush of white water connecting them. Here and there I caught a trout, including one or two at least eight inches long. They all came to the CDC Sparkle Sedge and I never felt the need to change my fly. It was not the sort of fishing that poses difficult problems of fly selection; I never asked myself whether the trout were taking swimming nymphs or emergers or surface flies; I never wondered whether I needed a pattern tied on a size 20 hook and there were no ticklish issues of presentation. There were fish rising and most of them took my chosen fly; there were other fish that only revealed themselves when they rose and grabbed it. It was light-hearted fishing but at the same time it bred very deep delight and it seemed, as I climbed from pool to pool and pushed my way round great slabs of rock, that I was rising above care. I slipped on a smooth ledge of rock on the edge of the stream and fell into shallow water. I climbed out and sat in the sun, laughing and knowing that very soon I should be dry again.

And then the climb was over and the stream was winding its sinuous way towards me over the floor of its lonely valley. There was a buzzard calling somewhere on the hillside, there was a fork-tailed kite floating high above me, there were the slow-moving shapes of sheep on the valley's rising slopes and there was a gentle drift of a few white clouds through the blue sky. Down by the water there was no breath of wind.

The pools were now much quieter features, mainly on the corners of the stream, with a dark slide of water round wide curves of the bank and with, on most of these corners, the marks and occasional splashes of rising trout. Fishing on along the wandering course of the stream and half-wishing that I could fish my way right to the source, at the same time acknowledging that I had neither the time nor the energy, I caught perhaps another half dozen trout, none of them longer than seven inches. Then, after about an hour, unless it was an hour and a half, I decided that I had reached journey's end: that it was now time to turn round and head downstream, except that, before doing this, I would sit on the bank for a while by one of the stream's small pools, feeling tired and happy and wondering once again how catching a few small trout could breed so deep and so grateful a contentment.

I have already said that, in following my stream up into the hills, I had seemed to be climbing above care. I now felt something else; that I had left behind the heaviness of Cwm Irfon and was breathing a much kinder and gentler and more refreshing air that had filled my heart with lonely delight. And the day, I realised, had also been without the tension that I so often find on the Wharfe and other rivers, a tension deriving from knowing that I need at least a brace of takeable trout for contentment. The way in which tension and anxiety dissolve as soon as that second such trout is drawn over the net is, of course, wonderful, and it breeds a deeper peace and a deeper fulfilment than came to me up in the high valley of my mountain stream. I had caught perhaps twenty trout; every one of them had been returned. There had been no bruising encounters with big fish lost, no moments of rapture with big fish caught and killed. The day had brought a succession of small pleasures which between them had produced this sense of delight and weary well-being. My mountain stream had been kind to me; sitting by that small pool of brown water I felt and savoured the loneliness, feeling too that I had spent the day in a beautiful and generous place where I had felt welcome and at peace.

There was peace down by the Washpool that evening, but it was a different sort of peace, a powerful but less tonic peace. The contrast between the two felt somehow complementary. I shall, I hope, be back at Cwm Irfon next year to breathe in its version of peace and then to go off in search of the gentler peace that waits for me along the steeply climbing banks and in the high, hidden valley of my mountain stream.

Chapter Nine

BIGGEST TROUT

I have mixed feelings about big fish. I do rather like them once I have them safely in the net, but the tension and anxiety of playing them, nowadays at least, is almost too much for me and losing them is traumatic, is a sort of bereavement, inflicting a wound that is slow to heal and sometimes leaves a permanent scar.

I can think of fishing days that were ruined by hooking and losing big fish; there was a trout on the Eden – I'm sure he weighed at least four pounds – that disappeared with my fly in his mouth after surging up and down the small pool where I had hooked him for what seemed at least half an hour but was probably no more than a minute or two. It was a loss that haunted me for days and, after something like twenty years, I can still remember the dreadful numbness that came over me when I was forced to acknowledge that the line had gone limp, that the rod was no longer bent. Perhaps like me, by the way, you find that it takes time for the dreadful truth of losing a big fish to sink in. Much earlier in my fishing life, towards the end of the second long vacation of my undergraduate days, there came my encounter with the monster of Clapham Beck, who almost certainly weighed nothing like four pounds but he was a big fish for the Wenning and its tributary becks, and he would have been a huge fish for the student who spent most of that summer fishing in the shadow of Ingleborough. I hooked him, anyway, on a corner of the beck during a huge hatch of blue wings. I cannot remember how long he was on for – probably just a few seconds – but I shall never forget the terrible bitterness of loss and how I struggled to confront what had just happened.

Perhaps the worst thing about losing a big fish is the emotional slump it involves: the sudden move from a tense and total engagement in the struggle to a sort of weak, un-sinewed and half-incredulous emptiness. Anyway, whenever I fished the Wenning in the weeks after this tragedy, I fished up the river impatiently, eager to reach the corner of the beck where I had hooked the monster in order to see if I could hook him again and this time hold on to him. There was never a sign of him and I am still wondering whether he weighed a whole two pounds.

I find losing big fish a little easier to manage when there's already a brace or more in my bag. Two summers ago I hooked something huge in Mile House Dub on the Wharfe. I played him until he was beginning to tire, until his runs were becoming shorter and less strong, until I could see the blurred and enormous form of him whenever he turned, but then, when I was beginning to think that he would be mine, the hook very gently removed itself from his jaw and left me feeling disappointed rather than heartbroken, because I could tell myself that there were already three good trout in my bag and there was every prospect of more. I should, of course, have preferred to catch him and I do remember that an element of my disappointment was unsatisfied curiosity, because I should never be able to establish whether he had in fact been as big as I had suspected while playing him, whether he had weighed a whole four pounds. In looking back over this loss, the beautiful three-pounder that I caught later the same afternoon may perhaps cast some sort of soothing glow over my recollection. But at the time it was those three earlier trout that helped me to come to terms with the loss of an exceptional trout.

Something similar happened at Driffield many years ago when at the end of a sunny and successful afternoon I hooked and lost what was almost certainly a very large trout indeed. He wrapped my nylon round a submerged post and that, of course, was that. There followed perhaps a few seconds of uncomprehending anguish, but then I sat on the edge of the beck and took from my bag the four trout that I had already caught, a brace of two-pounders among them; I laid these trout in the grass, gazed at them and was very soon able to tell myself that it would be ungrateful and greedy, when the day had given me four such lovely trout, to feel that it had been ruined by the loss of a fifth one, however big he might have been. And there was comfort too in the knowledge that the loss of this huge trout had not been my fault, that I was a visitor to the beck and knew nothing about that submerged post and could probably have done nothing to keep him from it even had I known of its lurking presence in the pool. Anyway, I remember driving home in good spirits.

I am probably an atypical fisher, given that, in my old age at least, I no longer want to catch exceptionally big fish. I have a friend who specialises in them, catching three- and four-pounders on the Wharfe throughout the course of most seasons. He seems to catch such trout almost as often as I catch pounders and his biggest trout from the Kilnsey water weighed somewhere between six and seven pounds. Peter searches out these big fish. I am happy to leave them to him and to spend my fishing days catching half- and three-quarter pounders, a few genuine pounders and even occasional trout weighing a whole pound more. The reason for this is that really big trout, it seems to me, disturb the emotional coherence of a fishing day, which sounds abominably pretentious but I still think it is true.

Fishing is an exciting as well as a beautiful activity. There is tension in casting to a rising trout, in watching your dry fly to see if it suddenly disappears or in following the tip of your line, hoping it will slide or dart forward to tell you that one of your spiders has been seized by a trout. Hooking a fish in response to these signs, feeling the sudden weight of him on the end of your line, these are thrilling and intensely satisfying moments in a fisher's day. Then there is the tension of the fight and, when things go well, the relief of capture and the sense of achievement that belongs to it. We fishers experience a wide range of emotions; this fisher can manage very nicely without the added intensity of emotion brought by contact with really big fish. I can cope perfectly well with the delight and disappointment of catching or losing ordinary trout (no trout are really ordinary but you know what I mean); I can wave goodbye to a pounder without feeling that his departure has put out the sun. If the struggle goes my way I can admire a pounder, in the net or on the bank, enjoying the calm and grateful satisfaction of success in contemplating his (modest) size and (incomparable) beauty. On the other hand it seems to me that there is an element of excess in our response – or at least in my response – to the loss or capture of enormous fish, which, it suddenly occurs to me, is probably why I have never really taken to fishing for salmon.

An ideal day's trout fishing should be a sort of composite experience, made up of numerous encounters with trout, encounters with contrasting outcomes, with one or two perhaps standing out as the high or low points of the day, but with neither of them turning all those other encounters into something trivial and irrelevant, which is what tends to happen when we catch or lose huge fish. Encounters with big fish are too dominant; they almost obliterate what lies on either side of them. They disturb the equilibrium of a day on the river. Soon I shall tell you the story of my biggest ever trout. In thinking of him just now I could not remember whether I caught any more trout on the day of his downfall. I had to consult my diary to find out that I did. You have already been told of the huge trout I lost one afternoon on the Eden; I can remember that, when this happened, there was already a trout of almost two pounds in my bag; I can also remember that he might as well not have been there. Big trout bring with them such strong emotions that they often leave room for nothing else.

The most powerful feelings of a fishing day should be the quiet ones: above all the feeling of peace that comes over you at the end of your day when you sit by the river in contemplative recollection of the day's events, and I think this peace is felt most deeply when it is accompanied by a profound sense of thankfulness, not for a single gift of extraordinary magnificence, but for a whole host of smaller gifts, gifts of surpassing beauty given, not just today, but on so many days and over so many years. These feelings should be with you through the course of a fishing day, but they will reserve their fullest and most welcome force for that time of reflection when, with fishing done, you sit by the Wharfe for a few minutes before telling yourself that it is time to go. They are the best gifts that a river can give to a fisher and, for me at least, I neither need nor really want a monster in my bag; I need no more than a brace of ten- or eleven-inch trout to feel the healing power of the fisher's peace.

I do not need, or really want to catch enormous trout any more. They are too disruptive. The thought of a five-pounder makes me nervous. Two-pounders I can cope with, even enjoy. I have caught a few trout of three pounds and they have made me feel very pleased with myself. But the fisher's peace that I frequently hold out as the river's best gift to us cannot close a day on which you have lost a five-pounder and I am not even sure that catching a five-pounder is likely to encourage peace to gather all round you at the end of your day.

*****

The biggest trout I ever caught came something like fifteen years ago. He brought me feelings of elation and pride and a huge sense of achievement. He was a sporting triumph and I am very pleased that I caught him but he did not bring me the peace that so often visits me on the headwaters of the Wharfe at the end of a day spent among seven- and eight-inchers, among half and three-quarter pounders and, if I am really lucky, perhaps a trout, or even two of them, weighing a whole pound. I wonder if this is because, in my old age, although I most certainly go fishing in search of trout, beyond this and more importantly I go fishing in search of a state of mind. This is why you so often find me sitting by the river and thinking about my experience of the fisher's peace. I make no apology for returning to this theme because different days seem to reveal different aspects of its depth and beauty. This chapter, anyway, is meant to be about big trout and so here is an account of how I caught my biggest-ever trout. It did not happen in the way such things are meant to happen.

I say this because I think the capture of your biggest-ever trout should be the culmination of a long campaign; you should have been engaged with him for at least half a season and have come to regard him as an old and supremely cunning foe, except that, in spite of the fact that he had so often mocked, despised and defeated you, in spite of all this, in spite of constant humiliation, you sometimes thought of him almost as a friend. You certainly spent lots of time with him.

He lived, anyway, on a corner of the river, under a high bank and beneath a willow with drooping branches that specialised in seizing your flies. To reach him you had to cast over a fast and broken run which seemed to promise your fly and line almost instant drag. When, by putting a rather skilful wiggle in your cast, you would have managed to avoid drag for just long enough, you did not always manage to avoid those drooping branches. Since you first spotted him, on a cloudy April afternoon during an untypically thick hatch of spring olives, and then sent your fly skating through his lair for the first time, you had spent long hours watching him eating flies before deciding that a little something-or-other might just do the trick. Sometimes it was a wet something-or-other, sometimes it was dry, sometimes it was halfway in-between. From time to time you managed that rather skilful wiggle with your first cast, so that your little something-or-other floated over him very enticingly and was, of course, disdained. The wiggle in your second cast was not always as successful, so that drag set in and for the time being put your opponent off his flies.

You would leave him and come back, sometimes after half an hour, sometimes a day or even a week later. Whenever it was that you returned to his corner, he was usually there, rising away steadily, pushing a huge snout out of the water every few seconds. He seemed to like his food. Now and then, after trying one or two subtler approaches, you resorted to shock tactics when, not forgetting to attempt the essential wiggle you flicked a huge Bottlebrush over him and waited for the explosion. When no explosion occurred you realised that the situation called for a Klinkhåmer, but the hanging abdomen of your perfectly tied and perfectly presented Klinkhåmer proved a resistible temptation. He saw through it straight away and he saw through the half dozen other flies that you drifted past him, until one of them lodged in a branch of the willow and your attempts to retrieve it dropped a twig on the tip of his enormous nose.

Spring turned to summer. Sometimes he was not at his feeding station and you wondered resentfully whether some other fisher had helped himself to your trout. Once you rose him to a tiny black gnat and were so surprised that you forgot to strike. Often your fly dragged before it reached him; once or twice he floated with it and then turned away. Sometimes you did not feel up to him, preferring the lesser challenge of more pregnable trout, but always you returned to his corner with renewed hope.

One evening there was a huge hatch of blue wings; your parachute B.W.O. fell beautifully and he complimented your incomparable skill by sipping it down; there was a huge boil on the surface of the water, with spray flying all over the place and flashing with rainbow brilliance in shafts of late sunlight. It was dramatic and it was beautiful, but the drama ended almost as soon as it had begun when your rod went limp and your nylon came back to you without the attachment of a fish or even of a fly. It was a situation that called for bad language or for throwing stones into the water and you thought it best to do both. You also gave up fishing and went home to seek comfort from Scotland's remedy for adversity; you brooded over a large glass or two, wondering just how big he was and wondering whether you might in fact have given up fishing for good.

Next morning you were, of course, back again. There were still a few spinners floating down the river. Yours floated over him and he ate it as though he had only just realised that he liked the taste of sherry spinners very much indeed and couldn't have enough of them. As soon as he was hooked he dived and then he ran and your line almost snagged in one of those drooping branches. There was no question of turning him and you realised that he must surely escape, but miraculously the line stayed tight, the rod stayed frighteningly bent and he made his own decision to turn just when the backing was beginning to show. Frantic hand-lining kept you in something like contact and then he ran again and so it went on, with three long runs and two or three shorter ones. You began to hope and at the same time you were seized by dread, because failure after so long a campaign and such a struggle would be a bitterness beyond endurance. Your heart was beating like a frantic hammer.

After those runs there were circles: slow, sullen circles that gave you plenty of time to see that he was huge. Once or twice he broke the surface and slapped the water with a swish of his monstrous tail. After those circles he hung there in the current, swaying wearily from side to side. Thinking that the moment had come you offered him the net, but he pushed away with the remains of his strength, attempting one last feeble run. You brought him in again; this time there was no active resistance, there was just the weight of him; you slid the net under him and he looked too big for it; he slipped over the rim when you tried to lift him and you almost panicked; somehow the second lift found a huge trout inside your net. You stumbled to the bank, completely drained and at the same time feeling like a god.

The spring balance told you what you knew already: that he was the biggest trout of your fishing life, although you would not have dared to guess that he weighed a whole five pounds. You wondered about putting him in a glass case; or you might turn him into the main course of his own funeral feast; but then, moved by a sudden and unexpected flow of mercy, you found that you had rejected thoughts of macabre feasts and bow-fronted glass cases. You eased the barbless hook from his jaw and then, with something like a lover's tenderness, you held him in the current while he slowly revived until, after a minute or two, you waved goodbye to him as, with breathing and balance restored, he swam slowly away and then disappeared. And now at last you knew for certain what you had half known all along; that he was no enemy at all but rather the best of friends. Time after time he had beaten you; just once you had got the better of him, which was more than enough and in future you would leave him undisturbed; you would see him rising on his corner, you would say good morning to him and, after wishing him well, you would go in pursuit of the three-pounder that lived in the next pool.

*****

That, it seems to me, is how you should catch your best-ever trout, although an acceptable, but on the whole less satisfactory procedure might involve another fisherman, a friend with whom you have for some time shared the secret of the corner and of the willow and of the huge trout living there. Your friend is a better fisher than you and on this occasion you have given him first shot at the monster, going off in search of mere pounders, which have come to net with some regularity in the course of a bright September morning. Returning to your friend at lunchtime you are feeling rather pleased with yourself; in particular you are feeling pleased with the trout in your creel that weighs a bare ounce less than two pounds. You are not surprised to find that your friend has never moved, for he is a determined as well as a very skilful fisher, the sort who refuses to admit defeat; he has, in fact, spent the whole morning refusing to admit defeat and he is prepared to spend the rest of the afternoon doing exactly the same.

You will have guessed what happens next. Your friend invites you to have a go. In spite of the fact that the monster is clearly smutting you cannot be bothered to change your fly, so you flick an Orange Partridge in his general direction and ten minutes later you have caught a five-pound trout. You try to be casual in your response to the miracle; you seem to feel something forced in your friend's attempts to be happy on your behalf; you may even detect a note of bitterness beneath the warm surface of his words, but he tries his best and he takes photographs of you and your trout before it is returned to the river. In the afternoon, he catches a couple of genuine two-pounders, you catch nothing at all and find that any sense of strain between the two of you has melted away. You are still the best of friends.

I think, on the whole, that I prefer the first way; its pleasures are deeper, purer and untainted by any element of *Schadenfreude*. You may prefer the alternative but you will, I think, agree that the capture of a great trout is most satisfying when he is known to be a great trout before he eats your fly; and the sense of achievement will be deeper still if success follows weeks and weeks of unsuccessful enterprise. It should be a triumph against the odds, a grand climax, a final victory after a long succession of defeats, which is not how it happened with me.

*****

I was on the Wharfe at the end of May. The water was dead low and the sun was very bright. It was eleven o'clock in the morning, already I was sweating and had retreated into the shade, where I was now sitting and telling myself that trout would be difficult to come by. It was towards the end of my week's fishing; earlier days had each of them brought a few trout, although most had been stock fish, with just a few of those slender-finned, broad-tailed, densely spotted wild and beautiful true trout of the river Wharfe. It seemed to me, anyway, as I sat smoking in the shadows, that a stock fish or two would be the best that I could hope for on a day of such low water and bright light. They might not be as cunning as the native fish, but they had been in the river long enough to be worth catching and I had just failed with two or three of them busy smutting in the slack flow of the long, lazy pool beneath the trees.

There was a gentle run into this pool, a soft ripple rather than a rough and broken stream; about halfway down it I spotted a rise, which looked to me like the rise of a decent trout. He might be a good pound and a half, and the unshowy neatness of his rising suggested that he had long ago perfected the art of seizing flies from the surface of running water; this meant that he was probably a wild trout, and the fact that he was coming up every minute or so indicated that he was not smutting; he was helping himself to the few pale-wateries that were floating his way. I put on one of my favourite flies, a small parachute olive with a Krystal Flash tail; the cast was straightforward and very soon I was connected to what was clearly an enormous trout. I will not bother you with the details of the fight. It was a long struggle; to me, at any rate, it seemed to last for something close to eternity. It was also a savage struggle, with a heart-stopping leap in the middle of wild runs and angry tail-slapping and violent head shaking; after the savagery, it became dogged and sullen, setting my arm shaking with the strain and tension of it all. He was a noble trout and he was unwilling to yield, but at last the net went under him and I splashed ashore with a huge shape writhing in the bottom of the mesh.

I thought of weighing him and then putting him back, knowing all the time that I was too primitive a fisher to show modern mercy of this sort. Would Skues, I asked myself, would Stewart have given such a prize back to the river? I knew they would not; nor would I and so I knocked him on the head. He did not weigh five pounds, but three pounds twelve ounces was quite big enough for me: three and three-quarter pounds of small-headed, deep-bellied, red-and-black-spotted wild river trout. He was the best and most beautiful trout that I had ever seen and the gloat, partially obscured by triumphant drifts of pipesmoke, went on for at least a quarter of an hour. It did not matter that he was a chance encounter, that casting over him had presented no special problems or that rising him had posed no ticklish questions of fly selection. He was the biggest trout that I had ever caught and that, together with his beauty, was all in the world that mattered to me.

I joined three friends for lunch. Andrew had caught and returned a two-pounder, Merlin had killed one of two and a half; I listened and looked and then, with a fine sense of timing, I produced my monster. There were gasps; there was loud acclaim; there were innumerable photographs; there was, so far as I could tell, no lurking jealousy; there was nothing but generous participation in the triumph of a brother-angler. In the midst of all this I thought of the glass case and decided that it would be too expensive. Instead of saving him for the taxidermist I decided to eat him, and the feast was celebrated with four other friends about a fortnight later. He had grown huge by helping himself to the Wharfe's bountiful supply of signal crayfish; his flesh was salmon-red; he tasted wonderful and, as I chewed away, I thanked him silently, not only for filling my belly but also for filling me with pride in his capture and persuading me to think of myself for the best part of a day as a high and mighty fisherman. It was not true, of course, but it was a pleasing fantasy, even though my faith in it soon faded. My next day on the river was a hopeless blank.

And there you have the story of my biggest-ever trout. You may feel that his catching was too easy. You probably feel that he should have gone back. Almost certainly you will yourself have caught (and returned) trout a whole lot heavier. All I can say is that during the years before the monster, I had caught plenty of trout over two pounds and not a few much nearer three. On the Eden I had caught one that I put in my diary at three pounds, but even at the time I knew that it was a lie; I knew that he weighed at least half an ounce less than three pounds. I had been dreaming of the first genuine and indisputable three-pounder for more than twenty years. Now at last he had come along and, whatever the circumstances of his capture, he would most certainly do. On reflection the only pity is that I was too mean for the glass case; for if now I could see him up there on the wall, I should be able to look at him each evening, remember the occasion that had put him there and then raise my glass to him in silent thanks, at the same time telling him that, whatever he thought of me, I could not help thinking of him as a chief benefactor and a very dear friend.

*****

The account you have just read was written shortly after the capture of my biggest-ever trout, who has, by the way, maintained his status through the intervening years. Several three-pounders have come my way since his capture but none has been as close to four pounds as he. I still think, by the way, that he should have gone in a case and been hung on the wall. If he were there now I should still – perversely perhaps – think of him as a friend and tell him so, but from time to time I should also tell him something else. This would probably happen most frequently when I had come home from the top of the Wharfe, from Yockenthwaite, Deepdale or Beckermonds, with a brace of trout in my bag. There would be dogs to run, dinner to get ready, there would be time for a bath and then, as soon as my glass was filled with *fino*, I should look at my friend on the wall and take a sip or two and then ask him to forgive me if what I was about to tell him caused offence, because I would then confess to him that the two twelve-inch trout that I had brought home with me from the high river somehow meant more to me than he did, in spite of all his strength and magnificence and all that sense of triumph and elation that came with his capture.

And then I should explain how I had been slow to realise this and had long thought that, unless an even bigger trout came my way, he would remain the crowning glory of my fishing life; but finally now the truth had been revealed to me and I was hoping he might be able to understand that, although between them the day's brace came to less than half his weight, although they were stunted troutlings when set beside him in the shining splendour of his very considerable bulk, they were in fact just as beautiful, perhaps even more beautiful than he, and they had brought me something much more precious than three pounds twelve ounces of trout; they had confirmed and strengthened the bond between me and my river and they had brought me a deep contentment and a still deeper peace, for I had sat with them lying in the grass beside me at the end of the day, looking at the river that had given them to me, and they had taken my spirit somewhere beyond desire or fear, somewhere where it wanted nothing more than what it found in the present moment. There had been a connection with something stronger and deeper than sorrow and pain, than loss and longing and death, and this was the source of that profound contentment and that perfect peace. It was a state of being that only came to me on the banks of the Wharfe and, although I could not take it away with me, I could take away something of its influence to bring light and comfort to my life away from the river.

I should explain all this to my biggest-ever trout and then, suspecting that he had failed to grasp what I had just told him and that I had consequently hurt his feelings, I should apologise to him and beg his forgiveness a second time. I should then finish by thanking him most sincerely for finding his way into my net all those years ago and I should get on with drinking my sherry and turn my thoughts to other things. You can only talk to a trout in a glass case for so long.

Chapter Ten

TYING FLIES

I hesitate (just a little) to write about tying flies because I am not very good at it, although I'm not particularly good at fishing and I certainly don't hesitate to write about that; in fact I can't stop myself. Returning to flytying, anyway, there are all sorts of techniques that I haven't mastered and there is nothing that I do really well, although I think my spiders are at least halfway to being decent specimens of their kind. I shall be writing about flies, not in an attempt to pass on, or impress you, with my expertise, but because they are an intrinsically fascinating subject. I am here referring to the ones we make rather than the ones that hatch and fly, although the naturals are, of course, every bit as interesting. I shall be writing about flies because both the man-made sort and the sort that live and die are central to the whole business of flyfishing and I have been involved with them for a long time. I also owe a lot to fishermen's flies; they have brought mc a great deal of fulfilment and happiness. This chapter is a sort of tribute to the central contribution flies have made to a largely contented life.

One of the intriguing things about artificial flies is that, if you did a survey, asking, say, a dozen equally successful fishers of a given river which flies they most favoured, I should be very surprised if each one of them didn't come up with a widely different selection. There might be some agreement about spiders; they would all be likely to favour the Orange Partridge, the Snipe and Purple and the Waterhen Bloa, but I fancy their choice of dry flies would show considerable variety. Anyway, I propose to tell you about the patterns that I rely on for most of my sport and say something about my rather haphazard development as a flytyer.

It is early March as I write these words and I am beginning to tie some flies for the coming season. Expert and enthusiastic tiers are at it all winter. I need the motivation of need to sit me down in front of my vice. I do enjoy making flies, although I lack the stamina of more driven and devoted tyers, but half the reason I do it is that several of the patterns that I like best are not available commercially and I am also thrifty enough to think that paying for things that cost virtually nothing if you make them yourself is something worth avoiding. Anyway, with a new season only a few weeks away I am trying to tie myself at least half a dozen flies a day and will now move into my favourite literary form and keep a diary for as long as seems appropriate, telling you about the flies that I have been tying and what I think of them and about some related matters. I shall give you the recipes if I think it a good idea.

2 March

I realised this morning, as I sat working at my vice, that there are flies and flies and that I like some more than others. I was busy tying a pattern of my own devising called Dry Simon. It is a fly that catches me lots and lots of trout; the only other pattern that comes anywhere near it, perhaps indeed outperforms it, is a relatively new arrival in my fly boxes, my version of a CDC Sedge, which I shall doubtless come on to before long and is really an F-fly with a few extra bits. Dry Simon, anyway, is a great catcher of trout but in spite of this he is a fly that I have never regarded with unqualified admiration

Dry Simon is, as it were, my baby, and I think I should probably explain why I am not exactly a doting parent. To begin with there is his name, for which I am, of course, responsible, although when the naming took place it seemed somehow inevitable that a fly developed from a much modified version of a wet fly called Simple Simon should in his name bear witness to his origins. Simple Simon is an even worse name that Dry Simon and I blame Courtney Williams, father of the original pattern, for the whole business (although I admire his dictionary of flies very much indeed, even if it is now out of date). It is the personification that I abhor. You may have noticed that I think of Dry Simon as he and you may have shuddered at this (I often shudder myself), but given the name, what else can I do? You cannot dismiss a creation called Simon as it.

I could have called him Catlow's Fancy and then it would indeed have been 'it' rather than 'he' and the name would have possessed the virtue of being fairly descriptive, since the fly in question is undeniably of the fancy sort and I am its originator. But there is a problem here: that I do not think we should commemorate ourselves in the names of the flies we devise; there is a self-advertising pride to it, a smack of complacency and conceit that I think is better avoided, although it is arguably less offensive than the ghastly personification which, applied to a hook adorned with orange thread and something flashy called Krystal Flash, with peacock herl and two garish hackles, is completely ridiculous and involves a sort of tasteless frivolity, a failed attempt at some form of wit or humour or cleverness. But it is far too late to change. Dry Simon he shall remain and I shall continue to cringe ever so slightly whenever I mention him.

The name is a mistake and then there is the look of him. He is very good at his job but he is far too flashy to be declared a tasteful or beautiful fly. He is a show off, an attention-seeker, a dandy. He would doubtless be much less effective if he were not so ostentatious, so overdressed and vulgar and there am I, by the way, surrendering to a positive orgy of personification. Anyway, the fact that he is an unabashed fancy fly, an attractor, means, or at any rate might mean to others, that catching trout with him is less satisfying than with a genuinely imitative pattern. Many fishers find their deepest satisfaction on occasions when they find the trout challenging and choosy until, after experimenting with a succession of patterns, they find the one that persuades them it is what they are eating and proceeds to bring them to net. You do not get this refined, quasi-intellectual pleasure with Dry Simon, you do not think your way to the solution of a problem. You stick him on the end of your line and not infrequently you get the obvious and somewhat more primitive pleasure of catching lots of trout. Fortunately I am an unrefined and primitive sort of fisher, so primitive in fact, so crude and unreformed that I still associate fishing with food. I have my reservations about Dry Simon but I am of course very grateful to him for so often making me a fulfilled and contented fisher.

I did not, by the way, intend to talk about names when I started this short account of my involvement with tying flies. But now that I've got started I can see there will be more to come, because it's not just Courtney Williams and I who should have known better; perhaps the worst thing about artificial flies is the appalling names they so often bear but perhaps I've said enough about this for one day, perhaps it's time to get on with tying a few more flies.

3 March

I knocked out a few more Dry Simons yesterday. This afternoon I have tied half a dozen Poult Bloas, flies that belong of course to the great spider tribe of the north, and spiders, even though I fish them less often than I used to (and probably not as often as I should), are still unquestionably my favourite flies. To begin with there is their economy of design and their spare beauty; then there is the further recommendation that they are straightforward and quick to tie; there is also their history, because the Poult Bloa, the Orange Partridge and the Snipe and Purple go back far enough into the past for their origins to be obscure. They have no named creators and form part of the common inheritance of all northern flyfishers. Whenever we fish with a team of spiders, we are re-embracing a great tradition passed down from generation to generation over several centuries. Spiders appeal strongly to my sense of history and to my imagination. When fishing the Wharfe I rarely tie on an Orange Partridge and, say, a Waterhen Bloa without thinking that, well over a hundred years ago, Pritt might have tied on the same flies and fished them through the same pool in more or less the same way; and Pritt, at a remove of roughly a century and a half, was almost certainly nearer to me in time than to the first appearance of his Waterhen and his Orange Partridge.

Next come the names, so simply descriptive, so straightforward, so devoid of affectation. Poult by the way means a young bird; bloa refers to a bluish or slate grey feather and is a pretty accurate description of the hackles prescribed for the Poult and Waterhen Bloas. Everything about spiders is somehow unpretentious, unassertive and reserved, rather like so many of the northern fishers who have caught so many thousands of trout with them down the years. I cannot, of course, include myself in this admirable company, because I am a fisher who cannot stop telling the world – or rather those bits of it willing to listen – what fishing means to me. Spiders, anyway, are wonderful flies;

it is not their fault that they are less effective than they once were and, even if they are generally less deadly than in the past, I am intending to tie more of them and fish with them more frequently this coming season.

5 March

There were no flies yesterday but this afternoon those that I tied were all either my much modified version of Courtney Williams' Simple Simon or what I call a hackle Coachman, although it isn't really. They are nothing like as beautiful as spiders; they lack subtlety and are rather too bright but they are often effective, especially in a coloured water, and you will meet them often enough in these pages. I think the trout take my Coachman for a drowned or swimming beetle. I am less sure what they think of Simple Simon, except that he seems to tickle their fancy often enough. Courtney Williams, admittedly talking about his original rather than my variant, suggests that he is taken for a shrimp. I am unconvinced but what matters is that trout take him and not infrequently with enthusiasm.

I tied four of each, which is about as many flies as I can manage at a single sitting, and I decided that Simple Simon is almost as garish as Dry Simon, with his orange silk, his green peacock herl body ribbed with silver or gold wire (it doesn't matter a fig which), with his double hackle of a black feather (from a magpie's wing at present) with a shorter feather from a white pheasant in front. What makes him ever so slightly less garish than Dry Simon is that instead of the glittering tail of Krystal Flash he has two rather less gaudy turns of flat gold wire. My Coachman is almost the same, except for no gold wire, and purple instead of orange silk, which completely transforms the look of him. He is almost in good taste and bears, by the way, almost no resemblance to the original Coachman or any of its numerous variants, for none of them are tied with purple silk and they all involve a red or brown rather than a black hackle. Perhaps I should claim the fly as my own and I should probably do the same for my Simple Simon, but then I should have to think of names for them, names that I should probably come to regret. Naming flies is a ticklish business and people very frequently get it wrong. Plain descriptive names are best and I can't think of suitable names of this sort for my not really a Coachman and my scarcely Simple Simon. Anyway, I almost always fish them together as a team of two. Sometimes the trout show a marked, even an exclusive, preference for one or other of them, sometimes trout are shared almost equally between them and there are times, of course, when the trout show not the slightest interest in either of them. On the whole I think my Coachman is slightly more successful but there isn't much in it.

While busy with these flies I looked back over my erratic development as a flytyer and realised that I couldn't recall when first I started. My first-ever trout, caught with a fly from the local tackle shop, is an imperishable memory and I should like to relive the catching of him on my death-bed, all ten inches of him, on a soft, still and cloudy evening in late September two days before I went off to university in London. I should like to see again the moist shine of him in the dimming light and the pock-marked butterbur leaves in which I wrapped him before climbing onto my bike and riding home exultantly. The memory of that first trout will never fade but there are no surviving impressions of my first ever fly and even if I could remember what it was and when it was tied, the thought of it would, I suspect, be unlikely to brighten up the last few hours of my life. I do not know what pattern of fly was the first that I tied but it must have been a dry fly because for years I fished nothing else and I fancy it came into being some time in my first university vacation, when I seem to remember that a vice and some basic materials were given to me as a Christmas present.

7 March

I tied a few more spiders this morning, Poult Bloas and my own Pheasant Tail Spider, which consists of a pheasant tail body ribbed with brown silk and a well speckled hackle from the middle of a grouse's wing. I like the look of this fly and the trout, in particular the trout of the Foston Beck, sometimes like the look of it as well. It pleases me, by the way, to make use of the birds that I shoot, not only by eating them, but by using their feathers to make flies.

While tying my spiders, anyway, I realised how surprising it is that I have made the half competent flytyer that I think I have become, because I have never really been any good with my hands. When things break or fall apart the only way I can get them mended is with a cheque book or by a friend; I could no more put up a row of bookshelves than I could design and build a satellite to orbit Mars.

I suspect that my earliest flies were misshapen things that came to pieces almost immediately on use. I can remember very little about them, except that for some reason I liked making their bodies from hackle stalks. I do know that I still bought most of my flies and I recall that the Grey Duster was a firm favourite. I remember too that I bought Courtney Williams' famous dictionary of trout flies in my first year as an undergraduate and constantly dipped into it, but I am pretty certain that I did not try to tie many of the patterns that caught my fancy; I used it more as a guide to buying flies and I certainly enjoyed (and still enjoy) the book for its own sake. It must have been at least ten years before I began regularly to consult the dictionary in search of patterns to tie for particular circumstances, and I think a few more years came and went before I added Simple Simon to my repertoire.

My first steps as a tyer of flies have left very few firm memories; my efforts, I guess were laboured and unpromising, they were also fitful for I do know that through prolonged periods of my seven years at university and then through my first half dozen years as a schoolmaster I tied no flies at all.

You will often have read that the deepest satisfaction in flyfishing is to catch trout with flies that you have tied yourself. These days most of the trout that I catch are indeed caught with my own creations, but when I catch a trout with a fly that a friend has given me or with one that I have bought it gives me just as much pleasure. I tie flies because I have achieved a modest competence in the basic techniques, although there are some that are beyond me. I tie flies because shop-bought flies are often inadequate and expensive. I quite enjoy tying flies but it is never too long before I have had enough. Once I have fiddled round with fur and feather and wire and thread for about an hour I must do something else. I may come back to it later in the same day but an hour at a time is about as long as I can manage. Just occasionally, by the way, I surprise myself by producing a fly that strikes me as being just as it should be and indisputably beautiful, almost a minor work of art. While admiring it in the vice or in the palm of my hand I half regret that, if it some day fulfils its purpose, it will be molested and despoiled by the sharp teeth of a trout with no aesthetic sensitivity, unless, to avoid this indignity, it goes up to roost on the branch of a riverside tree and stubbornly refuses to come back down. These exceptional creations do not appear very often. I hope that my sentences are shapelier than the majority of my flies.

8 March

I tied no flies today but while wandering round my shoot and scattering corn for pheasants in the hope that it will help them to stay healthy and breed successfully, I spent more time thinking about my development as a flytyer (what there has been of it) and I realised the truth of something that I have already mentioned: that what turned me into a regular practitioner was realising, as I became a better fisher, that it was only by tying at least some of my own flies that I could supply myself with what I needed. I think the first cause of this – some time in my early thirties – was one of Pritt's patterns: a fly called Little Black.

I remember reading praise of Little Black in an issue of *Trout and Salmon* and immediately feeling certain that, tied on suitably small hooks, it would be just what was needed on hot summer days of low water when olives were scarce and the trout were spending hours on end smutting in the shady pools and glides. It was. I tied my Little Blacks on Veniard's fine wire 16s – more like most makers' 18s – and they should have been tied on still smaller hooks, but even so there were times when with the help of Little Black I managed to catch three or four, sometimes even half a dozen trout that would almost certainly have stayed in the river in the days before Little Black appeared on the scene. I called this wonderful pattern August Black, by the way, because August was often the month when it was most needed. I no longer think it right to alter the names of established patterns and so the August Black is once again Little Black. The point here, anyway, is that I could only put Little Blacks in my fly box by tying them myself. It was the same when I read an article singing the fatal attractions of Kite's Imperial which for some reason the owner of the local tackle shop never stocked. There were other patterns which I could only tie onto my leader if they had been produced by the work of my hands. And because this forced me to spend more time tying flies, I enjoyed it more and got better at it.

And then I realised that the spiders I bought were almost always overdressed and often tied with the wrong materials and so I started tying my own spiders and so it went on. I bought fewer and fewer flies; I started modifying patterns to see if I could improve them and invented one or two patterns of my own (how many flytyers, I wonder, haven't done this?). Gradually I accumulated a larger stock of materials, finding incidentally that shooting supplied much that I needed, and before too long I was providing myself with almost all the flies that I used, which is more or less how it is today, although I am always happy to buy a few flies if I find myself in a tackle shop and spot some patterns that look likely to catch me a few trout. Tomorrow I think it will be time to talk about modern state-of-the-art flies and how I have taken a few halting steps towards turning myself into something like a modern fisher.

9 March

While tying flies this afternoon I listened to some of Mozart's wonderful piano sonatas. It is a combination of which I disapprove, because great art demands total attention and doesn't get it if you are doing intricate things with your fingers, but there are times when I give in to temptation, partly because I think Mozart's music helps me to tie better flies. Often it is exuberant, often dazzling in its intricacy, often playful, frequently profound, often too it is sad because a deep vein of melancholy runs through Mozart's music, but always it is beautiful and I fancy some of the beauty rubs off on me, or rather on my flies and I may well be talking rubbish, not of course about Mozart but about the effect of his music. I think, by the way, that Mozart would have made a first-rate flyfisher. He would have enjoyed the beauty of his surroundings and the intrinsic beauty of the activity itself; he would have enjoyed the grace and delicacy of flyfishing and the way excitement explodes out of peace. And music came so easily to him that he would have been able to compose piano sonatas and string quartets while casting his team of spiders upstream and even while playing trout. I am less sure about Brahms. He would have loved his days by running water, but I fear he would have been a clumsy caster and prone to play his fish too hard. Certainly he would have spent large parts of his fishing days not fishing at all but sitting by the river, dreaming of Clara Schumann or sunk in brooding reflection. I am uncertain about

Bach but there can be no doubt about Beethoven; he would have thought fishing a complete waste of time, which might well form an appropriate verdict on this paragraph, although I have enjoyed writing it. There must be some composers who fished and found inspiration in it. Someone should look into it. Perhaps someone has.

Anyway, the flies that I tied while listening to Mozart piano sonatas were IOBOS, which was probably a foolish choice because, however well you tie them, they can never be beautiful and the name is a complete disgrace. I have already insisted that we should not turn great music into background noise; there was additional disrespect this afternoon in tying the flies I chose to tie while at the same time half listening to surpassing beauty. I should have tied spiders instead.

IOBO is a smart-arse acronym for It Ought To Be Outlawed. I do not want to know who invented the fly but he clearly thinks that he has given the world something wonderful (he may well have done), and he also thinks that he has given it an ingenious and amusing name (which he certainly hasn't). It seems to me, when I contemplate this name and the appalling self-satisfaction lying behind it, that Courtney Williams deserves a posthumous knighthood for dreaming up Simple Simon. Compared with IOBO as a name, Terry's Terror represents the apogee of good taste. The IOBO is a sort of miniature Humpy, another name that deserves very low marks indeed, which reminds me all over again that too many flies have rotten names. Why does good taste go out of the window when flyfishers (including me) think up names for the patterns they have devised? Artificial flies deserve respect.

You know that I admire spiders for many reasons and that the unaffected plainness of their names is one of them. There are many other flies that, without any attempt at humour or cleverness, without any exhibitionism, just tell you what they are like or what they are made from. You cannot take exception to names like the Rough Olive or the Blue Dun or the Pheasant Tail. Red Tag is a sensible name, whereas the very closely related Treacle Parkin is a very silly name but not quite as silly (or pleased with itself) as Tup's Indispensable. I wonder, by the way, whether Skues was guilty of this lapse of taste. I don't like canon Greenwell's Glory – the name rather than the fly, of course, even if the canon was not himself responsible for it – and I disapprove of Oliver Kite's Imperial; both are irreproachable trout flies (which I doubtless use too rarely) but the names are self-important and boastful. I am almost finished with names, but what on earth is a Particular, with or without Lunn in front of it? And you will surely agree with me that Dog Nobbler is a ridiculous name, which brings me to the end of another paragraph that should perhaps never have happened but which I could not resist. And, given that the impulse was irresistible, I have been commendably restrained because it could have been a very long paragraph indeed. It could have been half a dozen paragraphs or even a whole chapter. I haven't even mentioned Miss Beautiful Zonker or the Marabou Bastard.

Returning to the IOBO, a name that I can barely bring myself to use, I had, of course, being a rather old fashioned sort of fisher, never heard of such a fly, until on the Eden one day (I was exercising the dogs instead of fishing) I met a pleasant but undoubtedly somewhat opinionated Australian who, for my benefit alone, delivered several brief but authoritative lectures, one after the other, on various aspects of fishing, and then he gave me two or three small flies of identical design that he insisted I should be using instead of the outmoded flies that he assumed were still living in my fly boxes. I rather think he told me that I should never need anything else and for some reason in telling me this he failed to tell me the name of his wonder fly. I cannot believe that I was told it and subsequently forgot it, because if the opinionated Aussie had revealed the name its supreme ghastliness would surely have stayed with me and I should surely have asked him the significance of the repulsive acronym.

When people give me flies I tend rather ungratefully to forget all about them; they lie abandoned in whichever compartment of whichever fly box I deposit them. And this, of course, is exactly what happened to the opinionated Aussie's flies, until a day in late September found me on the Yorkshire Derwent with the trout in an unusually picky frame of mind, rising persistently at something very small and on the whole refusing to rise at the flies with which I was trying to tempt them. By lunchtime I had caught half a dozen undersized trout and just one (barely) worth keeping. And the small trout, by the way, had not been risers; I had brought them up to Dry Simon in fast water. The afternoon, anyway, was if anything even more challenging than the morning and, with little more than half an hour to go, I had added two six-inch grayling to the day's tally of fish. It was then, while hunting desperately through my fly boxes, that I spotted the opinionated Aussie's flies lurking among a crowd of Black Gnats. They looked small and interesting; they were untested and they were, I decided, worth a try.

I tied one on and in the short time left to me I hooked a good trout that got free, left my fly in the mouth of a better trout and then, with its identical replacement, caught and returned a fourteen-inch grayling. I drove home telling myself that next season would find me supplied with a good number of the opinionated Aussie's flies. It was my friend, Andrew Moss, who knows two or three times as much about flytying as I do, who revealed the appalling truth about their name. It may well have been the shock of this revelation that discouraged me from tying any of them last year. Finally now I have persuaded myself that, although the name is repulsive and should itself be outlawed, what really matters is whether they catch trout and so, suspecting that they may well do just this when other patterns are proving ineffective, I have forced myself to sit down and tie half a dozen specimens of the pattern that I prefer not to name.

I dressed these flies on 18 hooks and they really look as though they might do business on days when the trout are gorging on small black things, although I may well have to go smaller, go down into the 20s. Undoubtedly the name is shocking but the design is ingenious and, like many modern flies, the fly itself possesses the great virtue of being easy to tie. The IOBO – I can't avoid it – looks infinitely suggestive of insect life and I am looking forward to giving it a go. I have tied some variants with white bits to make them easier to see in broken water but I shall say no more about them until the day comes when they fill my creel with trout extracted from a drought river, which will also be the day when I forgive them their name, although now that I think about it they are, of course, not to blame.

And now I have a confession to make: one that challenges my right to criticise or condemn even the most outrageous names imposed upon perfectly innocent artificial flies. I am already responsible for Dry Simon and have tried to excuse myself by arguing that I was following Courtney Williams' lead and had limited choice in the matter. I felt that it was my duty, I have told you, to acknowledge Dry Simon's origins in his name. I suppose this was questionable, especially when you consider just how very different he is from the fly that inspired his creation, but at the time it felt like some sort of justification, perhaps even a necessary form of recognition. Anyway, I have followed this with a truly scandalous violation of good taste. Halfway through last season I was tying flies one day and found that I had run out of the Krystal Flash from which I make Dry Simon's golden tail. My eye was drawn to a packet of green Shimmer and Shine – flytying materials, by the way, are also often given dreadful names – and I tied three or four Simons with these flashy green tails. They worked and I christened the variant Green Simon, which you will doubtless think fair enough. But then came temptation, which I resisted for a time, but it would not leave me; it kept nagging away and eventually I succumbed. It was the outrageous awfulness of it that somehow made it irresistible; it was as though I felt, having dipped my toe in sin with Dry Simon, that I might as well surrender completely and wallow in hopeless depravity. I reversed the elements of Green Simon's name; I called him Simon Green and, now that I have embarked on this path of shame, who knows where it might end?

11 March

I tied some more flies this afternoon and I am almost ready for a few days doing other things, not that I don't do other things as well as tie one or two flies. Anyway, just like the pattern that I prefer to leave unnamed, rather as actors reputedly speak of the Scottish play rather than of Macbeth, they were flies that made me feel almost an up-to-date fisher; they were F-flies in various sizes and colours and I confess that I had never heard of such flies until six or seven years ago when some progressive friends spoke highly of them and gave me one or two, which I looked at with secret disfavour before dropping them into one of my boxes and promptly forgetting all about them. But then, three or four seasons back, there came a late September evening on the Wharfe above Deepdale. It was a soft, still, cloudy autumn evening of the sort that I so love, the sort that seems inward-looking and absorbed in sad contemplation of the fading year. It is a very quiet sort of sadness and the pleasure that I take in it is perhaps self-indulgent, but on this occasion I could not enter into the mood because I could not catch my second trout, which with its coming would bring contentment and allow me to feel at peace with myself and the river and the season and the dimming day.

There was slightly more than a trickle of blue wings coming off the river and here and there in the little pools there were rising fish. Dry Simon had caught me a nice pounder in the afternoon but now, although surprisingly he can sometimes be very effective during a hatch of olives, he had failed except for a troutling or two and one or two more imitative patterns had failed completely, only managing to put trout down. I don't remember what it was that stirred the memory and brought F-flies to mind. Something did. I managed to find the compartment where they were living; I tied one onto the end of my leader and ten minutes later I had caught a brace of good trout on either side of the pound, meaning that I could now sit on a flat rock with my wadered feet trailing in the water and drink in the soft beauty all round me and the grey peace.

Just like the fly that should never dare to speak its name, the F-fly is simplicity itself to tie and can be very effective. You can tie them in all sizes and colours and I tend to resort to them when fish are rising and my usual patterns have failed. Today's half dozen flies were on 14 and 16 hooks with bodies of dull yellow wool. Presumably the F in F-fly is the first letter of its inventor's surname (Rajan Fratnik), which to me seems oblique and modest enough and therefore inoffensive. Both the F-fly and the IOBO – I've managed it – are fine examples of contemporary fly design: straightforward to tie, impressionistic and widely suggestive. I wonder what Halford would have thought of them. Skues would have understood and approved.

15 March

Today is the first day of trouting on some northern rivers. The Wharfe does not open until the 25th and I regard this slightly later date as the start of my season. I am happy to wait, especially because rivers this morning are too big for flyfishing and, anyway, the Eden, where the season does start today, has declined so far from its former glory that these days I barely go there. I find it too painful.

Mention of the start of the season, when the water is generally cold and it often takes a big hatch (a rare event these days) to tempt trout anywhere near the surface of the water, reminds me that March and April days on the river sometimes find me vulnerable to temptation and persuade me to do something that I should prefer not to do, something of which I am inclined to disapprove; for it is possible that, finding an absence of fly and rising fish, I shall tie a weighted nymph or even a beadhead to the end of my leader and search the pools with it in the hope of stirring some response from the trout.

I have never made my own beadheads; I don't know how to and I don't want to learn because I don't really want to fish with them. I dislike weighted nymphs. They are such unlovely things. When they are any size, moreover, they take away the delicacy that is one of the chief delights of flyfishing. Casting a heavy nymph seems to me rather like putting the shot with a fly rod, not that I have spent much time putting the shot without a fly rod. It is true that much lighter versions cast more or less normally but my third objection is that fishing with deep nymphs gives the trout no peace. I believe – most of the time at least – that when trout are feeding on the bottom of the river or down there having a rest they should be left alone. And if your nymph is trundling along near the riverbed I am not sure that you are really flyfishing at all. I rather think you might be ledgering instead.

The Skues version of the nymph is, it seems to me, irreproachable; it is really a chalkstream adaptation of the northern spider; it fishes where fishermen's flies have fished for centuries: near the surface of the water. I grant you the distinction is a fine one. Where should the line be drawn between near the surface and therefore commendable and too deep and consequently infra dig? Distinguish instead between method: wet flies and unweighted nymphs, thoroughly sporting; goldheads and the heavy brigade, disreputable. Some clubs have, I believe, restricted nymph fishing to the use of unweighted patterns. I think the Piscatorials are just such a club. On the other hand I know of one chalkstream club that has banned 'wet flies' but allows use of 'the nymph' come July. This is absurd and self-contradictory, because if a nymph is a fly at all it is most certainly a wet fly and how can fishing with, say, a Partridge and Orange be less legitimate than searching the deeps with a goldhead? And trout, by the way, take the Partridge and Orange for a nymph. Talk about drowned duns and spinners and February reds is nonsense. It is a nymph and has given me wonderful sport in hatches of spring olives (on the Wharfe), where the fish have sometimes much preferred it to the Waterhen, and of blue wings (at Driffield and Foston). Anyway, on the whole I am in favour of fishers being constrained by as few restrictions and prohibitions as possible. My personal philosophy as a fisher makes me feel ever so slightly guilty when I fish heavy nymphs and goldheads and it wouldn't bother me for my own sake if their use was denied me; it would remove temptation. But I have at least two dear friends who prefer the method to all others and I am not sure that I should want them denied their preference and their pleasure.

What persuades me to abandon good practice – not only and now that I think about it not even chiefly early in the season – is that I like catching trout much better than not catching them; and I particularly dislike not catching them when my friends are catching sackfuls; and sometimes, when this has been happening, the goldhead has been the obvious difference between their success and my dismal failure.

Three or four seasons ago I found myself fishing the Wharfe – alone as it happens – in a coloured water, falling and clearing but still on the big side for the fly. Simple Simon and my Coachman are sometimes deadly in these conditions but on this occasion after something like half an hour they had failed to stir a fin. I spent at least another hour trying out some other patterns; all were completely ignored and it was then that, quite suddenly, I was assailed by impure thoughts, by thoughts that should have been condemned and rejected just as soon as they rose up from some dark and conscienceless chamber of the mind. These monstrous thoughts were suggesting that it might be an idea to fish a little deeper, they were wondering whether there might be a goldhead or two or perhaps a couple of copper wire nymphs lurking somewhere in one of my fly boxes. Two hours without a fish had made me susceptible. A guilty search had soon revealed that there were no goldheads, at least I couldn't find any, but there were two or three copper wire nymphs tied – if that is the appropriate term – on 12s and 14s. They were probably relics of a brief and unsuccessful experiment twenty or thirty years ago; they were ever so slightly rusty. I promptly jettisoned my principles, tied one of them to the end of my leader and it started catching trout almost immediately. Moreover the extra depth that it gave Simple Simon meant that he started catching trout as well. I felt a trifle uneasy about this stratagem; I also felt that it was much better catching trout with a weighted nymph than not catching them without one. I caught lots.

Next we move to Shropshire's Rea Brook on a hot day in July, a day when, all through the morning and in the early part of the afternoon, there has been little fly and barely a sign of a feeding trout. The Rea trout are obliging creatures, usually willing, some of them at least, to seize a biggish dry fly even when they are not feeding on the surface. On this particular day they are in one of their less cooperative moods and I have struggled. At three o'clock I have only one trout in my bag and he is the only one that I have caught, the only one that has risen to my fly. It is now that an insinuating inner voice starts whispering about goldheads, asking me what harm there could be in trying one. In reply I tell the inner voice to get lost and that it is wasting its time because I haven't any goldheads, which I suspect is untrue, because I think there were one or two in a small consignment of flies recently given to me by a friend. In claiming that I have no goldheads I am pretty certain that I am deceiving both myself and the inner voice, which anyway ignores my deceit and continues its insidious temptation until, two fishless pools later, I decide to find out if my friend's gift includes a goldhead or two. It does and very soon one is attached to the end of my leader. Ten minutes later I have caught a brace of trout from the same small pool: a good pounder and one more than half as big again, which is almost a specimen fish for the Rea. He may even be the biggest fish that the little river has ever given me.

From Shropshire I drive into Wales to the deep, twisting, very green and very beautiful valley of the Irfon, joining friends to spend a week fishing the river and some nearby streams. I shall probably tell the story in a later chapter. All I shall say here is that it turned into the week of the grayling and the week of the goldhead. Ten years ago, incidentally, the Irfon was almost dead, poisoned by acid run-off from the surrounding conifer plantations, but the work of the Wye and Usk Foundation has brought it back to life, which shows that it can be done. Anyway, I fished a short length of the Irfon three or four times, never for more than two or three hours at a time, and the same small goldhead, given to me by a friend who said it was all the fish wanted, caught between forty and fifty grayling. I don't think I caught a single one of them on a different fly.

I have been given more goldheads by kind friends and I confess that last season I bought half a dozen pheasant tail nymphs. It may be that they will never be used but I rather doubt it and I should probably stop telling the world that I disapprove of them because the world is likely to condemn me as a hypocrite. But the truth is that I do disapprove of them, even though I sometimes fish with them. I am a sinner who acknowledges and condemns his sin but sometimes finds its appeal irresistible. It is really moral frailty rather than hypocrisy. Temptation will come on a day when I have fished for several hours without any hatching flies, a day when dry flies and wet flies, when the Simons and F-flies and IOBOS and spiders have caught me nothing, a day when I have turned back to patterns that I once favoured and found them ineffective; and it is then that trout-hunger will drive me to desperate measures in the form of goldheads or copper wire nymphs and I rather hope they don't work because it will make me less likely to turn to them more frequently. At the time I shall be hoping for the opposite result and I shall be very pleased if they put trout in my bag, especially if it is the first trout of another season. But I should much prefer to feel grateful to an Orange Partridge, to Dry Simon or my Coachman or even to Simon Green.

20 March

I have yet to fish and I shall be tying no more flies until I need them. I have, I think, an adequate supply for the start of the new season. In the past day or so I have tied some CDC Sedges on 12 and 14 hooks and a few soft hackled dry flies on 12s. The CDC Sedge is an F-fly with the addition of a body of yellow wool palmered and hackled with ginger cock feathers. The palmered body is ribbed with fine silver wire and I generally use brown thread. It is a very effective fly indeed and I do not think it is taken for a sedge, not at least when it is on the end of my leader, because in my old age I never fish in the evening and I have never caught a trout with it that was feeding on hatching sedges. I think it suggests a wide variety of insect life and I think trout find its undoubted buzz attractive. Rising trout often take it eagerly and it can also bring up fish that are not obviously feeding on or near the surface. I also tie a version – inevitably, you will probably tell yourself – with Dry Simon's tail of Krystal Flash. It is sometimes very successful.

I tie my soft hackled dry flies with orange thread, with a body of brown or grey wool or fur, two or three CDC feathers for wings and a well mottled partridge hackle. They are specifically a fly for the upper Tees, where they sometimes work very well indeed and seem to have the ability to bring up monsters a whole eleven and even twelve inches long. I think it is their mobility that appeals. They seem less effective on my other rivers. I do not know, by the way, when soft hackled floaters first appeared and who it was who first tied them but, like the majority of modern flies, they are easy to tie and impressionistic rather than strictly imitative. Anyway, they were the last patterns of my early spring flytying campaign. I have enjoyed it but I am glad it is over.

*****

I shall finish this chapter with a few general remarks about our flies and with a true story from my recent past. And far the most important thing to say about our fishers' flies is that for me they are objects of almost sacred wonder, demanding deep reverence and profound thankfulness, which is of course because in catching trout for me they give me so much more. It is a marvel to me that the Orange Partridge and the Waterhen Bloa – not to mention Dry Simon and the abominably named Simon Green – somehow manage to persuade trout to eat them, but the even greater marvel is that catching trout through so many years has been a continuing source of such joy to me, a joy that I should never have experienced without the help of artificial flies.

I owe artificial flies very much indeed, especially the ones that have put trout in my bag. It may well be that, writing as a flydresser of limited expertise, I have already said more than enough about them. Many of the fishers reading this book will know twice as much about flies, especially modern ones, and tie them twice as skilfully as I do. But please allow me, before I finish, to make a few observations on fashion in trout flies and then finally to tell you my already promised short story from my recent fishing experience.

Patterns come and go. You will all be able to think of flies that were once in almost every fisher's boxes but are now virtually forgotten. Some of this is doubtless commercially driven, because fishing magazines need articles to tell their readers about new flies that are guaranteed to catch scores of trout, and novelty possesses its own sort of charm for fishers, because most of us like to experiment. Many of these supposedly indisputable bag-fillers will themselves be forgotten in twenty or thirty years but I am not suggesting that advances have not been made. The last forty years has seen very genuine progress in producing a range of flies better designed and more effective than the old models they have largely supplanted. The Klinkhåmer, for example, represents a huge step forward in fly design; the widespread use of CDC feathers is another such example and the growing awareness of the importance of emerger patterns (of which the Klinkhåmer, of course, is one). In my early fishing years there were wet flies, dry flies and, in the view of us northerners, newfangled things from down south called nymphs. Nowadays even novice flyfishers are aware that trout eat duns sitting on the surface of the water or trapped in the surface film or in the act of hatching or stillborn or crippled; the emerger covers many more of these eventualities than the traditionally hackled dry fly. I am not an expert and I need to shut up or I shall make a fool of myself. But the point I want to emphasise is that flytying is a progressive art (or science) and that, on the whole, modern flies, based on a greater knowledge of the trout's feeding habits, also on a greater understanding of the 'triggers' that persuade a trout to swallow a fly, are better at catching trout than their predecessors.

There has been real progress but it is also true that flies come into and out of fashion for no sensible reason, unless I am the only fisher who thinks for a season that he has found the fly of flies and, when next season comes along, decides that it can't hold a candle to the pattern that has now won his heart. When, for example, did I last fish with a Grey Duster, which many years ago was undoubtedly my favourite fly? In the past most of my fishing friends were, like me, devotees of this fly. One or two of them still use it, tied on tiny irons, for smutting trout but it is not a presence in virtually every fisher's fly boxes as it was thirty and forty years ago and I guess that most fishers who still turn to it now and then are fishers with more years behind them than those that lie ahead. Kite's Imperial is another case in point. There was a time, something like thirty years, when it was often my dry fly of first choice and, something like thirty years ago, virtually every dry fly fisher was loud in its praise. It was the standard pattern for large dark olives and was a fine general fly as well. It caught heaps of trout and I suspect that today it is not much fished. I suppose the modern approach to trout flies thinks that the profile a fly presents to a fish is more important than fine details of dressing. We regard the Klinkhåmer as a style rather than a fixed pattern, we dress Klinkhåmers in many sizes and many colours and it is the same with F-flies. It would be possible to produce versions of both the Imperial and the Duster in Klinkhåmer or F-fly styles, turning them into emergers. I seem to remember that a parachute Grey Duster was sometimes very effective for me in the past and I have some parachute Imperials but can't recall whether I have ever used them.

The Imperial and the Duster, anyway, are just two examples of great flies that seem to have dropped largely out of fashion, undeservedly. Fancy flies, I think, have fallen from favour as a whole class (not with me, of course) and they shouldn't have; in fact I think the sad decline in ephemeropterans means that fancy flies are more important than they used to be, with the trout more likely now to eat miscellaneous items of food. But how many of us ever tie on a Treacle Parkin or a Red Tag these days? I think there is some snobbery here; the scientific approach to flyfishing is in vogue and I think many fishers now tend to look down on fancy flies as crude attractors rather than impressionistic suggestions of insects at some particular stage of their development. Personally I rather enjoy the not infrequent days when the trout are smutting away and yet find the unexpected appearance of Dry Simon, floating over their noses in all his vulgar splendour, irresistibly attractive. But then I would enjoy it wouldn't I? because I am a vulgar sort of fisher.

Spiders have maintained their status, even though they depend on hatching olives and even though olives now hatch much less abundantly, but in many fields of endeavour there is a tendency for the old to be ousted by the new in the name of progress and this is certainly true of flytying. As I have already insisted there has most certainly been genuine progress in the matter of artificial flies and I am already, as they say, behind the curve and need to catch up with foam duns and shuttlecocks and half a dozen recent innovations. Much ingenuity and intelligence has gone into producing the modern generations of trout flies, but there are times when the trout mock intelligence, ingenuity and modern theories of fly design. This chapter has gone on long enough. I want to end it with a brief account of three days when the trout made a complete fool of me and my attempts to tempt them onto the hook until in despair I tied on a fly as a sort of last resort that I thought was almost bound to fail.

It was July. I had fished the Foston Beck on Monday and Tuesday and caught only one trout. I had looked for them where I could usually find them and seen no trout at all. I did not doubt their presence; I was sure they were there, hidden in the weed or down among the roots or tucked under the banks. Wherever they were they were unwilling to show themselves, except for a fish here and there, visible over the chalk in deep water and unmoved, unimpressed by whatever I showed them. Even a half-guilty resort to goldheads provoked no response. Once or twice a trout appeared from nowhere to inspect temptation and find it resistible. The one fish that I did manage to catch came to a speculative cast with a largish Klinkhåmer. I had to be content with this single fish, although I was, of course, very far from content. One fish from two long days' fishing was, for me, at least three fish too few.

After those disappointing Foston days there was a day at Driffield, where there were plenty of trout on show and they were rising as well, at least in the late morning, helping themselves to a steady trickle of blue wings. The trouble was that I could not catch any of them. I tried Klinkhåmers dressed to represent smallish olives, I tried F-flies dressed with blue wings specifically in mind. Neither provoked so much as an inspection. I found a few Imperials and tried versions with both conventional and parachute hackles. They were ignored. I thought the profile of one of my larger IOBOS might persuade a trout to take it. I was mistaken. I have already told you that when blue wings are on the water a Partridge and Orange will often put trout in your bag and has on occasions been very successful at both Foston and Driffield. On this occasion it was entirely unsuccessful. I didn't expect a small CDC Sedge to work and in this at least I was spot on. I tried one or two more patterns that might reasonably be expected to appeal and they lacked even the beginnings of any attraction. Desperation finally tied a Dry Simon to the end of my leader in the hope that shock tactics might save the day. Something like twenty minutes and half a dozen disdainful trout later Dry Simon admitted defeat and told me that it was time for lunch.

Wine was a comfort but I should have preferred it to be a celebration. The afternoon was almost an improvement on the morning in that a biggish trout splashed twice at Dry Simon and another trout appeared from under the weed and almost swallowed a small IOBO, but that, unfortunately, was it. The clubroom of the Driffield Anglers, like lunchtime wine, is always a comfort, because it breathes out peace and is filled with soft light and quiet dignity and the love of fishing; it is somewhat less of a comfort when you are sitting there and entering a blank against your name in the guest book, especially when the blank means that you have now fished three long days and caught just a single trout. I told myself, as I looked through the window, down over the lawn to the line of the beck, that adversity comes to all fishers and has to be patiently endured, hoping at the same time that the fourth and last day of my visit to East Yorkshire would bring an end to this present dose of it by bringing me a few trout.

This last day was spent on the delightful Yorkshire Derwent in the delightfully named Troutsdale. The Derwent was fished by several distinguished anglers of an earlier generation, most notably perhaps by Eric Horsfall Turner: fishing writer, master angler and inventor of the famous Eric's Beetle, a fly which I often used with good results in the past and should perhaps start using again in suitable conditions. The day in question, as it happened, did not strike me as a day for Eric's Beetle, even on a stretch of water frequented by its originator, for I seemed to remember that it had served me best in water falling back from spate and the Derwent was low, low and clear, most definitely fishable but low enough to suggest that catching trout might not be easy. Catching trout was very far from easy and by lunchtime, when I felt in desperate need of whatever drops of comfort red wine might be able to offer, it seemed to have turned for this fisher into a lost skill or a forgotten art. I normally take pleasure in the success of my fishing friends, but I have to admit that, as I sat with my host Oliver on a bench by the river and talked of the morning's sport and of other things, I almost wished that Oliver had not managed to catch himself a nice brace of trout; I almost wished that Oliver could perhaps have lessened my pain just a little by sharing my failure.

Anyway, I sipped my wine and undoubtedly it brought comfort of a sort, and it might have been the wine that, in defiance of recent experience, insisted to me that there was still hope. It may also have been the wine that told me to forget all about Klinkhåmers and F-flies and IOBOS and all the other flies that I had tried in the course of the morning, turning my mind instead to three or four compartments in one of my fly boxes, where lived an assortment of – mainly very small – dry flies given to me many years ago by the late Michael Thornely, one-time headmaster of Sedbergh School. They were already old flies when I got them almost twenty years ago. I guess they were tied in the 1940s and 1950s of the last century although they could easily be older still. They are definitely not the sort of flies that the progressive fisher attaches to the end of his leader, although many of them are undeniably minor works of art: beautifully proportioned artefacts with delicate quill bodies and tiny, very delicate split wings. They are old and old-fashioned and many fishers would declare then hopelessly outmoded. I have no idea why I suddenly thought of them – unless of course it really was the influence of the wine – but, having done so, I seemed to remember that occasionally in the past one or two of them had caught me a difficult fish or two on the Wharfe and the Eden.

And so it was that with the wine finished and the grim prospect of the afternoon stretching ahead of me, I sorted through the headmaster's flies and, finding a very small Wickham's Fancy, decided to give it a go. Why I chose this particular fly I have no idea, unless it was the lingering influence of the wine. Anyway, it was dressed on something like a size 20 hook; my 3lb nylon was far too thick for the hook's tiny eye and so I was forced to tie on a short length of some inordinately expensive fluorocarbon stuff, a material in which I had little faith because several times in the past it had let me down with breakages and slipping knots. There was cold comfort to be drawn from reminding myself that it was unlikely to be put to the test because I was exceedingly unlikely to rise or hook any trout. Should the miracle occur I prayed that it would serve me better than in the past and set off upstream with what hope I had pinned to the ancient and very unfashionable – but beautifully tied – dry fly that some irrational impulse had attached to a foot or two of suspect and very modern fluorocarbon.

It was not long before I found a fish rising at something invisible, probably smut. As soon as my Wickham's Fancy floated over him a substantial nose stuck itself out of the water. I failed to connect, of course, and moved on with a silent curse, gloomily convinced that I was doomed to drive home at the end of the afternoon with a heavy heart and an empty bag. Round the next corner I found another rising fish; his response to the appearance of my fly was just the same and, thank God, my response was different because this time I raised my wrist at the right time and, at the end of a lively contest, I drew over the net a trout of something like a pound and a half. I was very relieved because small flies are, I think, somewhat more likely to surrender their purchase on trout flesh, but it had held its grip tenaciously and the fluorocarbon had stood a fairly stern test and now at last I had proved to myself that I could still do it, could still catch a trout. I knew that, if only I could catch one more of them, I should drive home a happy man.

I came to a footbridge over the river and the pool beneath it. There were several fish busy under the far bank. They had been busy there a few weeks earlier when I had also been Oliver's guest on the Derwent and I had tempted them with big dry flies, which experience told me were likely to do the trick, but on that occasion they had let me down; the trout had only splashed at my Klinkhåmer and nudged the two Simons. I had pricked a couple with the CDC Sedge but none had been firmly hooked. On that occasion, after resting the pool for a time, I had tried smaller flies: size 18 F-flies and IOBOS and my smallest versions of Spring Black, but these had also failed completely; perhaps they had not been small enough. Now, anyway, it was the turn of an ancient Wickham's Fancy to see what it could achieve. It floated over the lowest of the feeding trout and provoked a boiling rise, an indisputably genuine rise, which I missed. I am usually a good striker; this time I think I was too eager for the brace.

I missed the next fish too but he came again and I hooked him; and the hook stayed in his mouth and my fluorocarbon did what it needed to do, which meant that a good pounder was landed and knocked on the head and thereby made the brace, turning this fisher, who had so recently been morosely contemplating his complete inability to catch any trout, into a most profoundly contented and deeply thankful fisher, convinced beyond doubt that his chosen sport was the most wonderful activity known to man, which of course it is. I had, I suppose, still believed this during those three and a half days of frustration and failure. A tiny Wickham's Fancy, anyway, a fly at least fifty years old, had now confirmed and strengthened this belief, making it unshakeable, as firmly rooted as a mountain, a belief that would, I felt sure, hold fast even if I never caught a trout again, even if the future held nothing for me as a fisher but an endless succession of blank days.

The brace was already enough for me, but not for my Wickham's Fancy. It floated over a dimpling rise; it disappeared and a big trout was bending my rod. He weighed something like the first fish. The WF, as I was now calling it, soon hooked another trout that threw the hook and then it caught another that weighed well over the pound. And then Oliver appeared and it was time to finish and, as we walked down the fields together, I began to ask myself questions about the events of the afternoon, questions that recurred from time to time as I made my contented way home. And, by the way, the Yorkshire countryside looks incomparably beautiful, even through the dusty, bird-dropping-and-dead-fly stained window of a filthy Land Rover, when, at the end of four unusually difficult fishing days, the driver of the Land Rover is heading home with two brace of trout in his bag.

My questions concerned the WF and they wondered why the trout of the Derwent had shown no interest in the flies that should have interested them (little black things) or in the big, bright flashy flies that so often caught their fancy, but had attacked a small WF as though it was the one fly they had been longing to see for the whole of the season. I remembered something that I had not remembered when deciding to see what the WF could do for me: that it used to be recommended as a sometimes useful pattern for smutting trout. I determined to experiment on the Wharfe and elsewhere. I wondered if the appeal of my WF had been more a matter of size than pattern. Some of the flies that had failed so miserably in the morning had been small enough but, tied on 18s rather than 20s, not quite as small as the WF. I was uncertain whether size alone had been crucial but I was confident that a significantly larger WF would have been significantly less successful. And, by the way, in one matter I experienced a total change of opinion. I was now a devotee of the very expensive fluorocarbon sold by Orvis as Mirage and subsequent use has confirmed that it is superb. It is very thin, very strong and very supple; it holds a knot onto nylon securely and it holds angry and quite heavy trout with apparent ease. I am a convert, although I do not use it all the time. I reserve its use for low water and bright sunlight and shy trout and I also use it when I fish with small flies. The fluorocarbon that let me down, by the way, was of a different brand.

I remember that I was late home from that September day on the Derwent and that it was almost ten o'clock before I raised a glass of red wine to my lips, wine that was most definitely a celebration as well as a comfort. The occasion, it seemed to me, demanded toasts. There was a toast to Dr. Wickham and then I remembered that some thought it was a different Wickham, a Captain Wickham, who had invented the WF and so there was a toast to him as well, just in case. There was, of course, a toast to the WF itself, to the fly that one or other of the Wickhams created. I was not sure why a small version of this fly had been so stunning a success in the afternoon but, I reflected, as I sat for a time over my claret – and this is the point of concluding my thoughts about flytying with the little story that I have just told you – I reflected on how, for all the undeniable advances that thoughtful fishers and tyers have made in recent times, flyfishing and flytying is very much an imperfect science and the response of trout to our flies is still sometimes bafflingly unpredictable. I acknowledged progress but realised that the new does not always make the old obsolete and then, with my glass almost empty, I realised that I had left my most solemn duty unperformed and so with my last drops of wine I drank a reverent toast to the former headmaster who something like twenty years ago gave me a box full of very old-fashioned dry flies. May he rest in peace.

Chapter Eleven

A FISHER WHO SHOOTS

Almost every morning in autumn and winter finds me out feeding pheasants on my little shoot at High Park. I enjoy it very much indeed and soon I shall tell you why, but the reason I mention it now is that this morning, a soft morning under cloud in the middle of November, while wandering round the feed rides and feeling pleased to see a good number of pheasants waiting for their ration of corn only two days after my second shoot, this morning I asked myself why it is that I never, or very rarely, go fishing for grayling after the end of the trout season. It is a question that I have asked myself many times before.

The reason for its latest recurrence was that a friend had been in contact with news of several successful and clearly delightful grayling expeditions to the Ure. This week's succession of mild and gentle days must, I imagine, have been almost perfect for enjoyable sport. It seemed strange to me that I did not, like Peter and several more of my friends, prolong my fishing season by fishing for grayling on quiet autumn days. Only the other day another friend told me that the stock of grayling on the upper Eden was now at last recovering from the ravages of Storm Desmond in 2015. Why, I wondered, did I not take my rod and try to find out whether my friend is right, especially as I think grayling such lovely and graceful creatures, lovelier and more graceful than many of the trout each season brings to my net, though never quite achieving the noble beauty of my noblest and most beautiful brown trout? And, by the way, it occurred to me this morning that, except in the matter of size, one grayling does look much like another, whereas no two trout look quite the same. I like variety and I like to observe and enjoy the differences between trout. I like their individuality very much.

One reason, anyway, that keeps me from going grayling fishing was immediately plain to me; it was what I was doing while thinking this matter through. Feeding my pheasants takes me about an hour and a half. Add running the dogs and an extra quarter of an hour or so spent training my young puppy and more than two hours has already gone from the day. Of course this leaves time to go fishing, though there are often odd jobs to do round the shoot and, even if I go home as soon as I have finished with birds and dogs, I am ready for coffee and half an hour's rest.

But I could, of course, easily combine pheasant care and fishing; I do it in August and September and I have friends who are happy to see to my pheasants when I am away fishing for a few days and who would be just as happy to do it if I wanted to be off early in search of sport with grayling. The truth is that, once October comes along, I become preoccupied with my shoot and with shooting in general. I am certainly a fisher who shoots, because I find much deeper satisfaction and fulfilment in waving a rod to and fro than in swinging a gun, but I still love shooting very dearly, which helps to explain why I am a fisher who puts away his rods at the end of September and turns to his dogs and his guns.

It is also a matter of where I should have to go to fish for grayling, or rather a matter of where I cannot go, because the Wharfe at Kilnsey never carried a big head of grayling and now they seem to have abandoned our water altogether, driven away perhaps by a succession of drought summers in the nineties of the last century. The Kilnsey water, so high up the river, was always marginal grayling territory but until those savage summers came along, most seasons put something like half a dozen of them in my net and I have just remembered that the first fish I ever caught on the Wharfe was a big grayling. It came on a cold April morning in long-distant undergraduate days when I was fishing the river near Buckden on a day ticket bought at the village pub. It was that same day, incidentally, that first brought me to the Tennant Arms, then the headquarters of the Kilnsey Club, for a pint of beer on my way home. I was allowed by the landlord to look into the room then reserved for Kilnsey members and was immediately filled with a deep longing to become a member myself and to sit there in the room by right at the beginning and end of fishing days.

The grayling, anyway, that those earlier Kilnsey summers brought my way – all caught during the trout season – were very welcome and much admired. I even caught a handful of small ones way up the river towards Yockenthwaite. And I know perfectly well that, if the Kilnsey water supported a thriving population of grayling, I should certainly devote at least a few autumn days to fishing for them, because this would for a time preserve my contact with that wonderful length of the Wharfe that means so much to me. There is still a fair head of grayling much lower down the river round Ilkley and Myddleton. My friend Peter would probably be able to give me a ticket or two for the water but the motivation to make use of them is not there. I prefer to go shooting or to potter round my own shoot and give time to my dogs.

I think another reason for this reluctance to go fishing once trouting is over is something that I have already mentioned:

my sense of seasonality, my feeling that different times of the year are made for different activities. In particular it seems to me that spring, summer and September are the right time for flyfishing, the right time for trout, whereas October through to the end of January is the right time for shooting, the right time for pheasants and partridge and duck. February and early March, incidentally, is the right time to rest from sport and relax: the one time of the year without any pressure to perform. Not everyone shares this conviction about the appropriate seasons for fishing and shooting. Grouse shooters will tell you that they are at it in August, and undoubtedly a grouse moor is a wonderful place to be, with either a gun or a flanker's flag, on bright days in August and September; salmon fishers cast lines with snow on the ground and with ice coating the rings of their rods, grayling fishers, of course, insist that winter is a fine time for catching fish and coarse fishers, rarely flyfishers, agree with them wholeheartedly. I acknowledge that there will be those who disagree with me but I cannot help thinking that the best time for flyfishing is in the six months of the trout season, whereas shooting belongs most appropriately to late autumn and winter. It is partly a matter of when our quarry is in order for sport and the table, but flyfishing surely is most enjoyable on soft and gentle days, while days of wind and sharp air often provide exceptional sport with the gun.

But there is something else and this is perhaps more important than any sense of seasonality or than my involvement with shooting. It does not involve a new and startling insight into the nature of things. I have not discovered a hidden truth that changes the way we should look at our lives. No! I simply think that choosing not to fish for approximately half the year means that its other half, when I go fishing as often as possible and wish that I could go fishing even more, is made more special and more rewarding than it would be if I fished throughout the year. The spring reunion with my rivers, when I find myself standing once again by pools and runs that have been flowing through my imagination all winter long, welcoming them back into my life and impatient for the gifts I am hoping they will give me in the months ahead, this reunion is precious and wonderful. It seems, and is, marvellous to be fishing again and the first few trout of the season bring a very special sense of wonder, as I marvel with new eyes and a new heart at the shining, spotted beauty of the creature that I have just drawn from the water, at the same time relieved and deeply thankful to discover that trout still matter as much to me as they did at the end of last September. And the delight, the joy of fishing through the spring and summer is surely heightened by the knowledge that there will be an end. It is precisely this knowledge that explains the emotional intensity of September fishing, when of course I know that the end is now very near. September is my favourite month and I love September fishing best of all. It is this approaching end, this imminent separation that so deepens my experience of and response to September sport.

I thought something along these lines, anyway, as I wandered round the shoot this morning, but I did not find that I wanted to leap through the winter and find myself on the threshold of another trout season. I wanted to leave my fishing appetite to grow through the intervening four or five months so that, when April did at last come along, I should be really hungry for fishing and for trout and everything that they bring me. In the meantime I wanted to enjoy my shooting and the deep pleasure of wandering round High Park every morning with a bucket of wheat, scattering food for my pheasants and looking round at what each morning gave me to see and to enjoy.

*****

I was there again today under a bright sky. Many of my trees are bare now, although the oaks are still carrying most of their foliage, which has darkened to a deep and glowing russet; elsewhere the bright remnant of the leaf hangs yellow and orange on birches, aspens and hazels. The weather has been largely dry for the last ten days and under the trees I walk on a dry and rustling carpet of leaves. I can hear hen pheasants squeaking their plaintive response to my whistle; I can hear the patter of their feet on the leaves. Jays, busy with the last of the acorns, depart with rasping calls. Magpies fly off with a cackle, while I tell them that the Larsen traps will be ready for them in spring. Sometimes a wren surprises me with a brief snatch of sound. Occasionally a dipper sings its sweet song down on the beck; they seem, by the way, to sing right through the winter; it is as though, hearing the music of water all round them, they must from time to time pay it the tribute of imitation. Robins, dunnocks and chaffinches hop round on the ground, keeping their distance and helping themselves to grains of corn. Pigeons clatter from the trees. Cock pheasants clear their throats. Sometimes a red squirrel looks at me from a tree before darting jerkily away along the branches. The blue sky is filled with the movement and nervous chatter of fieldfares which, in response to my approach, flock away from the hawthorns and the red berries that drew them there.

It takes about an hour and a half to feed my pheasants. It is a most delightful way to spend an hour and a half, a time full of interest, full of beauty, full of peace. It brings a contact with nature that I value very highly, a restful and stable sort of contact without the intrusion of any predatory thoughts or the emotional fluctuations of sport. It is an undemanding sort of pleasure, bringing an easy peace, a peace that does not depend, like my fisher's peace, on prior performance. It does not wait on achievement. It more or less greets me on my arrival at High Park every morning and then it walks round with me from place to place and keeps me company. It is a shallower peace than I find on the banks of the Wharfe but it is very welcome and it helps me to think, which is why, knowing this morning that before too long I should be sitting down in front of my laptop in an attempt to make some progress with this chapter, I gathered my thoughts on why it is that I am a fisher who shoots, on what it is that makes shooting a pleasure and a delight to me and makes fishing something much more.

I immediately knew that the centrality of water was of fundamental importance. There is, to begin with, its alchemic beauty, the way it takes the brightness of sun and sky, takes the forms and shapes that rise above or lean over it and transforms them into shining water-images, into flowing patterns of light and shadow. Water is an impressionist and undoubtedly makes great art. And the sound of it is, of course, endlessly soothing and, although we do not always seem to hear it when fishing, because we are so absorbed in the practice of our sport, I think it seeps into us and works unrecognised therapy. Water, moreover, is an element where we do not properly belong; in fishing we reach into water and draw treasure from a different world. This brings some sense of mystery to fishing, and I believe that this deepens the power of the hold that it has on us.

Next, it seems to me, there is the quietness of fishing. Shooting is full of loud noises. Fishing is accompanied by the slip and slide of water, by the whisper of your fly line and by the singing of birds and the sounds of the fields. Sheep may bleat, cattle may low but these sounds are somehow part of the peace. Fishing, moreover, is essentially a solitary activity. It is true that some fish with ghillies or guides but most of us fish alone and this, together with all those soft and comforting sounds, makes fishing, for me at least, seem like a sort of meditation, a sort of retreat, in which the soul is absorbed and soothed and at the same time enlarged by its intercourse with all the elements of the fisher's world. There is nothing quite like this in shooting.

Perhaps flighting comes nearest, when the silent wait by water as the light thickens and night takes slow and irresistible possession of earth and sky, reconnects us to the rhythm of nature: something which our moderns lives have lost or at least often choose to ignore. In my old age I go flighting much less than I used to, because it is not the best medicine for stiff and creaking joints. When I manage to rouse myself and wait for the night by one of my ponds, I feel for a time that I have entered a more primitive, an elemental world, governed by the coming and going of darkness and light.

I have already told you that I prefer to fish alone. Sometimes too I shoot alone, less often than formerly because I have found that on the whole I prefer to share my own shoot with my friends. Right at the end of the season in the last week of January I still sometimes wander round High Park with just a spaniel for company; there is a delightful informality to days of this sort but their mood is very different from solitary fishing days. It is a joy to shoot over an eager spaniel, to direct him into a jungle of gorse and to see the gorse move and shake in response to his drive, to admire his disdain for things that sting and scratch, for briars and brambles and thorns. Working a good dog is a deep pleasure, but it is not a pleasure that brings a meditative peace, anymore than the bark of a shotgun encourages quiet reflection.

I associate my best fishing days with a gathering intensity of stillness. This cannot happen on a shooting day, even with just yourself and a dog. There is too much push and bustle about them, there is the sound of your whistle, the sound of your voice and the much louder sound of your gun. A rough shooting day is full of nervous expectation and success, I think, brings a sense of exhilaration rather than the deepening sense of peace that belongs to the progress of a good fishing day.

As well as running my own shoot I am a member of three other small shoots, where shooting is essentially a collaborative and social activity. We depend upon each other and our dogs for sport, and the sport is important but the company matters just as much. A large part of the pleasure of organised shooting comes from intercourse between friends, from the warmth and quality of the *craic*. And here I am drawn back to dogs, for we shooters love our dogs and often find as much satisfaction in working them as in pulling the triggers of our guns. I have a half-gun in a delightful Saturday shoot. One Saturday I beat, the next Saturday I shoot and I sometimes think that I enjoy the beating days slightly more than the days I spend standing in a line of guns.

Piscator non solum piscatur runs the motto of the Fly Fishers' Club, which I paraphrase as 'there is more to fishing than catching fish', and, of course, I agree. There would be no point in this book if catching fish were the only thing that mattered, because manuals of instruction would be the only sort of fishing books worth writing or reading. Indisputably there is much more to fishing than just catching fish but I am not the sort of fisher who can declare a fishing day that has brought no fish to net a success, declaring it so because the sun has shone and the birds have sung sweetly and the flowers have been bright along the banks and all nature has seemed fair. A day without trout is a failure and sends me home frustrated and unfulfilled. There is much, much more to fishing than catching fish but, for me at least, catching trout is essential for contentment, catching trout is the key that opens mind and heart to the wonderful gifts that we fishers are given together with the wonderful gift of those trout.

Shooting days are somehow different. I have driven home from some of them without ever firing a shot and nevertheless pronounced the day a success, and I have already told you that there are those days when I leave my gun at home and prefer to work my dog in the beating line. I enjoy shooting pheasants but a single pleasing bird is often enough for me. The other day I was shooting with friends and on the first little drive I killed a high and very fast crossing hen; immediately I knew that if the day brought me no more chances I should still fell well contented at its end. When the end did come and I had still only pulled the trigger twice – that high hen had been a second barrel kill – I told myself that the company had been first rate, that the weather had been kind, that the day had been spent in beautiful places and had brought me a memorable bird and was sending me home with a brace of pheasants and had in every way been thoroughly enjoyable.

With fishing it is different. A brace of trout in my bag means a successful fishing day but, even with the brace of trout secured, I am eager to catch, though not necessarily to kill, more of them. I never seem to get enough of catching trout, whereas when I am shooting I do not really want to kill more than half a dozen birds and there are days when, if the morning has put pheasants over me and I have killed five or six, I give my gun to a friend for the afternoon and join the beaters.

I am beginning to think that this difference reflects the very different process involved in shooting a bird and catching a trout. Shooting a bird involves hitting a target; success or failure is more or less instantaneous. Catching a trout on a fly involves a process of imitation and deception and is also a matter of observation and interpretation; it comes, moreover, in stages; it takes time and success is uncertain until the trout is finally drawn over the net. Catching a trout is a much more complex and protracted business than shooting a pheasant and this, I think, is one reason why I find it so satisfying, why I am so keen to do it as often as possible and so slow to tire of its repetition.

The quietness of fishing, the delicacy of it, the flowing water at the heart of it, the slowness and loneliness of it, the beauty of its practice and the beauty of its surroundings: all this and doubtless much more makes me feel that going fishing draws me deeper into sport and at the same time into something more important than sport, making a deeper and more nourishing connection with the life of nature than I find in going shooting.

Shooting, it seems to me, although it is much more than an entertainment, because it is – or should be – about providing food, shooting is nevertheless much more like an entertainment than fishing. Shooting is often exciting; a good day is exhilarating and invigorating. At the end of a good day's shooting I feel a happy sense of fulfilment and a feeling of satisfaction that I have played my part in the success of the day. I also take deep pleasure in the beauty of the places where I go for my sport and in the taste of the game that I bring home with me.

Shooting is an extension of normal life into a particular sphere of activity; it is full of varied and at the same time complementary pleasures and my life would be much poorer without it. Fishing, on the other hand, at least my fishing, is a withdrawal from common reality into a quiet world of water and fish where I find things that I find nowhere else, neither in shooting nor in any other activity or occupation. This thing, whatever it is, is felt most powerfully on calm September evenings as I sit for a time by the Wharfe in grateful recollection of the day's sport before getting up and stowing my tackle and driving home. It is felt as a stillness, a stillness of the soul. I am not really sure what it is, but I know that it is wonderful and that it returns me to everyday life feeling contented, grateful and restored. And this, I believe, helps me to understand why I have come to think of myself as first and foremost a fisher: a fisher who also happens to shoot.

Chapter Twelve

THE BECK

I like the beginnings of rivers, particularly the beginnings of the Wharfe up at Yockenthwaite and Deepdale. I like the two becks that make the Wharfe, waters so small that a younger man than I could cross them with a single bold leap. I have fished with you on the Tirry in the north of Scotland, a river that is little more than a burn, I have told you of my deep affection for the Rea, a river small enough to be known as the Rea Brook, and I have tried to share with you the joy that I find in fishing a tiny stream that tumbles down from the hills at the head of the Elan Valley in Wales. I like becks and the beginnings of rivers almost wherever I find and fish them but undoubtedly it is the beginnings of limestone rivers, of the Wharfe, of course, above all that I like best; for the colours of the rock that shine through them, for the delved pools with their promise of better than average trout, for the wealth of fly that comes sailing down their pools and for the flowers that bloom all along their banks: blue bird's eye primrose, shining yellow kingcups, spiked orchids and

205

late-summer harebells. I like the high waters and the headwaters of limestone rivers; I like the becks that form them and the beck that I like best, even more than the becks that unite their waters to make the Wharfe, is a beck that I last fished almost twenty years ago and think that I shall probably never fish again.

It is still there for me, no further away than the Wharfe itself. Friends of mine still fish it three or four times in the course of most seasons and still catch trout from its runs and pools. I have not promised that I shall never go there again with a fishing rod but I think it unlikely. I may be moved by a sudden longing to return to its banks, but it is a longing that, if it comes to me, I shall probably try to resist because I do not want to disturb or tarnish the memories that belong to it.

I am almost surprised by what I have just written because part of the richness of a day spent on the Wharfe is that present experience rubs along with and is enriched by the memories of an association stretching back more than fifty years. And every day adds to my store of memories and deepens my affection for my beloved river. The sense of continuity is very important; on my beck the same sense has been broken and I think this is one reason why I avoid it. I think that in going there I should be going in search of the past and fear that I should be unable to find it and would in this way find a wealth of precious memories tainted by renewed and unsatisfactory contact.

And the beck is surrounded by associations beyond itself. The fishing rights are held by a pub where, four or five times a year, I used to spend a few days, sometimes as long as a week. Almost invariably, if suitable conditions for fishing the beck coincided with one of my visits, I would head off eagerly up the beck and spend the day in its steep-sided valley, in the hope of catching one or two of its trout. The pub is still there but the couple who owned and ran it are not and one of them is dead. Robin was a character and it was not a performance; it was who he was and I liked him. I like his wife, Elspeth, too and I liked the way they ran their pub and, now that they are no longer there, I no longer want to stay at The Falcon, although I am sure that it is still run well enough and welcomes those who spend time under its roof. My friends still stay there and speak warmly of the hospitality that they find there.

I could buy a ticket to fish the beck, but I suspect that I never shall, because Robin and Elspeth and the special atmosphere of The Falcon were part of the pleasure of a day on the beck. They were there at either end of it and a day without them would, I am sure, feel incomplete and unsatisfactory. And so it is that, unless a sudden and unexpected impulse takes hold of me, Cowside Beck will flow though my memories rather than through present experience, a place where others fish but where I no longer go except in recollection, which is how I now propose to revisit the beck, reawakening those same memories in loving tribute to the days I spent there and to all the delight and all the beauty that I found there.

*****

One of the pleasures of staying at The Falcon was waking up in the morning and realising that I was there and at the beginning of a fishing day. On the whole it seemed to me that the right time to wake up at The Falcon was about eight o'clock. It took the kettle about five minutes to boil and took the tea about five minutes to brew. Then it took me about fifteen minutes to drink my first cup, while lying in bed, listening somewhat inattentively to the news and feeling relieved that I was not part of it. The second cup was drunk between strokes of the razor and often tasted somewhat of shaving soap. This second cup lasted about as long as the first and usually the tea pot gave me half, or at least some portion of a tepid third cup to drink during the five or so minutes that it took me to put on clothes and shoes, which left me time before breakfast to stroll down through the village to the old bridge over the Skirfare, time to lean over the parapet, gazing at the water while blowing plumes of smoke from the day's first pipeful onto the morning air.

Often in summer there was no more than a shallow slide of water over the rock and moss; sometimes it was a wild surge of foam and brown water. Sometimes the smoke from my pipe hung and curled and drifted on the morning stillness; on other mornings the wind almost snatched it from my mouth and swept it suddenly away. A thin trickle under the arches, anyway, usually turned my thoughts to Kilnsey and the Wharfe, of which the Skirfare, of course, is a tributary; if the trickle was really thin it sometimes turned them – in those days – to a long rod and a tin of worms. Intemperate winds always irritated me, even if they were upstream, setting me thinking of places where I might perhaps find some shelter and some pleasure in casting a fly. Those wild surges of brown water always sent me back to The Falcon in a gloom because they meant that the day had turned from a fishing day into one of disappointment and deep frustration.

Over the years I stood on the bridge in every sort of weather and with every sort of water flowing beneath me. Most usually I suppose there was something like a manageable breeze blowing down or, much better, up the river; more often than not the water was on the low side but offered the prospect of enjoyable sport with the chance of a trout or two. But just occasionally, in a typical year perhaps on two or even three mornings in the course of the season, as I stood there on the bridge gratefully sucking in the day's first mouthfuls of smoke – there are times by the way when I find myself wishing that I still had not renounced the pleasures of my pipe – just occasionally anyway, as I stood there smoking on the bridge, I felt a gathering sense of expectation, because as I stood and gazed and smoked, I realised that there had been just enough rain overnight, or that the water had dropped back just enough from yesterday's spate,

I realised too that the morning was calm or one blessed with a gentle breeze from the north-east and that all this meant that conditions seemed more or less perfect for a day on the beck.

Just to make sure there would now be a short walk to a much smaller bridge right on the edge of the village, a bridge which was little more than a bump on the road with a wall on its either side. It was and still is, of course, the bridge that spans the beck and, on those expectant mornings twenty and more years ago, as I stood there smoking and looking at the beck below me, I was asking myself if it was telling me the same message that the river had told me just a few minutes ago. Once or twice I seem to remember that they disagreed with each other, probably because the rain that had refreshed the river had somehow missed the fells where the beck was born. But almost always beck and river spoke with one voice, telling me that the day ahead of me was going to be one of those rare and special days spent along the margins of Cowside Beck.

Conditions had to be right for the beck and I never thought of fishing it except when staying at The Falcon. This meant that there were seasons when I never fished the beck at all. It was obvious from the start of our association that it needed leaving alone in low water, that it needed fresh water for successful sport and I very soon learned that the wind was also a crucial factor, because the steep sides of the beck's narrow valley, once you came between them, turned what, in the open fields of its lower course, had seemed no more than a mildly irritating breeze from the south or the west into a howling downstream gale that robbed flyfishing of all its pleasure.

For a good day on the beck you needed a fresh and falling water with calm air or a light breeze from the east. Part of the charm of fishing the Wharfe up at Yockenthwaite and Deepdale is that, because most seasons bring long periods when the conditions there are unsuitable for sport, my days on the high river are for this reason alone special days. Opportunities to fish the beck came much less frequently and made the days I spent there seem like red letter days even before my first cast had been made. There were, of course, days that seemed no longer to deserve such honour when the evening brought me back from the beck with only a single trout or with none at all, but there were many more that returned me to The Falcon in the evening feeling privileged to have spent another golden day in the beck's very generous company.

I never took my fishing bag with me when I set off up the beck. There were high walls to cross and there was much ground to cover, for I often found the best sport way up the valley not far from the beck's source. In the days before I finally acknowledged the usefulness of a many-pocketed fishing waistcoat I slung a small rucksack over my shoulder, stuffed with a thermos and a pack of sandwiches, a spare reel and some spools of nylon. Sometimes I wore a waterproof, sometimes a sports jacket; whichever of these it was, its pockets held a pipe and a pouch of tobacco and at least two boxes of matches and I forgot to mention that my rucksack carried, in addition to the contents I have already mentioned, yet another box of matches inside an old tobacco tin. This was an emergency supply in case I dropped the other boxes in water or wet grass or fell in the beck myself and found that sodden matches denied me the consolations of tobacco. This was something that had happened once or twice earlier in my fishing life and I knew that it was something to be avoided, especially on those high and holy days when I was able to fish the beck. I have never, incidentally, spent a day on the beck since I finally gave up smoking a dozen or so years ago.

Once or twice I thought about fishing the beck in walking boots rather than waders. It would certainly have made the walking more comfortable and most of my fishing was done from the bank. I think it would have worked but, although I often considered it, always in the end I pulled on my thigh waders and so, looking I suppose like a hybrid walker-fisherman I would, with my preparations complete, stamp off up the lane behind The Falcon, with eight feet of Hardy's Palakona Perfection swaying above me in rhythm to my steps, and let myself through the narrow gate which opened into a wide pasture, a pasture where years and years ago there was a mill pond. I used to walk along the flat ridge of the old dam, watching rabbits scurry ahead of me over boggy ground that had once been under water. I would look for signs of the breeze, looking for smoke from the chimneys of the village, following the plumes rising from the bowl of my pipe or, in August and September, watching the drift of thistledown on the air. Always I would look up at the sailing clouds above me and I would be hoping that smoke and thistledown and sailing clouds were all telling me the same message: that the breeze was gentle and coming from the same direction as when I had been standing on the little bridge over the beck an hour or so past. If this was the case, which it usually was, I would feel comforted and reassured, I would leave the decaying embankment of the old mill pool and walk down to the edge of the beck. It was time to make a start.

The beck ends its short journey from its beginnings on Darnbrook Fell in a relatively open world, winding through almost level fields in the crazy way streams so often do when released from the confining walls of a narrow and steep-sided valley; something like a reeling celebration of freedom on escape from captivity. And, whenever I was standing by the beck at the start of a fishing day, the water was up and lively, which was of course why I was there, flowing with such vigour and such a voice that it added to the air of festival and made me very happy to be there among it all.

I suppose, by the way, I might have expected that revisiting the beginnings of days on the beck, with the sense of delight and exhilaration that belonged to them would make me question my renunciation of them. They were very special, and I am now asking myself whether I should make a few more of them, or perhaps just one of them, returning to the beck just one last time to see again its lonely and beautiful pools and say farewell to them all, hoping that they will send me away from their valley with a farewell brace of trout.

Returning, anyway, to the past I almost always made my first casts in the bathing pool, almost always with a pair of spiders, perhaps a Greenwell and an Orange Partridge, unless perhaps it was Poult Bloa and August Black. It is a place where the beck tumbles over a high limestone shelf into a broad and irregular basin, a rushing confusion of strong currents, glowing darkly, flecked and lined with foam. It was not an easy place to fish. Drag was often a problem and the trout were inclined to grab at my flies without taking a proper hold, although there were days when this first pool gave me my first trout. Usually he was a good one and it was, of course, a comfort to find success so early in the day, to find after only five minutes that already I was half way to the brace. And just writing about fishing the bathing pool at the start of a day on the beck is making me question all the more why I have cut myself off from what I found there. It would surely be good to return to the Bathing Pool and see if perhaps I could manage to catch the day's first trout from its rushing currents. It seems foolish to deny myself, not just the bathing pool, but the whole lonely and lovely world of the beck with the wonderful sport that can sometimes be found there.

There were days when the Bathing Pool was kind to me; more often I felt only the brief pluck of a trout or two followed almost immediately by the frustration of a slack line. Sometimes there was recompense waiting for me in the next pool, where the beck turned against the steep bank that carried the climbing road on its way to Darnbrook and Malham. The trout of this pool seemed more inclined to take a firm hold of my flies. There was a wall to cross here. Beyond it the beck flowed down to meet me in a swift succession of sudden twists and broad curves and sharp corners. On every turn there was a little pool, full of the promise of trout; it was a promise not infrequently fulfilled. A little further upstream the beck flowed for half a field's length in an approximation to a straight line. Here there were small pockets of water behind rocks and boulders, there were brief glides beneath the tussocky and often undercut banks. Almost anywhere I felt that a trout might be waiting to seize one of my flies.

It was fishing in miniature, a sort of fishing that I have always loved. On a summer morning of slow-drifting sunshine and slow-moving white clouds, with the beck full and lively and bright, with the wet earth breathing out the fresh smells of limestone country, with swallows and martins chasing each other through the washed sky and dipping down onto the water to pounce on the beck's flies, with all this and with the further blessing of finding the beck's trout on the fin, it often seemed to me that I was surely enjoying the best fishing in the whole world. I cannot help now wondering whether I should go back to find out if it is still so.

It was miniature fishing but it did not always bring miniature rewards. Once I took a trout of 2lbs from the beck and trout on either side of a pound were by no means uncommon. I caught most of my better fish on the higher reaches of the beck, once the steep slopes of the beck's valley had closed in. Further down I found sport with half and three- quarter pound trout and between them there were always five- and six-inchers, telling me that the beck was healthy, that its trout were breeding and repopulating their home.

The lower stretches of the beck were a delight; as well as fishing the little pools as carefully as possible I never ignored those sheltered pockets behind boulders and those glides under the banks; I just brushed them with my flies and from time to time a fish would pounce and, after a brief struggle, come splashing into the net unless he won the struggle and with it won his freedom as well. The beck itself was narrow but, down there on its lower reaches with almost level pastures on its either side, there was a feeling of space for the fisher along the banks. I could look down its course to the tall line of trees on the banks of the Skirfare. Often the steep roofs of the village houses were gleaming in the morning sunshine and, even on a bright summer morning, some of them would be sending white columns of smoke up into the blue sky.

As I stood by the beck I could raise my eyes to the high crest of the escarpment on the other side of the river, looking beyond those white outcrops of rock to the darkly glowing spread of the grouse moor beyond and, way up there almost on the horizon, I could make out the square of the stone hut where the guns took their lunch on shooting days. All round me at a distance were the sloping lines of rising and falling ground with the sense of width and space that so often comes with the meeting of two valleys.

In these lower reaches the beck seemed part of the world beyond itself and I would often pause and rest for a time before I moved on to leave this wider world behind me, something which happened when I scrambled over the third of the walls that stood in the way of my upstream progress. I seem to remember that almost always I caught my jacket in the loose and rusty wire that ran along the wall top and how, after freeing myself, I then half slid, half jumped down to solid earth on the other side, relieved that my rod tip was intact and that both ankles were still in working order. There was an almost desolate sense of pleasure in acknowledging that, now that I was over this wall, the mood of the beck and its valley had suddenly changed and taken on the loneliness of a wild and unfrequented place.

This was because the steep side of the beck's valley had suddenly closed in on either side of me, because the beck itself now flowed, no longer where it chose, but where the high and confining slopes allowed passage between themselves. The wide expanse of the grouse moor had disappeared, the roofs of the village houses could no longer be seen, the sky was reduced to a wide ribbon of light between the felltops. The beck had now taken me to itself and, even as I write these words, it seems to be offering to do it again, to take me there where everything that I see – the rushing water, the pale bent, the shapes of sheep moving over the rough pastures, the wheatears bobbing in clumps of reeds, the jackdaws shouting from the shadowed cliffs – where everything that I can see and hear is of the world of the beck: a withdrawn and secret world so that it seems almost a stolen pleasure to be standing there, an intruder into a place where I do not belong. But, in remembering that feeling, the pleasure no longer seems stolen or illicit because becks, of course, are made for fishers, becks welcome the fishers who love them and it now feels to me as though my beck might even be longing for my return, might even be insisting that I should find my way back into its secluded, secret and very beautiful world.

Over the wall there was a long straight pool running along a tumbledown wall that somehow held back a long and rising limestone scree. I always fished this pool carefully and more than once it gave me trout of about a pound. I fished the next, much shorter pool with equal care, which brought me to a place where the back turned and flowed beneath a natural wall of rock, the steeply sloping ground above criss-crossed by a maze of sheep tracks. Almost always there was a pull or two on the line here if not a trout in the net, and then, fishing my way along a stretch of boisterous, boulder-strewn water flowing aslant the narrow pasture, I came to Cliff Pool, the most striking feature of the whole beck, where a high and dripping face of limestone falls sheer into the water, throwing shadow over the stream and making the deep pool a dark place even on a bright morning.

It was here that I caught the only two-pounder that the beck brought my way. I remember that it seemed too big for the place that it had come from; I think I enjoyed the pounders and three-quarter pounders that Cliff Pool gave me on other occasions more than this monster that I suspected did not even belong to the beck because it looked to me as though it might just have begun its life in one of the stock ponds down at Kilnsey. Anyway, whatever the truth of this, ritual demanded that, once I had fished Cliff Pool, I sat down on the grass, put a match to my pipe and rested for a while before fishing on. And I think it was now, sitting there with a couple of trout in my bag, sitting there with most of a long day and most of the beck still ahead of me, that delight and contentment often deepened into a sort of lonely rapture. And I cannot help wondering whether, should I return to Cliff Pool, this same feeling, at once so powerful and so serene, would be there to take possession of me all over again.

Beyond Cliff Pool the beauty of the beck and its valley is a haunting and very precious memory. I can still see the beck itself flowing beneath sheer walls and hanging cliffs of white rock, where dark yews had found purchase along broken ledges, where squabbling jackdaws cackled while above them swifts soared and swooped on sharp wings, screaming in the giddy joy, in the ecstasy of their flight. Just to be there, I used to tell myself, down there on the floor of the valley, with all this surrounding me, with bright springs gushing over the green grass, with wagtails fluttering from rock to rock, with a dipper darting upstream and singing the bubbling song that seems his tribute to the flowing water which gives him life, just to be there would have seemed an undeserved happiness, but to be there with a fishing rod in my hand, with a light breeze on my back, with olives hatching from the stream and with trout rising to eat them, this was a blessing beyond my deserts or expectations.

The two pools in the middle of all this looked unexceptional but they both held big trout and from both of them I caught fish well over the pound, unquestionably the beck's own. In the higher of the two I was once broken by what I feel sure was a monster, bigger, I am convinced, than the probable alien from

Cliff Pool. You know that I have gone off exceptionally big fish, partly, perhaps chiefly because of the blank horror that comes from losing them. The loss of this particular fish darkened the day to which it belonged, which my diary tells me was a bright and productive day that would otherwise have shone in the memory.

Once I had fished both these pools it was always time to sit and smoke again. On the day of the great trout's loss I doubtless sat there brooding while sucking in gloomy mouthfuls of smoke. More often, somewhere beyond the noon of the day, I would smoke for a while, then put my pipe away and lie back in the rough grass to allow that feeling of rapture first experienced at Cliff Pool to take an even deeper hold on me, lying there with the music of the beck in my ears, with the raucous laughter of the jackdaws pealing through the sky, with the warm air soft on my face and with slow patterns of cloud and sunshine drifting over the floor and the sides of the valley. And more than once, I can remember, I raised myself on one arm to relight my pipe and look round me in wonder, knowing as I blew smoke gratefully onto the air, that I wanted only this: to be alone by the beck with a leash of trout in my bag, with a rod lying beside me, with a soft breeze blowing and with a bright sky shining in that band of light above the towering cliffs. I think these brief periods of solitary repose have brought the most nearly unalloyed if not the deepest happiness of my whole life, which is, I suppose, why I am now asking myself whether I should set off up the beck in the hope of finding it again.

Except for the Bathing Pool and Cliff Pool there are no names for any of the beck's features and I never felt tempted to give my own name to any of its pools or runs; I felt that the anonymity, the unrecognised presence of these same places seemed somehow entirely appropriate. It was almost as though, when fishing the beck, I wanted to fancy that I was the first person who had ever fished there and that I might never return.

Names, it seemed to me, would have destroyed this illusion and this deterred me from supplying them. They would have robbed me of that feeling of discovery whenever I fished the beck and, after leaving the Bathing Pool and Cliff Pool, came between the limestone cliffs and all that I found there, seeing it all with the marvelling vision of first sight and then pressing on with eager eyes towards the beauties – and the trout – that lay ahead.

When I had fished the two pools above Cliff Pool I always stopped to rest and smoke for a while. Usually I also ate my sandwich and drank from my flask of tea. Sometimes I dozed for a few minutes or even for half an hour. Before too long, anyway, it would be time to start fishing again: along a short length of turbulent water where trout grabbed a fly with lightning speed and were so often too quick for me, until the high wall of the valley returned right to the edge of the beck in a rough pillar of mossy limestone.

Climbing round this I would gaze at another line of cliffs, deeply overhung and again lined with sombre yews, cliffs that retreated from the beck before disintegrating into a tumbled chaos of shivered and broken rock where countless rabbits had made their home. It was now that, for a time at least, some feeling of space returned, for I found that I had entered a wide moorland bowl, with green and circling slopes, with welling springs and standing pools of clear water. Standing in lonely elegance halfway up the long lift of the ground was a small circle of sycamores, with a few single trees dotting the slopes elsewhere.

The sense of space had returned, but it was a sense of lonely and unpeopled space for, although there was a road just over the horizon on one side of the valley, there was no feeling of human proximity; it was a space for the wind and the curlews, for the browsing sheep and the teeming rabbits, for the beck that flowed there and for the lone fisher who had come there along its banks.

Before long the beck turned gradually to the right and soon there was nothing left to call a valley, merely a narrow cleft where the beck flowed on its hidden course and where hawthorns and rowans found shelter from the Pennine wind. Here I found an intimacy to the loneliness, and there was mystery too, for the beck now flowed mainly over the living rock, over ledges, slabs and shelves of white and yellow limestone, with one or two places where the bed disappeared in huge holes: great, dark peaty gaps where the bottom seemed a wild and distant surmise. Always here there was the hope of a surprise, of a three- or four-pounder or something even larger; it is a prospect that would no longer hold much attraction for me but almost twenty years ago it was a real hope: the hope that a lurking giant would remember the diet of his youth and, yearning for times and pleasures past, would take one of my flies and find too late that it contained a hook. I never came across such a trout but I caught good trout from those high pools of the beck and, with or without them, I always marvelled at the secluded beauty of their upland home.

There were places so beautiful that always they struck me with the beauty of first seeing whenever I came to them. And always, although I had been there many times before, I gazed upon them with new eyes and repossessed them with deep gratitude.

There was a pool with a single rowan standing graceful sentinel at its head and, although there was nothing particularly striking in the scene, it somehow embodied the lonely and very lovely spirit of the place, with the beck flowing secretly between its steep sides, with a broken and mossy wall across the water, with the rock gleaming through from the bed of the stream and with that single tree standing there and hung, in August and September, with red or with reddening berries. Some way above all this was what I took to be the deepest of the beck's many pools: a dark and yawning hole of unfathomable mystery. I never caught even a six-incher there but I never doubted that trout much longer than six inches were down there brooding somewhere in the deeps.

There was an arched cave on one side of this pool, through which a bubbling spring of water gushed into the beck. Beyond the cave I could see the same spring splashing and foaming down the hillside, rushing down from white falls perhaps a hundred yards back; and all along its course the lime-laden water had laid down a smooth and gleaming deposit, building and shaping a raised channel for its brief and impatient journey to the beck.

There were rocky gorges with ferns pushing out their long leaves from every crevice and crack. In places the beck was forced into deep limestone runnels barely a foot wide, flowing as a gleaming cord or a smooth and sinuous vein of swift water. There were yellow steps and slabs: miniature falls with water-delved pools beneath them. Above the beck there were often narrow ledges of rock which offered precarious passage to the pools and runs beyond. There were rowans and thorns, clinging to the steep sides, leaning branches, leaves and berries over the water beneath them. And the best of it was that I had not come there just to look, which would of course have been good enough, but I had come with a fishing rod in search of the spotted trout that made the beck their home. And, whenever the line darted forward or to one side, whenever in response to this I lifted my wrist and made contact with a trout, whenever this same trout was drawn splashing over the net, always my heart was moved by an impulse of excitement and delight. I have written all this in the past tense, but those pools, those runs, those slabs and ledges, those leaning trees in blossom or berry, they are all still there and the spotted trout too and there is no reason why I should not go among them again, no reason at all unless I decide that it is best to leave them a memory rather than to turn them back into living experience.

I never fished right to the source somewhere above Darnbrook Bridge; I was uncertain whether I had permission to go so far although I suspected that no one would care much if I did. Anyway, I always stopped three or four pools above the pool with the little cave and the gushing spring, struggled up the steep, bankside slope onto the open moorland above, before resting and smoking for a time and then heading back towards Arncliffe and The Falcon. There were days when it was only at that point that I realised I was hungry and that there were uneaten sandwiches in my rucksack, so absorbed had I been in the beauty of the beck and by the fascination of fishing for the trout that lived there.

The speed of my return always surprised me, for in fishing my way up the beck I seemed to have fished my way a whole world away from the place I had left behind after breakfast. Pub and village and human company seemed very distant from the fisher who almost unwillingly began his journey back towards them. But this journey was finished in less than an hour, although it took at least twice as long if the most enticing of the beck's pools persuaded me to fish them again.

Some way below Cliff Pool, anyway, the brown or purple slopes of the grouse moor hoved into view as I looked beyond the beck's valley for the first time in many hours. The last of the morning's three walls to be crossed now turned into the first; once over it I caught sight of the steep roofs of the village with those columns of smoke rising through the quiet evening air. The high sides of the beck's valley now retreated, the beck itself began to celebrate its freedom with all those sudden twists and turns and corners and I would make my way along the banks with rabbits fleeing ahead of me, with my rod swaying behind me, while swallows chattered in the sky and sometimes dipped down onto the water to take the first of the spinners that would fall more thickly as the evening wore on.

I would retrace my steps along the line of the old dam and then, leaving the beck to the rabbits and the swallows and the sheep, I would go through the little gate into the lane and saunter down to The Falcon, thinking how precious to me were the high places of the beck, how great a privilege it had been to spend a day with them again and how delightful it was to be returning to the Falcon after long and lonely hours in the hills, returning to display my catch on the platter in the hall, to drink tea and smoke for a while before lying in the bath and listening to the news. Then it would be time to drink two bottles of Guinness before dinner and wondering whether, with dinner over, I should forget coffee and go down to the river for the evening rise. Sometimes the coffee won, more often it was the river and the evening rise.

If I did return to The Falcon and, if I did spend a long day on the beck, there would no longer be any question of the evening rise; it would be coffee and conversation followed by a stroll down to the river before a pint or two of bitter and then bed. Writing this homage to the beck and the days that I spent there has made me question the decision that I made ten or a dozen years ago: to leave the beck flowing through my past. I make myself no promises but I think it would probably be best if I kept the beck as a memory, a memory of a particular time and particular circumstances and particular people.

Nowadays, even if the beck itself fulfilled all my expectations, the day on either side of it, without the friends who once belonged there, would be unsatisfactory and incomplete. And so I shall try to leave the beck to others, finding some sadness and much deeper comfort in the recollection of golden days along its banks.

Chapter Thirteen

FISHING IN THE
TIME OF COVID

To begin with, of course, there was no fishing in the time of covid. March arrived and brought daily briefings, announcing the spread of the virus in Europe, particularly in Italy and then in Spain. I seem to remember that this caused some anxiety but our daily intercourse was nevertheless more or less normal and there was no general expectation that we would be forced to make drastic revisions to the pattern of our lives. My friends, Andrew and Kelvin, were still planning to come and stay for a couple of nights towards the end of the month before we began our season together on the Wharfe. The thought of fishing was very comforting; I was busy tying flies and telling myself that every day brought me a day nearer to that first day on the Wharfe which, even if it gave me no trout, would be a precious day of reconnection. Meanwhile the weather, with its sunshine and warm air and light winds, made it hard to believe that, with this early coming of spring, anything other than kind days lay ahead.

I find it increasingly difficult to find my way back to the mood and atmosphere of those days, but there was surely a gradual change, a darkening, with the advice from politicians and the scientists with whom they were now surrounding – and protecting? – themselves, ever more insistently urging caution and the avoidance of unnecessary human contact. It was still advice rather than instruction, but I agreed with my friends' decision that, given the circumstances, it would be inappropriate for them to drive the long road from Essex to Cumbria and for us then to fish together on the Wharfe. I think I still intended to go fishing myself, because it seemed to me that I could drive to Wharfedale, fish there and then drive home again without posing any risk of infection either to myself or to anyone else.

And then very suddenly our lives changed almost beyond recognition. I had been expecting further restrictions; I was not expecting so drastic a curtailment of our freedoms and it came as a shock to me that fishing had suddenly turned into a forbidden activity. I was shocked but I can't remember disapproving. I know that I felt the lack of my rivers and should have loved to go off in search of the season's first trout, but I nevertheless accepted that no fishing was a price worth paying if in any way it could hinder the spread of covid-19.

They were unsettling and jumpy times. Fear and anxiety hung in the air like a miasma, spread by those daily and ever-climbing figures of infection and death. New words entered our lives, new images of shrouded, masked figures struggling to save lives in hospitals that were already almost overwhelmed. No one knew what to expect. Perhaps worst of all was that people had suddenly become a threat to each other, a danger to be shunned like lepers back in history, except that now we were all lepers. Ordinary human intercourse had suddenly turned into a sin.

It was like nothing that we had known or lived through before and we were emotionally unprepared for the privations that it imposed and the pressures that it bred.

For many it was, of course, a time, not just of uncertainty or fear, but of pain and sickness, of death and loss and grief. I can remember insisting to myself that it was no time to feel deprived because I could no longer go fishing. I was, in fact, no longer sure that, in the middle of so much suffering, I even wanted to go fishing. Perhaps I felt that somehow it would be insensitive as well as irresponsible.

But I did have an escape; I did have a place where I could find comfort and something close to peace. I was missing my rivers very much indeed, missing everything that I had found on the banks of the Wharfe and the Tees, but I could go to High Park, where I ran my little shoot, and there I found something precious, something almost as precious as I found on the banks of the Wharfe.

It took the Land Rover less than five minutes to make the short journey to High Park where, after first of all running the dogs, I let out and fed the hens before collecting their eggs for my own use and for (socially distanced and outdoor) distribution to neighbours and friends. It was after this that I took the opportunity to exercise myself in my own fields, in a place where there was no risk of any dangerous human contact. I might talk to Gordon, the farmer who grazes my land, at an appropriate distance. I might do the same with Tony, the retired keeper who was then helping me on the shoot, but it was all out under the sky and, anyway, all three of us were to differing degrees nervous of proximity. We regarded other people, even friends, suspiciously, fearfully. Only two years away from the first lockdown, I think we have already forgotten just how anxious so many of us were in our contacts with our fellow men.

And this is why High Park was so important to me because, denied any human intimacy, I could connect with something almost as important to me. Every morning I walked my boundaries with the dogs and, while Fred and Zac investigated spreads of gorse and beds of rushes and tangled confusions of bramble and briar, I drank in the unfolding miracle of spring (and what a spring it was!). On a morning in late March I heard the chiming of chiffchaffs ringing out again for the first time that year. Soon afterwards I welcomed the sad and lovely song of returning willow warblers and very soon there seemed to be one singing in every tree. And every day the air above my fields throbbed with the calling of curlews and every day I could watch them floating through the sky. Every day too the blackbirds sang more sweetly and every day cock pheasants were proclaiming themselves alpha males more insistently.

I watched hares doing in April what they are meant to do in March. I saw more and more bees buzzing and bumbling through the grass; I saw the first butterflies of spring – peacocks and small tortoiseshells – spreading out their wings to the touch of the sun, which shone down day after day, shining kindly with the restrained warmth of spring, shining on the primroses now opening their flowers more thickly along so many of my banks and under my hedges, on the celandines that were starring the grass more abundantly every day, on blackthorn blossom now whitening along the still leafless branches in warmer, brighter places, a whiteness so intense and so dazzling that every spring I wonder all over again how a bush that bears such blossom was given such a name.

There came a day when I walked for the first time beneath wild cherry blossom, which shares its bough with the unfurling leaf: subtler, lovelier perhaps than the blackthorn's so striking simplicity. In the course of a week the big wood turned into a green sea of dog's mercury and pungent wild garlic; the hawthorns, the honeysuckle and the elders began to put on green, the pussy willows turned yellow, while the catkins on the hazels were still scattering their pollen onto every breeze. And by now, in shady places, anemones and violets were shining white and blue beneath the trees.

I could not look on all this, I could not breathe in the spring air and the brightness of the sun, I could not drink in the wonderful sounds of spring without responding with something close to joy and, of course, with deepest gratitude. Beauty cannot be other than a comfort, even though sometimes of a complex sort. But there was something else that affected me as well, because every morning, in the forty minutes or so that I spent at High Park, I encountered a realm of nature that knew nothing of covid-19, a place where covid-19 posed no threat and had no meaning for the life that I found there. And so for a time I felt that its threat and its fear were held at bay or in retreat, which meant that I returned home feeling refreshed and reassured and better able to face the further course of a lonely day.

A glass or two of wine with my lunch, a pleasure normally resisted on days that were not fishing days, became essential medicine. Then it was time for a brief siesta. For the rest of the day the dogs were given the limited freedom of my back yard, although I confess, without it is true any feeling of guilt, that I took them out again briefly before going to bed. After lunch and about forty minutes' rest, anyway, I opened wide the back door where, seven or eight steps below my yard gate, Swindale Beck flowed on its way; it was good for me to hear the music of running water, together with the sounds of the dippers and wagtails that lived on the beck and together with the sound of the blackbird that was so often singing his heart out on a rooftop over the water.

In the afternoon I tied flies and dreamt of fishing, I sat at my laptop and tried to make progress – not very successfully – with this book. I read and cooked and even from time to time did a little housework, until at last seven o'clock came round, meaning that it was time to sip and sniff my way, with something like sacramental reverence, through two very slow glasses of sherry, followed by dinner and red wine and, before too long, bed.

It was a way of living. It would have been intolerable without that daily contact with a world beyond covid at High Park. It continued for weeks, until there came a point when, in defiance of the letter of the law, I began to return to High Park in the afternoon, because in doing so I knew that I was doing others no harm at all and was doing myself nothing but good. I repeated the boundary walk, sometimes the other way round, or did some work on the shoot or did both. I no longer cared whether I was out for forty minutes or four hours. I felt much better for this, although I often wondered how others were coping without the sustaining beauty and the precious release that I found out there on my little patch of freedom.

And so it went on from day to day and from week to week, with my hair getting longer every day, and, although High Park continued to bring nourishment and comfort, I began to long more and more for the comfort and nourishment that I found in fishing. There was no immediate prospect of their restoration and so I continued to walk my boundaries at least once a day. I ran the dogs in the meadow now, to avoid them disturbing pheasants on eggs or other ground-nesting birds, then I put them back in the Land Rover and walked my boundaries alone. Sometimes, when this was done, I set off through the bluebells, orchids and anemones in the big wood where, reverting to the practice of distant childhood, I spent half a morning or half an afternoon exploring bushes and banks, peering into holes and crevices in search of birds' nests. You will be relieved to hear that I was no longer in search of eggs for my collection; I was in search of beauty, hoping to find and admire the exquisite craftsmanship that built the nests, hoping to marvel at the shining and wonderfully varied beauty of the eggs or of the birds that might be sitting on them. I discovered that I no longer had the eye (or the back) that I had for this business as a boy of nine or ten, but I found the nests of robin and thrush and blackbird and wren. I looked and marvelled and very soon passed on.

A beck flows through the big wood, then down one side of the meadow before turning a wide corner and leaving my land. I have always been in the habit, when passing the bigger pools, of peering into the water, where sometimes I can spot the shapes of as many as half a dozen small trout, hovering there and then darting for cover under the banks. It is a sight I have always loved, because of course I love trout wherever I find them, but until that covid spring it had never inspired any predatory thoughts, any urge to bring a rod to High Park and try to catch a trout or two. I regarded my little portion of the beck as a sanctuary where trout could swim in safety without the danger of any interference from me. But now I began to ask myself whether perhaps, if fishing my rivers continued to be impossible, I might after all fish for the troutlings of High Park. I told them that any I caught would most certainly be returned and I also kept deciding to wait a few more days or another week. In the event my trout remained unharassed, because I felt that to break my promise, made when first I came to High Park, a promise to leave them to live in peace under my protection, would be an act of callous betrayal.

I never fished at High Park, and never will do, but in that first covid spring another sight that turned my thoughts to fishing (where of course they often found themselves without the encouragement of any external promptings) was the yellow spread of kingcups in a damp corner of one of my fields, for it reminded me of a spot on the Wharfe, a spot at the bottom of a favourite pool where in spring the kingcups grew thickly along the edge of the water, a spot where I had sometimes chosen to eat my sandwich and drink my lunchtime glass of red wine; and, if this had happened at the end of a May morning that had brought me a trout or two, and if, while I sat there, the river was flowing brightly under the sun, with the kingcups shining all round me, then the man sitting among them had, I could remember, been feeling as happy as any mortal man could reasonably hope to feel.

I saw the kingcups at High Park and acknowledged their shining beauty; at the same time the sight of them brought a sharp pang of regret because they reminded me of the kingcups that would be shining along the margins of a river where I could not go. By now I was longing to be fishing again, and I no longer felt any reservations about this; I was thirsty for my rivers, hungry for trout, pining for the feelings that rivers and trout so often bring to me.

There were mornings at High Park when I sought distraction by making a mental note of all the birds I could identify by sight or sound. The cackling of magpies and the hoarse cawing of crows failed to fill me with delight; the mewing of buzzards was not exactly music to my ears. But the songs of many birds, of course, are very beautiful indeed. Over the years I have wavered but that spring I finally decided that the three I like best are those of the willow warbler, the curlew and the blackbird. I heard all three in abundance on those morning walks round High Park. I also love the twittering laughter of swallows and, at the end of the first week in May, it worried me that I had barely heard it and seen no more than two or three of the birds that make it. But the song thrushes were loud; often I saw little parties of long-tailed tits flitting and squeaking through the branches above me. Robins and dunnocks sang sweetly, great tits and blue tits made the noises that they always make. Pigeons cooed quiet comfort and, although I could not go fishing, everywhere at High Park I was surrounded by the peerless beauty of spring, by the beauty of the young leaf and the blossom on cherry and crab, by the yellow splendour of the gorse, by flowers scattered through wood and field and by all that sweet symphony of birdsong.

It often moved me very deeply and only partly because I was so eager to see and hear it all by the banks of the Wharfe as well.

I can remember a day that found me, almost at the end of my morning round, standing beneath a young and still leafless ash tree listening to what I felt certain was a garden warbler, until I spotted the bird and saw at once that it was a blackcap, and I remember how the song was so fluent and beautiful, and how the bird singing it was so delicate, so fragile and so lovely, and how both song and singer were surrounded on all sides by such wonderful and complementary beauty of sight and sound, that I sat straight down on the bank and burst into floods of tears. I think I was weeping for the incomparable beauty all round me, weeping too for the uncertainty, the frustration and the deep sadness of the times. They were tears of gratitude, they were tears of sorrow, they were tears of longing and I felt better for letting them flow.

Those lockdown visits to High Park were most wonderful therapy and they taught me all over again or more likely emphasised something that I had known all along: that what made me a fisher and a shooter was my love of nature; and how the love that sent the ten-year-old boy scouring the countryside in search of nests and eggs was the same love that now sent the seventy-year-old man off to his rivers or out under the sky with his gun and his spaniel in search of fascination, fulfilment and nourishment for both body and soul.

High Park and what I found there kept me sane. But High Park could not give me what I find by running water. During covid my lunchtime glass, followed by the evening's somewhat more generous allowance of sherry and red wine were both a deep comfort. But they could not quite supply the same comfort and delight that I found in sipping the contents of my beaker while sitting by the side of a river with a brace of trout already in my bag. I sometimes think that fishing gives me an excuse for lunchtime wine (which before covid was almost never allowed at home) but in truth I have always known that, if I have spent the morning in search of trout and put two or more of them in my bag, I do not need an excuse to fill my scratched old metal beaker with a generous measure of wine, because it seems almost my duty to fill and raise a glass in honour of the river's bounty. And I am telling you this now because, in that first covid spring, we fishers were finally given back our rivers halfway through May. In grateful response to this I went fishing just as soon as I was allowed and did my lunchtime duty with the beaker for the first time since the end of September, and then I did it again five times before the end of the month. It was wonderful, even though it was not on the Wharfe.

The committee of the Kilnsey Club delayed opening the river a few days until they could arrange a zoom meeting. Meanwhile I discovered that the Strathmore water on the Tees above High Force was definitely open with tickets available from the butcher in Middleton; and so it was that, almost two months into the season, I finally found myself on the banks of a river, found myself on the banks of the Tees at about half past ten on a bright day just after the middle of May (they were all bright days that spring) with a gentle breeze, with covid-19 no more than a dim and unthreatening memory because my heart and mind were brim-full of the hope of trout.

An hour later I had caught four trout; two had been ten-inchers and so I sat down by Cronkley Bridge to do my duty with the scratched old beaker, drawing it from my bag together with a half bottle of wine. It was a day of high celebration and I had decided to allow the holiday allowance of three rather than two beakerfuls so that I should be able to perform my duty for a little longer, performing it in honour of the tumbling currents and restless pools of the upper Tees and, of course, in honour of the trout the river had given me. I also raised my beaker in honour of Cow Green Reservoir at the river's head, because it was the reason why the currents were still tumbling and why the little pools were still restless and disturbed. It had been a very beautiful spring; it had also been very dry. The Wharfe was already down on its bones and the Eden was lower still.

Given the conditions and given a choice between the Wharfe and the Tees, I might, in spite of my devotion to The Wharfe, have decided to fish the Tees and, if so, Cow Green would most certainly have been the reason.

I was sitting there, anyway, beside the Tees, which was flowing brightly on its way in the sunshine. I remember lifting my eyes to the heather hills all round me and wondering what would be happening up there when August came along, whether the warm, dry spring would produce an exceptional crop of grouse and whether shooters and keeper and beaters and flankers like me would be allowed to gather together with our dogs to perform our respective roles and enjoy the sport together with its wonderful setting and the pleasure of each others' company. I also wondered whether August would find me caring for another generation of pheasant poults at High Park or whether continuing restrictions would leave the pens empty and give me more time than I should have chosen to go fishing. Yes, I remember wondering whether there would be any grouse shooting and whether I might just have to live through a whole winter without any pheasant days, but in truth they were no more than passing thoughts because I was too full of the immediate present to worry about what might happen or not happen whole months ahead. What mattered was that I was sitting by the Tees with a brace of trout in my bag and that there would be more fishing in the afternoon, which would in all probability bring me some more trout and might even deepen the unqualified contentment and the unclouded happiness that had taken possession of me.

There was, of course, more fishing and there were five or six more trout and every one of them was a joy. There were curlews in the sky, there were sandpipers along the margins of the water, there were lapwings tumbling over the rough fields, with redshank above me whistling their shrill disapproval of my presence there. And all this was a part of my joy but the fishing and the trout were its heart. It is our love of the life of nature that makes us shooters and fishers. It was this same love that had brought me such comfort in those weeks of lockdown at High Park, but there was something more, something even more precious here on the Tees, for here there was a different and deeper level of involvement.

In walking my boundaries at High Park, watching and listening and marvelling at the beauty of it all, I encountered a world where covid-19 had no place and this perspective was deeply comforting, and yet it always felt that I was an observer, that I was looking on. But now, here fishing on the Tees, I was no longer a spectator, because I had entered and myself become a part of that world, part of nature's endless drama as a fisher in search of trout, a hunter in search of his quarry. And in doing this I had for a time put myself beyond the reach of covid, beyond the fear and anxiety and gnawing anxiety that it inspired because I was so completely absorbed in my fishing that there was no room for anything else. Mind and heart belonged exclusively to the pursuit of trout and to the world of beauty in which it was taking place.

And so it continued throughout the summer, on the Tees, on the Wharfe, on the Foston Beck and on the Rea. Three or four times a week I found, in my fishing world, a place where the daily statistics of disease and death had no meaning. You will perhaps think this callous but I think you are wrong, because it was not bred by indifference to suffering and loss; it was rather that when I went fishing I entered a world where covid had no purchase; I left covid behind me together with all its consequences and I think the fundamental contrast that I experienced between these two worlds made me better able to feel and understand the pain of the pandemic when I returned to it.

Going fishing unquestionably made me far more resilient; the comfort, the release, the absorption, the nourishment that it brought made me better able to bear the continuing strain with which we were all still living. Undeniably it was wonderful therapy. If it was a sort of escape, it was an escape into something real rather than an illusion and it helped me, in the time of covid, not to ignore its cost, but to live in good hope of the coming time when covid would be gone or would have lost its sting. There has never been a time when fishing has mattered more to me or when I have felt more grateful that God in his kind wisdom made me a man to find part of the meaning of life along the margins of running water.

Chapter Fourteen

WHAT'S IN A TROUT?

A few years ago, a friend who no longer fishes gave me his complete set of a now-defunct magazine called *Salmon, Trout and Sea Trout*. Why, you may be wondering, have I just mentioned this? Because, leafing through various issues from the early 1990s, I came across an article by a well-known northern fisher and master flytyer, an article in which he referred to catching trout as his 'fix' and told us how desperate he became when denied it for more than a few days together. I was not happy with this metaphor and almost immediately realised that I have myself often described fishing as an addiction or as a fever and a disease. I knew why I had used such language, because the urge to go fishing often seems irresistible, but I didn't really like thinking of something as life-enhancing as fishing in terms of illness and compulsion. I didn't really approve of applying to fishing, however light-heartedly, the vocabulary of physical and mental disorder (it should surely be seen as therapy rather than sickness) and it seemed even worse to compare the deep fulfilment to be found in catching trout with a chemically induced state of mind, the craving for which destroys lives and families.

Anyway, throughout this book I have been trying to come to some sort of understanding about why this whole business of catching trout means so much to me and why, after fifty years spent catching trout in fair numbers, I find an even deeper satisfaction in catching them now than I did as a young fisher when they were caught much less frequently and were therefore individually much more important. I hope that I have managed some insights but it seems to me that there is always more to be seen and more to be said. Yes, I acknowledge that there will be fishers who think that I have already said far too much about my love of the river Wharfe and the trout that I catch there and the feelings, especially the precious peace, that the river so often gives me, feelings felt on other rivers but never with quite the intensity that belongs to them when they visit me on the Wharfe. Well, they can take comfort from my solemn promise that this is most certainly my last book. In this last chapter of my last book, anyway, somehow stimulated by my disapproval of those metaphors that I and others have so often used to evoke the powerful hold fishing exercises over so many of us, I am going to try to draw together some of the various strands and themes and thoughts that have come to me in the course of my fishing life and in the course of this book, doing this in the hope of binding them together in something like a coherent conclusion that will shed some final light on why the arguably trivial business of going fishing and catching trout has become so central to my well-being and my happiness.

Shortly after reading the article mentioned in my opening paragraph, I found myself in the middle of a savage drought, down in deepest Shropshire on the tiny Rea Brook. You have been there before with me; it is a stream that flows, or seems to flow, through the middle of nowhere, which is one of the reasons why I am so fond of it. It is the perfect river for a heatwave, because there is delicious and restoring shelter to be found in the shade of the tall willows and alders that rise all along the tangled banks. And, if those tangled banks and leaning branches claim a fishing fly or two, it is a price worth paying for the blessing of the deep green shade beneath those whispering green leaves and for the cool comfort they bring to fishers of the Rea.

Anyway, I was there beneath the trees and I was baffled and delighted to see just how much water was flowing between the banks. It was the second half of July and there had been no rain worth the name since the end of April. I had at last been forced to abandon the Wharfe; I had found a substitute river in the reservoir-fed Tees, except that there is no such thing as a substitute for the Wharfe, and now I was on my leisurely way to Wales, where I expected rivers to have virtually disappeared (they had). I had also been expecting, on reaching the Rea, to look over Duddlewick Bridge and immediately decide that fishing would be useless or merely symbolic or a necessary ordeal to be suffered until the effects of two glasses of wine had worn off and I felt it fit and proper to drive over to my friends' house in Ludlow.

My first sight of the Rea immediately confounded these expectations. Yes, the water was low, but it was the sort of water that, back home in the north, I associate with a week or perhaps even a fortnight without rain. It was low but it was undoubtedly a river where a fisher might hope to catch a trout or two, a river challenging me to make sustained and serious efforts to do just that. There must, I thought, be huge reservoirs of water stored deep somewhere under the Brown Clee Hill.

I fished the Rea that afternoon; I caught a trout or two and I lost a trout or two and I fished the little river again the next day, when by lunchtime I had caught and kept a good trout of almost a pound, returning two or three smaller fish. It goes almost without saying that my lunchtime pork pie – Griffiths of Ludlow, by the way, indisputably make the best pork pies in England – it goes almost without saying, anyway, that my lunchtime pork pies, in fact a brace of them, were washed down with two glasses of red wine and that, given the heat and humidity of the day, the pies and the wine were followed by half an hour's siesta in the green shade. It may in truth have been forty minutes, perhaps even an hour.

However long it was it came to an end and it was back to business with rod and line. I had soon spotted a rising fish. The fly was cast a foot or so above him and a minute or two later I had caught a most beautiful trout weighing an ounce over the pound, which is a big fish for the Rea. Nearly all trout, the wild ones at least, are very beautiful; the trout of the Rea are as beautiful as any that I know. I am, of course, biased and partial; otherwise it is just possible that I should declare the trout of the Rea more beautiful even than the wild trout of the Wharfe. It was, anyway, while marvelling at the beauty of this trout: at his red and his black spots, at his yellow belly, his amber fins and the red rim of his full and perfect tail, it was while I was lost in wonder at the shape and the shimmer and the moist shine of him that I suddenly thought of that article and considered whether my trout had just given me something comparable to the false euphoria of an addict's fix and whether the whole business of catching the incomparable beauty before my eyes had brought passing relief to an addiction or a fever, and of course I knew, at once and emphatically, that the answer was no. I sat down for a few minutes before fishing on and while I sat there and while I fished on through the afternoon, I kept asking myself why that beautiful trout had meant so much to me and how it had managed to make me such a happy man.

One or two reasons were obvious. His capture had helped me to feel that I possessed something approaching competence in a pursuit that I regard almost as a vocation. He was moreover a good fish for his river and he had also made the brace, which for me, as you know, means contentment. If the rest of the day turned into a disaster, with missed fish and lost fish and monsters throwing the hook, I should at least be able to tell myself that I had caught a brace of trout, that I had done what I had set out to do and deserved to be called a fisher.

There were also circumstances peculiar to the capture of this trout that brought particular satisfaction, the most important of which was that I had hooked and lost him the day before. On both occasions he was rising two or three yards above a thick trunk that had fallen right across the river and the only way to cast to him was from a position just downstream of this obstruction. You will immediately know what happened on his first hooking; he dived under the trunk before I could stop him and promptly broke me.

Next time he didn't get a chance. I held him hard near the surface, trusted my tackle and before long he had surrendered to the net. It is good to catch a trout that defeated you yesterday; this one had also come to a change of fly, something which often persuades me – for a time at least – that I am an astute and observant fisher. His rising, anyway, had suggested that he was eating something just below the surface, perhaps some sort of beetle, and so my dry fly had been replaced by my hackled version of the Coachman, which as I never tire of telling you should be called something else because it bears virtually no resemblance to any of the many variations on the Coachman theme. The misnomer had clearly not bothered my trout; he had grabbed what he thought was food without first asking what it called itself or whether it deserved its name and he had realised the deceit too late. These two facts, anyway, that he had escaped me the day before and that I seemed to have understood the message of his rising, these two facts between them increased my sense of achievement in catching him, especially as he was a trout that belonged to a summer without rain when trout had been more than usually hard to come by.

These were special considerations; a universal of the fisher's calling is his involvement with the world of nature, which of course immediately brings me back to beauty, to the incidental beauties of moor and field and riverbank, with the flowers and trees that grow there and the life that lives there, to these incidental beauties and to the central and captivating beauties of water and trout. These beauties are an inestimable blessing but there is much more than the response to beauty in our involvement with nature because, as hunters, we are drawn deep into its life; we become participants in the endless and necessary drama of predation and through this we establish an unsentimental and sustaining connection with the natural world, a connection that grips and fascinates and fulfils. This connection, moreover, is made through a rod that weighs a few ounces and a line that ends with a gossamer length of nylon. The delicacy and refinement of flyfishing turns it into something like art and makes taming the force and energy of an angry trout sometimes seem almost miraculous.

Humans were made to hunt and there can be little doubt that part of the fulfilment we find in catching trout comes from the satisfaction of this ancient and abiding urge. And this, I suppose, is why we are constantly being told, mostly by fellow fishers, that the appeal of our sport is atavistic, taking us back, according to Howard Marshall, 'into pre-history to shake hands with the cave man'. I am unconvinced. Stone Age men painted pictures on the walls of their caves but we do not think that Raphael and Rembrandt were consciously following their example in an attempt to re-establish some sort of contact with our first fathers. Stone Age men doubtless made Stone Age music in worship and celebration, in expression of sorrow and joy, but no one to my knowledge has ever suggested that Mozart, when writing, say, his sublime clarinet quintet, was somehow groping his way back to the beginnings of the race. Men have always been driven by the urge to create and we have always been driven by the urge to hunt. They are constants of human nature; in going fishing I do not believe that I am doing something regressive any more than I believe that Shakespeare wrote plays or Brahms wrote music in some sort of endeavour to re-forge a link with their most distant forbears. Artists make art in the spirit of their own times. Fishers go fishing in the same way. What, after all, would Stone Age man have made of catch and release? Men have always fished and have always been conscious that countless generations fished before them. The sense of tradition is an enrichment but it is no half-conscious need to establish some sort of bond with my Stone Age ancestors that drives me to rivers in search of trout. I go there to make a particular sort of connection with nature and to draw nourishment from this most precious involvement.

Arthur Ransome comes to the same conclusion in his essay 'Back to the Stone Age'. He is sceptical about the fisherman's resumption of Palaeolithic life, although he does suggest that he steps back through the centuries, 'climbing down his family tree' and returning 'not to the Stone but to the Golden Age.' I am not myself conscious, when I go fishing, of a longing to find my way back to any earlier or more innocent age, nor really was Ransome, who made these suggestions in a spirit of speculative whimsy and was surely right when he says that we do not go fishing in search of any past age but to establish 'a relationship with nature which is valuable in all ages.' This is indeed why I go fishing and why I so love catching trout, because it brings me into a relationship with nature that I find only by rivers with a fishing rod in my hand. I make contact with nature in many other ways, walking the dogs, wandering in the hills, watching birds, releasing and shooting pheasants, flighting duck, flanking on the local grouse moors and occasionally shooting grouse myself. This is all very precious to me but there is something about my intercourse with rivers and trout that takes me deeper into nature and brings me deeper healing and reassurance, deeper comfort and nourishment. It is the reason why I have written this book.

It is time to leave the Stone Age and its inhabitants, except that I should just like to point out how unlikely it is that they all conformed to a single type, living only for the joy of chasing bison and mammoth over hill and dale. One of the most striking features of us humans is just how different we all are and I cannot believe it was otherwise with the men and women of the Stone Age. Surely there were cavemen who hated the whole business of hunting, even though they acknowledged its necessity and went out dutifully with their flint-headed spears, cavemen who were secretly terrified of mammoths and bisons and would have much preferred to stay at home with their wives or mothers, cleaning the cave and doing the cooking in readiness for the bloodied hunters' return. I have already mentioned Stone Age artists and the exquisite images they have left us on the walls of their caves; it is not, I think, unlikely that some of them found their art more fulfilling than the dangerous, exhausting and very messy business of hunting savage beasts armed with lethal horns and tusks. Surely too there were cavemen poets in love with words rather than with tracking animals through the forest in snow and wind and rain. I don't know whether Stone Age musicians had instruments at their service, bone flutes and whistles perhaps, or whether their music was just for the human voice and whatever sort of rhythm section was available, but I am sure they experimented with different patterns of sound and pitch and beat, finding their true vocation in this rather than in the excitements and challenges of the chase. Doubtless too there were cavemen obsessed with sex rather than with hunting, as well as lazy, listless or depressed cavemen who weren't much bothered with either. And there may well have been cavemen who found other cavemen more attractive than cavewomen and there may even have been cavemen who wondered whether they were in fact cavewomen cruelly trapped in the wrong body (and vice versa). I think my point – if I really have one – is that, as with their descendants through all generations, there were surely all sorts and conditions of cavemen (and women), all with different temperaments and interests and tastes. We demean our remotest ancestors if we assume that they were all the same. Doubtless necessity made most of the men into hunters but for some, their hearts and minds would have been away in a different realm of contentment or creation or desire; they were cavemen just going through the motions of the hunt while the experts and enthusiasts did the tracking and read the signs and got on with the job. And I find, after all, that I do have a point, for what it's worth, which is merely this: that, in reaching back with Howard Marshal through history and pre-history to the beginnings of the race, you might find as a fisher hoping to make contact with a kindred spirit, that you were shaking hands with the wrong caveman. I think I had better leave it there and return to my trout from the Rea.

I mentioned catch and release, suggesting that the men of the Stone Age would have found it difficult to understand. They would have found no such trouble with the way I treated my trout from the Rea, because I knocked him on the head. Nowadays I give back to my rivers many more trout than I kill, but this one was unlucky. I wanted to provide tomorrow's breakfast for myself and my friends; my brace would do the job just about perfectly, not least because the trout of the Rea, as well as being (arguably) the most beautiful trout that I know are indisputably the sweetest tasting that I have ever eaten. The trout of the Wharfe taste delicious, the trout of the Rea taste even better, a claim that must be true given my inordinate affection for the Wharfe and everything to do with it. Anyway, my trout from the Rea went in my bag because he was destined for a plate. At the same time I told myself that if the afternoon brought more trout – it did – they would be returned now that breakfast had been secured.

Providing food for oneself and for others brings deep satisfaction. Ask farmers and gardeners and they will, I feel sure, confirm this claim; and I think, by the way, that they are unlikely to claim any special feeling of kinship with the first tillers and planters of the land. Fishers like me, anyway, fishers just primitive enough still to think of fishing as an activity connected with putting food on the table, acknowledge the need to exercise restraint in wild waters but at the same time believe that the taste of trout and the nourishment they provide is an important part of the justification and pleasure we derive from catching them.

I have probably left unsaid most of what needs to be said but a brief summary of what catching trout means to me goes something like this. Catching a trout gives me the pleasure all sportsmen find in success. Sometimes a particular trout brings the particular pleasure of particular circumstances. Catching a trout fulfils the hunter in me and draws me into a fruitful and fascinating relationship with nature and also helps to meet a basic human need. Flyfishing is a refined and beautiful activity, which catches (edible) beauty from the infinite beauty of water in places full of surrounding and complementary beauty. No wonder then that catching a trout often fills me with a very deep belief in the goodness of creation and in man's duty to preserve and cherish and where possible restore his very precious and fragile and threatened inheritance.

*****

It was a trout from the lovely Rea Brook that inspired those thoughts on catching trout, but I must turn now to the Wharfe, where catching trout matters more and means much more to me than catching the trout of any other river. Very soon I shall share with you a day on the Wharfe, the last day of the season a year or two ago, a day that helped me to see why the Wharfe and its trout have so powerful a hold on me. But, before revisiting this day, I should perhaps explain in a more general way how my attitude to the trout that I catch, wherever I catch them, has developed over the years, how I regarded them in early years as prizes, as edible trophies, the reward of my (very limited) knowledge and skill, how for a time they possessed the power to convince a clumsy novice angler with most of the rudiments still to learn that he was in fact already a mighty fisher. In those days undoubtedly the more of them there were the greater was my satisfaction and, of course, the bigger they were the better I liked them, although in those days I had more often than not to be content with few trout of no great size.

I think that I was always moved by the beauty of trout, but there came a time when I began to take a more considered and much deeper delight in the spotted and shining beauty of a wild trout; I realised that a perfectly proportioned specimen of twelve ounces or half a pound (or indeed a mere five or six inches), fully and slender tailed, thickly spotted and amber finned, was an altogether finer fish than a bloated stock fish of one and a half or two pounds. I came to regard trout as living works of art, as things of sometimes indescribable beauty. I still killed a proportion of those that came to net and, as you found when you joined me on the Rea, I still do because I still sometimes want to possess the beauty that lies before me in the grass, wanting also to take it home with me and eat it myself or turn it into a gift for one of my friends.

And trout are still for me the hunter's prize and I still look on them as miracles of beauty and they still provide food for me and for my friends. But they are now much more than this because every trout that I catch, at least every wild trout and especially the wild trout of the Wharfe, as well as meaning to me everything that I have already mentioned, is also a deep comfort and reassurance, for it is telling me that the river I love so dearly, although undoubtedly hurt by many forms of human interference, is still strong and clean and fertile enough to turn eggs into trout. When I fish right at the top of the Wharfe, up at Deepdale and Beckermonds, I catch among a few larger trout lovely red spotted ones of six and seven inches; I catch them down on the river's main beats as well and, although these graceful troutlings cannot bring me the contentment of the brace, they tell me their wonderful message of a deep-down power, even in wounded nature, to breed life and beauty in running water, in the water of my beloved river Wharfe. And mention of Deepdale and Beckermonds brings me back to that last day of the season a couple of years back and how it taught me something of why catching a trout on the Wharfe is for me a different, a more complex and much richer experience than on any of my other rivers.

The days that led up to it were full of rain and the Wharfe, when I checked the level online every morning, was full of far too much water. Every morning I acknowledged bitterly that fishing was out of the question. It was still too big when I checked it early on the season's last morning and, if it had not been the day that it was, I should immediately have abandoned any thought of going fishing. The river was certainly too big but on the other hand the graph told me that it was falling and the forecast for the rest of the day was good. Reluctantly I decided that, however fast the Wharfe might be falling, it would not be able to fall fast and far enough to make fishing feasible in the afternoon and so I went off to feed my pheasants, intending once this was done to spend the day on the shoot wiring stiles, doing a few other odd jobs and feeling disappointed.

Feeding my pheasants takes just over an hour; by the time I had done it any idea of odd jobs and wiring stiles had been rejected, because I knew that I could not leave the Wharfe unvisited on the season's last day, even if it meant no more than driving to the top of the river just to have a look, before turning the Land Rover round and driving straight back home. I thought this would almost certainly be what happened, but it was just possible that I might be surprised and find a river that had fallen far enough for me to fish. It was just possible; it was also very unlikely. I scarcely doubted that my journey would be wasted, although I realised that, even if the Wharfe was too big for sport, I should be able to thank the river for all that it had given me throughout the season. This would help to make my journey seem worthwhile and I might also drink a (single) glass of wine in the river's honour and pour a drop or two (no more than a drop or two) as a farewell libation into the swollen stream. If against the odds I found a river fit for fishing I should, of course, drink the three glasses of wine that tradition demanded on the season's last day.

You have driven the road to Deepdale with me on an earlier last day of the season and you have found me looking anxiously at every watercourse on the route up Mallerstang, then down the first miles of Wensleydale and up over the hills and down into the beautiful beginnings of the valley and the river that I most love. On this last morning of the season, a year or two later than that other one, the infant Eden looked high but just fishable. Whether I should want to fish the Wharfe if I found it in a similar state was a good question, because just fishable rivers rarely give good sport and I thought that I might prefer, as my last memories of the season, to recall two or three recent days when both the sun and the river had shone and when the Wharfe had been kind to me, rather than to fish a just fishable river, catch nothing at all or just a few midgets and then return home feeling that my last meeting with the Wharfe had been cold and unfruitful. The Ure above Hawes looked as the Eden had looked. In Hawes itself I turned right, to head up over Cam Fell and down into Langstrothdale. Gayle Beck looked slightly more promising, but then it was a much smaller stream than the headwaters of the Eden and the Ure, much smaller too than the beginnings of the Wharfe.

As you drop down into Langstrothdale, which is what the first few miles of Wharfedale call themselves, you can see the silver line of Oughtershaw Beck wandering through the fields below you. I could not tell how high it was running until I came to the tiny hamlet from which the beck takes its name, where the stream flows close to the road and allows fleeting glimpses of the water between the houses and the trees. It looked big and boisterous but, although I could not be certain, it did not look muddy or brown. Once through Oughtershaw you climb over a steep shoulder of land and then, as soon as the road begins to drop again, you see the Wharfe something like a hundred yards away; again it is an imperfect vision but it did seem to be telling me the unexpected message that I might after all be able to go fishing. The road continues to drop and draws ever closer to the Wharfe; soon I was driving with the river flowing beside the road only a few yards away, flowing impatiently it was true but at the same time telling me unambiguously that it was much better than just fishable, that it was on the high side but falling and clearing all the time, full of the deep almost purple glow that comes from the peat when the mud has gone and the river is fining down. I thought that it was also telling me that I should fish wet flies upstream, Simple Simon and my Coachman, and I was very eager to make a start, but first there was my pious duty to perform by drinking those three beakerfuls of red wine: a solemn and essential ritual to mark the last day of the season and the separation that would come with its passing. It was a ritual of celebration and sadness at the same time, mingled on this occasion with profound and grateful relief that the river had fallen so far. I could not help wondering whether the Wharfe had done it just for me: in acknowledgment of my devotion, so that I should be able to mark the last day of the season as it should be marked: not only with three beakerfuls of red wine but also by going fishing and by catching the season's final brace.

It was while drinking my wine that I realised just how important the brace was going to be, not only – or indeed chiefly – because I should not have another chance to catch a brace of trout until next spring came along: much more because I was hoping to drive away from the river and from the season feeling that the Wharfe had been generous to me on our last meeting of the year, feeling profoundly grateful for this and also for the river's bounty over the last half year. Failure on this last day of the season would be a sharp disappointment, because I wanted my parting with the Wharfe to be a sweet sorrow.

It was a grey afternoon with no wind, but the stillness was much more than the absence of wind; it was a presence beneath the cloud, a gathered and powerful grey calm. It was undoubtedly an afternoon deeply touched with melancholy and not only for a fisher conscious that his fishing was nearly over for the year. There was fading and decay everywhere in the brown and untidy spread of bracken over the steep fields, in pock-marked leaves hanging motionless on the trees, in dead flower heads and long, leaning stalks of pale, withered grass. It was also a very beautiful afternoon, beautiful in the potency of its stillness, in its soft colours and in its sadness; and it was a beautiful afternoon for casting a fly onto flowing water, and every cast that I made was made in the knowledge that before long I should be making the season's last cast of all.

I caught a trout almost as soon as I started. He was a rising trout and he pounced on the Coachman just a soon as he saw it. My fly had fallen perhaps a foot wide and he moved at once to seize it. He was a good fish for the top of the river, perhaps an ounce or two over the pound and he may well have been moving up to the spawning beds from somewhere downstream, although there are resident trout scattered through the pools at Yockenthwaite, Deepdale and Beckermonds as big and indeed much bigger than he. This statement, by the way, was probably mainly an excuse to make another mention of those lovely and evocative place-names.

I was half way to my brace, anyway, in less than five minutes. Thereafter fish came at well-spaced intervals. The river was quiet but now and then the line slid forward and I had soon caught another trout. In the end, there were four of them, two to the Coachman, two to Simple Simon and they were all welcome and all beautiful but none of them made the brace because they were all just too small to kill: eight- or nine-inchers rather than stretching to the whole ten that permits a Kilnsey fisher to kill a trout. I came to a rock pool on a bend just below the meeting of the becks and the beginning of the river. I began to search the water and suddenly the line darted upstream and I knew as soon as I had hooked him that if he stayed for the net he would go home with me. He was eleven inches long and he was all that I needed. I fished on to the river's first restless pool and then I sat for a while by the beginning of the Wharfe, conscious that it was now almost over, that my relationship with this river would, except in my mind and heart, be interrupted for half a year, that I would not stand or sit on the banks or wade the water in search of trout until another spring brought me back in the hope of another season's first brace.

It was while sitting there in the grey stillness with the sound of the river hanging on the air all round me that I turned my mind to something that I have known for years and mentioned a few paragraphs back: that the trout of the Wharfe mean much, much more to me than the trout from any other river. I thought of the Rea and how much I loved, not only the river, but also its wild and very beautiful red-spotted trout. I thought of favourite beats on the Foston Beck and how beautiful they were together with the trout that swam there. Undoubtedly I loved both the beck and its trout. I love all flowing water clean and lively enough to give trout a home; I love trout wherever I catch them but there is something different about the trout of the Wharfe, something that sets them apart from and raises them high, high above the trout of all other becks and rivers and streams.

There is, of course, an obvious reason for this: that since the Wharfe means so much more to me than any other trout stream, so the trout that I catch there will mean much more as well. I acknowledged this while sitting by the river with the season's last brace in my bag, but at the same time I knew it was an incomplete explanation. I gazed at the water for a time, delighting in its rich peaty glow, in its soft music and its sliding flow, and perhaps it was this that made clear to me something that I have long felt but never fully articulated, even to myself, for I realised that, although I may on several occasions have talked about trout as the gifts of whichever river they come from, this view of them applied most properly to trout from the Wharfe, for when I caught trout from the Rea Brook or the Foston Beck (or anywhere else) I looked upon them first and foremost as my achievement, as my prizes won from the water, precious prizes because they were beautiful and because I had caught them and made them mine. Of course I loved the streams from which these trout came but what the trout themselves told me most clearly was that by catching them I had proved that I was a fisher worthy of the name.

On the Wharfe, I now realised, it was different, because on the Wharfe I thought of the trout that I caught not with any – not at least with much – fisher's pride, not chiefly as the reward or demonstration of my fisher's knowledge and skill but, much more importantly, as the river's gift to me, the gift of grace unless perhaps they were gifts given in recognition of my devotion and love. And because trout from the Wharfe were of the river's giving they produced, rather than self-satisfaction, a deep sense of grateful contentment and a profound reverence for the river from which they had come. I realised that catching trout on the Wharfe was for me a sort of spiritual experience and it will perhaps seem sad to some that a man can have such feelings towards a river and its trout, but to me it seems like a blessing almost beyond words.

I probably sat by the river for ten minutes or so and then I wandered off downstream through the grey and now deepening light past browning and yellowing leaves. There was the sound of the water in my ears, while my eyes followed the slip and slide of the river's flow and its more restless passage between confining rocks and stones, and this sound and movement somehow deepened the surrounding stillness. Just above the lip of a pool I saw a trout rise and was minded at first to leave him in peace. The brace after all was already in my bag and, on reaching and fishing the river's first pool, I had decided that my fishing was over for the day and for the season; but suddenly I knew that I could not deny myself the chance of this one last trout; and the line fell quietly and then slid forward and he was hooked and he was seven or eight inches long and very soon he had been given back to the river.

And that was it, except that I sat by the river to gut and clean my two fish, doing what I often do before I get out the knife by laying my brace in the grass and drinking in its beauty for a few minutes. Those two trout were the Wharfe's most recent gifts to me and, while gazing down at them, I saw how every trout that the Wharfe gives me is yet another in the countless succession of them stretching back fifty years, fifty years with bright images of trout woven everywhere into the fabric of my recollection, to those first and not so frequent trout of my undergraduate days.

Every trout that I catch forms another link in those most welcome chains that bind me so inextricably and so tenderly to the river that I most love. And every trout that I catch from the Wharfe does something else, because it reconnects me with the young student who caught his first trout from the river all those years ago, telling me that what mattered to him now matters even more to the elderly man that he has turned into, telling me that the same love of fishing has survived dark times and been deepened by them and that the joy of catching trout has grown stronger and deeper too. Every trout that I catch up at Deepdale or down at Spout Dub or Watersmeet, every trout from any beat of the Kilnsey water, re-establishes the bond between me and my young self; and it strengthens another bond, the one between me and my river, by deepening my love for something that I have already loved for more than half a century.

When you have lived for seventy years you will probably have fallen out of love with things that once seemed essential to your happiness; you may well have fallen out of love with some men and women too; almost certainly you will have known the uncomprehending pain of bereavement; you will also have said farewell to places that mattered much to you and found that there are things you once did and found delight in doing and now can do no longer or no longer want to do. There will have been gain as well as loss, but there will have been change, and here is one reason why the river Wharfe and its trout mean so much to me, because every trout that I catch on the Wharfe speaks to me of something very precious that has stayed the same, of a compound something, formed from a pursuit, a river, a relationship, that has flowed through most of a lifetime and altered only by enrichment. This sense of continuity is a gift as precious and wonderful as the trout that my river gives me; it brings a feeling of wholeness and coherence and enduring love and is a prime element of the Wharfe's best and greatest gift to me: the gift of peace, given to me by the river through the mediation of two or three trout and felt in all the softness and strength of its healing power when I sit by the water at the end of a fishing day, at one with myself and the river and all the beauty around me, possessed by a feeling of fulfilment and thankfulness that wants nothing beyond itself, a feeling of profound and perfect contentment that I felt in all its fullness on that evening of the last day of September as I gazed at my trout and then cleaned them before walking slowly back to the Land Rover to stow my tackle and drive away.

I may have helped you to understand why every trout that I catch is such a blessing and why every trout from the Wharfe is a blessing beyond compare. If not, I think that I have at least helped myself to see some way into the mystery. As I drove home that evening, anyway, over the darkening hills, I hoped that there were more blessings waiting for me in years to come, praying above all that in whatever time remained to me, my beloved Wharfe would be able to give me just a few more trout and with them its best and greatest gift of peace.

Also published by Merlin Unwin Books